**Vertical Cities Asia
Internationa**

Volume 1

Everyone Needs Fresh Air

School of Design & Environment,
National University of Singapore

World Future Foundation

Copyright © 2011
School of Design & Environment
National University of Singapore

Printed in Singapore.

ISBN 978-981-07-1419-2

Publisher
School of Design & Environment
National University of Singapore
4 Architecture Drive
Singapore 117566

www.sde.nus.edu.sg

Designed by Vikas Bhatt Kailankaje
Printed by First Printers Pte Ltd

Cover photograph: Glynis Hong Tinghui
Typeface: Linotype Univers
Paper: Stora Enso LumiSilk

All rights reserved. No part of this publication may be reproduced in any form or by any electronic or mechanical means, including information storage or retrieval systems, without permission in writing from the publishers, except by a reviewer who may quote brief passages in a review.

The publisher does not warrant or assume any legal responsibility for the publication's contents. All opinions in the book are of the authors and do not necessarily reflect those of National University of Singapore or World Future Foundation.

VERTICAL CITIES ASIA

INTERNATIONAL DESIGN COMPETITION & SYMPOSIUM

EVERYONE NEEDS FRESH AIR

CONTENTS

Symposium Papers

14	In Search of the Best City Measures: Ten Propositions
26	Design Approach for High-Rise and High-Density Living in Tropical Asian Cities
42	Gridding Manhattan
54	The Vertical Reconstruction of Living Space
60	Multitasking Spatial Infrastructures: Slender Urbanism and Mobility Models
82	Lessons from High-Intensity, Mixed-Use Urbanism in Singapore's CBD
92	ONE City
96	Key Issues in the Design Approach of Megastructures
104	Urban Breeding Grounds in Chinese Greenfields
114	A Conversation on Architecture South of the Border
126	The Edge of Vertical
136	Muddy Skies in Construction: Paper and Projects by Mark Anderson and Peter Anderson

8	Introduction
156	Design Competition

Design Competition

160	SymbioCity
168	The Wall
178	Boundless City
186	Village City
194	Compact Paragenetic Ecology
196	Agropolis
198	AgroCity
200	Osmosis
202	Democratic City
204	VertiCO Urbanism
206	Bamboo Commune
208	MODO City
210	Park City
212	Hover
214	Delicate Canyon: Interdependent Urbanism
216	Dragon's Nest: Above the Valley Fog

218 **Appendix**

Event

Participants

Image Credits

Introduction

HENG Chye Kiang
Professor and Dean, School of Design & Environment
National University of Singapore

This Vertical Cities Asia initiative is the result of a happy confluence of favourable conditions in the face of challenges posed by Asia's rapid and massive urbanization.

In March 2009, I set up the Centre for Sustainable Asian Cities (CSAC) at the NUS School of Design & Environment to synergize the efforts of my colleagues in the departments of Architecture, Building and Real Estate (in collaboration with our counterparts in other NUS faculties and universities) to further our research in the area of sustainable high-density living. We have been doing this for many years, albeit from different disciplinary perspectives, methodologies and concerns.

Coincidentally, at about the same time (in February 2009), the World Future Foundation (WFF) was registered in Singapore as a philanthropic charity to pool the "collective intelligence, wealth, professional networks and knowledge" of "public-spirited entrepreneurs, scientists and professionals . . . to create a peaceful, equitable, prosperous and sustainable environment for the future generation". An initial meeting with Mr Lu Bo, Managing Director of WFF, followed by a subsequent meeting with Dr Feng Lun, chairman and founder of WFF, in the middle of 2009 and his visits to CSAC as well as our laboratories led to our determination to collaborate on the research and design of sustainable high-density cities.

When WFF suggested, towards the end of 2009, that our staff and students worked on the design of a high-density township to house a hundred thousand people within a square kilometre of land, we were excited by the prospects and challenges of planning such comprehensive high-density environments. Meanwhile, Singapore had completed in the same year, an iconic residential cluster called The Pinnacle@Duxton with a floor area ratio (FAR) of about 9, with some 1,848 apartments on a 2.5 hectare site. We deemed the design challenge posed by WFF feasible, especially in the tropical context although the project would be larger in scale and more complex. However, to up the ante, we proposed to WFF that instead of NUS working on it alone, we would invite, finances allowing, other schools from around the world to participate in this very meaningful exercise. This would provide a platform for researchers and students from across the different continents to discern the realities of Asia's fast-pace high-density urbanization and formulate appropriate sustainable solutions.

The circumstances for such an undertaking were compelling. Since 2009, more than half of the world's population have been living in cities. The phenomenon of global climate change and the ever-increasing ecosystem degradation only remind us of the environmental imperative that cannot be ignored by cities which stand in the front line of the global agenda of sustainable development.

The challenges faced by cities in Asia are great as Asia is home to more than half of the world's urban population. Moreover, Asia accommodates an increasing number of megacities with more than 5 million inhabitants and it has many cities with the highest population density in the world. Asia and Africa are the two regions with the fastest pace of urbanization. Rampant urbanization is usually accompanied by the problems of urban sprawl, traffic congestion and pollution that also threaten the prospects of biodiversity, greenery, liveability and the general well-being of urban inhabitants. Urban sprawl has led to the loss of agricultural land that further exacerbates the threat of food security already made evident by climate change. In China alone, there is a loss of 883,000 ha (or 8830 km^2) of farmland over the last five years!

The question then arises: Should cities continue to be built in the same manner with its attendant problems or can new models of urban architecture be explored that orient towards a new paradigm of sustainable and land-efficient urban growth?

Through this series of Vertical Cities Asia symposia and international design competitions, we hope to provide a unique platform for researchers and students from across the world to debate and investigate the planning and research of such a paradigm and spearhead an international effort to confront the realities of Asia's fast-pace high-density urbanization, and formulate appropriate sustainable solutions for very high density compact cities.

In this regard, we are delighted to have formed a consortium comprising some of the leading schools of design across the three continents of Asia, Europe and the United States—Chinese University of Hong Kong, National University of Singapore, Tongji University, Tsinghua University, University of Tokyo, Delft University of Technology, Swiss Federal

Institute of Technology (ETH) Zurich, University of California (UC) Berkeley, University of Michigan, and University of Pennsylvania—to undertake this effort, made possible by the generous support of WFF.

    This book, launched in conjunction with the exhibition of the inaugural edition of the Vertical Cities Asia programme, brings together not just the design competition entries from the participating universities, but also the reflections and contributions of the faculty and jury members during the accompanying symposium. The design entries of the student teams from the participating universities have been, to iterate the inaugural event's theme, a breath of fresh air. Although each proposal presented an argument for the ideas and programmes that inspire the design; seen together, they are an argument for a multiplicity of approaches and for generating a vibrant debate. The spectrum of design approaches and breadth of ideas were also evident in the papers presented at the symposium. This is the first volume of a series of books that will address the various dimensions of high density compact cities that will be published in the near future with the support of our collaborators and sponsors.

    I would like to take this opportunity to record my gratitude to the World Future Foundation, especially Dr Feng Lun, for generously supporting the Vertical Cities Asia programme. My gratitude also goes to Beijing Vantone Citylogic Investment Corporation for sponsoring the publication of this book and the organization of the exhibition. I would also like to thank the Deans and Heads of the schools for their support of the programme, as well as the student teams and accompanying faculty for engaging fully with the topic and theme. Last but not least, my special thanks to the students, staff and faculty of the School of Design & Environment and its Department of Architecture for their help, in one way or another, in organizing all aspects of the programme: design competition, symposium, exhibition, publication and the logistics.

SYMPOSIUM PAPERS

In Search of the Best City Measures: Ten Propositions

Joaquím SABATÉ BEL
Professor and Chair of Town Planning
Polytechnic University of Catalonia
Barcelona

Introduction
There is a remarkable tradition that stands for a close relationship between good architecture or good city form, and the precise dimension of their elements. It defends the existence of well-defined rules that link the parts with the whole city, smart rules that were applied from ancient times until the present.

This paper discusses some of these arguments, checking how designers have long sought for measures that assure the good shape of the city, its best performance, hygiene, safety and beauty. Among these rules, density has quite recently become one of the most relevant attributes to describe the form and characteristics of a city. Therefore, Vertical Cities Asia has proposed a project set on a main parameter: a density of 100,000 people per square kilometre. It is certainly a remarkable high density.

But is it too much? To extent should a given density determine the urban form? I would like to share with you ten propositions regarding these questions.

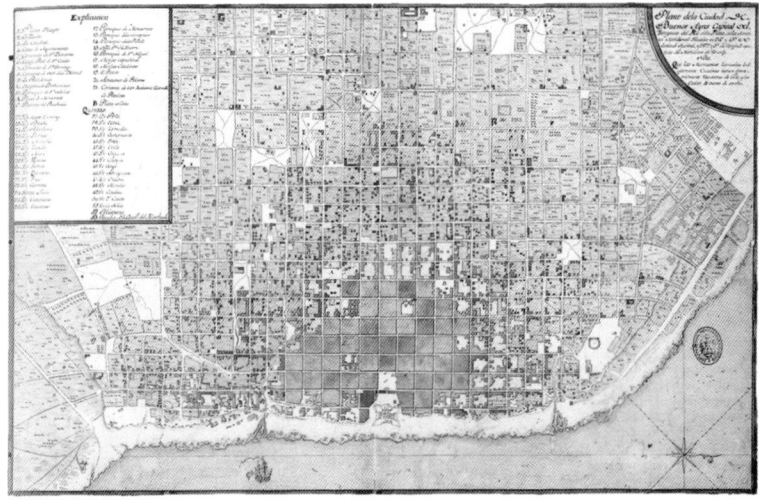

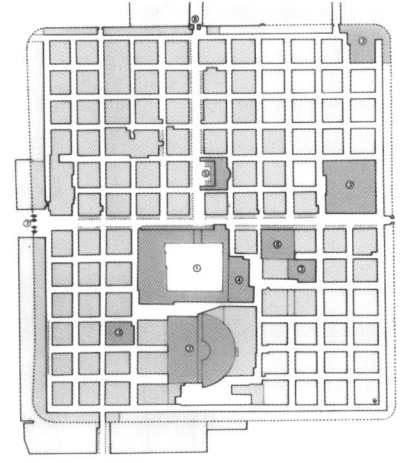

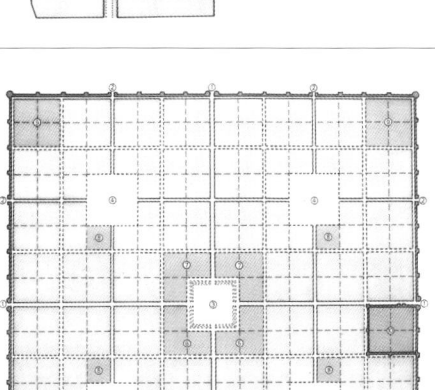

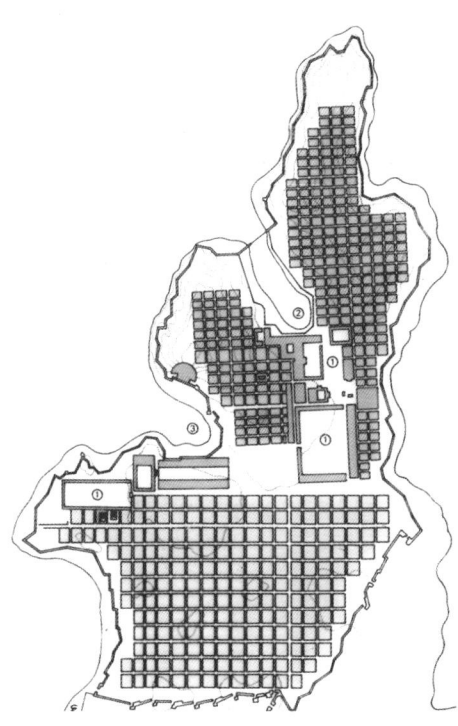

Opposite page
Fig. 1   Buenos Aires, end of eighteenth century.

This page
Fig. 2   Tamugadi-Timgad 100 aC.
Fig. 3   Eiximenis ideal city 1383 aC.
Fig. 4   Mileto 475 bC.

1. Discovering the most suitable proportions between the parts of a building or a city has been a continuous aim in the history of architecture and urbanism.

Diverse proposals have defended a close relationship, a confidence in an accurate mathematical and geometric connection, between the parts and the whole city, following specific guidelines to guarantee good architecture or a good city form.

This aim is quite common in classical studies, but also in the most recent ones by Lionel March and Leslie Martin, or using the powerful *Spacematrix*.[1] The goal to find the best measures runs along many rich cultures from the field of architecture to the construction of towns. You may recognise it in Plato's Dialogues, or in his book about the Republic;[2] in different medieval treaties; and in the background of all the extensive colonisation processes in France or Spain.

A theoretical desire is implied, but also a rich field of experimentation. I am not going to discuss who was the first to search for these magic measures, or to design regular cities, whether China or Mesopotamia. In fact, the most ancient cities tried to be quite regular in shape, based on precise grid patterns, and many of them searched for ideal measures.

Regular geometric patterns became quite common features in classical Greece, where the concept of Hippodamian layout first appeared;[3] but also in the Roman camps; in some Middle Eastern Arabian cities; in the fortified French *bastides* in the thirteenth century;[4] in the cities along the *Camino de Santiago*; in the Spanish villages after the Christian Reconquest, and obviously in the great epic of the foundation of cities in Latin America from the sixteenth to eighteenth centuries.

With the great European Town Extensions of the nineteenth century the discussion about the best measures of streets and blocks extended further to a broader scale.

2. Some of these projects relate to the most appropriate street, block and building parameters with some desired urban attributes, like hygiene, safety or beauty.

Perhaps the engineer Ildefons Cerdà with his broad scientific studies to support the town extension (the *Eixample*) project for Barcelona was one of the first to show this concern.

The reasons for his 20-, 30- and 50-metre streets, 113-metre by 113-metre octagonal blocks, and interior courtyards of nearly 3,000 square metres have been widely discussed. Quite often, he has been criticized for worrying too much about street intersections, proposing

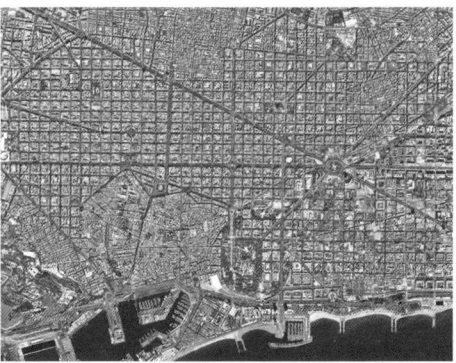

blocks that are too wide or neglecting architecture.

The question still remains how different Barcelona would have been if Berlin, Buenos Aires or Manhattan type of urban blocks had been employed?

Many researchers have tried to find the secret reasons for the peculiar dimensions of his project, which are so strange that they should be considered key design decisions. They have speculated about the mysterious origin of the form of the block and its measurements.

We discovered twenty years ago that the Cerdà tested quite different measures, before designing his 113-metre by 113-metre blocks. We further discovered that he consciously decided the dimensions of his project not considering astronomic, magical or geometric criteria, but trying to optimise the efficiency and mainly the habitability of the new city, evaluating and providing the volume of air that every dwelling occupier needed (30 cubic metres per hour), through a complex mathematical formula.

A few decades later, German professionals like Stübben, Baumeister or Eberstadt wrote impressive studies, where they formulated the discussion on the shape and dimensions of urban layouts, or the most appropriate and most logical depth of blocks from the point of view of economy and hygiene.[5] Nevertheless not one of their treaties achieved the scientific level and precision of Cerdà's contributions.[6]

3. The dimensions of urban tissues are quite relevant to guarantee their quality.

Thirty years ago, we analysed more than a hundred city foundations and town extensions—all of them based on regular grids—over a long time span. Measuring the width of the streets, the depth of the block and the area of the basic module, we tried to answer some intriguing questions:

Would it be possible to find some regularity among these projects, some significant relations between these parameters?

Figs. 5–9   Aerial view of Barcelona's town extension (*Eixample*)

Would it be possible to find some precise measures that guarantee more efficient, healthier or even more beautiful cities?

Our analysis concluded that the shape and dimension of streets and blocks, typological features of the buildings, and the resulting quality of the city are quite closely related. It was possible to discover quite precise intervals where these street and block dimensions implied better urban scores regarding health, efficiency or even beauty. We also found that some categories of cities gave priority to different attributes. Following this argument, one of our main goals as urban designers should, like being at the tailor's workshop, be able to choose precise measurements.

4. Some cities score well in this kind of "league tables", including Barcelona's *Eixample*, regarded by many international observers as one of the greatest pieces of urban architecture.

In 1859, the Cerdà interpretation of the grid implied a dimension of modern rationality, a mixture of order, discretion and homogeneity that generated empathy with the Catalan society. But did their specific dimensions that contribute to this?

Today, the central *Eixample* covers 819 hectares, with half of this area occupied by roads, open spaces and public facilities, and the other half by private zones. We can roughly say that there are about one-third roads, one-third open spaces and interior courtyards, and one-third public and private buildings.

The streets of 20 metres and avenues of 30 metres width define 498 quite regular octagonal blocks, and 10.235 building plots, that are also quite regular.

In the *Eixample*, there are 308,340 residents and there are around 264,500 others who work there daily. This implies an average density of 323 jobs per hectare, a figure only found in quite specialized and dense central areas.

The residential floor area covers 56 percent of the total built surface, and the non-residential areas, including public buildings that generate a lot of activity, the remaining 44 percent. These proportions are quite similar to those of high-value central areas where there is significant residential use.

Such a high concentration of people and jobs is supported by a high floor area ratio of more than three square metres of floor space per one square metre of land.

There have been recent attempts to measure the amount of information of different cities.[7] In the *Eixample*, this amount of information (diversity) shows its centrality. According to its scores over six "bits" of information per individual, the *Eixample* can be considered the greatest area of centrality in Spain. It has been built as a complex ecosystem that is comparable, in relation to natural systems, to tropical rainforests or coral reefs.

The *Eixample* radiates activity around it and extends the urban complexity along some streets. Interruptions in the linking of activities are shown by "holes" that reflect lower levels of urban diversity. A so-called "22@ District" is currently under development. When completed, this enlarged *Eixample* is expected become one of the most important urban area in the world in terms of activities related to information technology.

One may also add the enormous flexibility provided by the grid system, which allows the urban fabric to host diverse architecture and an intensive network of public transport and services. All these characteristics make the *Eixample* a paradigm of contemporary urban planning. Its functional mixture and urban complexity provide a great level of urban sustainability.

5. High residential densities and high intensity of activities have not always been regarded as positive urban features.
A high concentration of population in nineteenth century industrializing cities was considered to be one of the major causes of fires, illnesses, epidemias, deaths and social turmoil.[8] Therefore in this period, density was introduced as a powerful tool to analyse the quickly growing and often overcrowded cities and their problems. After decades of increased public intervention by both the city and the state, density has evolved into an instrument used to search for alternatives and to control urban parameters in order to guarantee air, light and privacy to every home. Although this has become a common opinion today, it has become clear that more than ever, we need minimum densities to support facilities and public transport to guarantee social coexistance and urbanity, as part of the set of ingredients needed to produce more sustainable urban environments with potential for vital human interaction.

This shift from prescribing *maximum* to propagating *minimum* densities can be illustrated referring to two famous planners: Raymond Unwin and Jane Jacobs. At the beginning of the twentieth century, Unwin claimed that nothing was to be gained from overcrowding in cities; and he proposed a maximum density of 30 houses per hectare.[9] Fifty years later, Jane Jacobs warned that inner city slums were not the only issue faced by America, but also the bland, low-density suburban areas. She suggested that a minimum of 250 dwellings per hectare was a necessary condition for a vital and participatory city life.[10]

Left
Fig. 10　View of a typical street at Barcelona's *Eixample*

Below Left and Right
Figs. 11,12　Buildings at Barcelona's *Eixample*

Bottom
Fig. 13　View of a typical corner at Barcelona's *Eixample*

Fig. 14,15 Buildings at Barcelona's Eixample

6. The general consensus today is that high densities are more sustainable.

In many occidental cities, the dramatic increase in space consumption during the last century has become a crucial problem in urban agendas. There are some clear trends in the wealthier societies: the number of inhabitants per dwelling unit decreases, dwellings become larger, and cities become less dense. It is generally acknowledged that the sprawl of people and of activities have dramatic effects such as the increase in vehicular and goods traffic, energy consumption, air and noise pollution, and the fragmentation of ecosystems. Public transport, local amenities and services also become less viable.

Currently, urban development can follow very different trends. It can evolve explosively and be out of control; or it can obey strict public rules; or it can occur through negotiations between private and public actors. However, whatever the political, economic and technical balances will be in the near future, some urgent issues such as urban density will require substantial responses. One century ago, the overcrowded English industrial cities provoked some reactions (Garden City Movement and the limitation of densities). Today, this type of overcrowding, extreme poverty and human misery have moved from Manchester to Manila.

Demographic, social and economic trends have resulted in low densities and created new problems driven by overconsumption of resources such as transport, goods, energy and space. Clearly, high density is not the total solution to these problems, but we do know that low densities contribute to private car dependency, increase of carbon dioxide, reduced social contact and less urbanity. The densification of our cities has become one of the main requirements to achieve a more sustainable city, and a priority in our urban agendas.

7. The fastest growing cities in the world have quite high densities, but urban residential density and activities intensity may have some limits, and need additional parameters to guarantee urban quality

Barcelona's *Eixample* has quite a high density of people and activities. Like in so many other dense cities, this has caused excessive car use, high levels of air and noise pollution, visual intrusion and a low proportion of open

Fig. 16 Transport-related energy consumption
(gigajoules per capita per year)

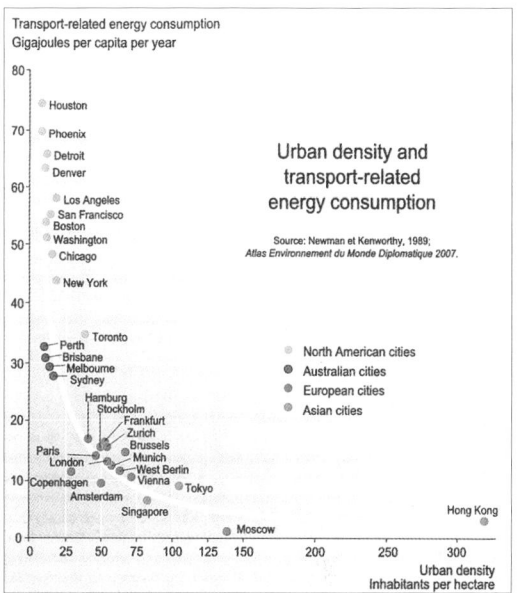

spaces per inhabitant. Barcelona's gross density is 376 inhabitants and 323 jobs per hectare, but although this might be considered as being quite high already, it is only one third of the density proposed by the Vertical Cities Asia competition, which is a density never before achieved at the scale of an entire city.

All the entries in the competition have therefore done a great effort locating this amount of people and jobs in only one square kilometre; even if we admit that several of these proposals have compromised a larger area (the five square kilometres of the entire reference site). Meanwhile, although net density achieved 1,000 people per hectare, gross density only scored one-fifth of this figure. Still, even in these cases it represents a density higher than in the densest cities in the world.

Although urban growth follows a variety of patterns, the current tendency is to increase the concentration of population and the intensity of their activities. A new generation of megacities with over ten million people is developing, mainly across Asia but also in some parts of Africa, North and South America.

The pace of urban change can be measured by the amount of people who will be added to each city every hour by 2015,[11] or by the increasing international air journeys, that bring cities into closer contact, and at the same time highlighting the differences between them. In megacities, this pace becomes more and more accelerated, and the human concentration becomes higher.

If we look at New York, Shanghai, Mexico, or the many fast growing cities in the world, we discover that they are achieving quite high densities. However, in these cases the highest gross average density comes only to 9,610 people per square kilometre in New York. In Shanghai it reaches 24,673 people within its urban core, and 37,600 people per square kilometre in the Barcelona's *Eixample*. Yet this is just one third of the density proposed by the Vertical Cities Asia competition.

8. High density is not enough to achieve positive scores; it should be always accompanied by a really efficient public transport system, and by strict open space requirements

Density matters, but it seems that there have been until now some limits

Fig. 17 Building Intensity and Coverage   Fig. 18 Gross Floor Area and Network Density

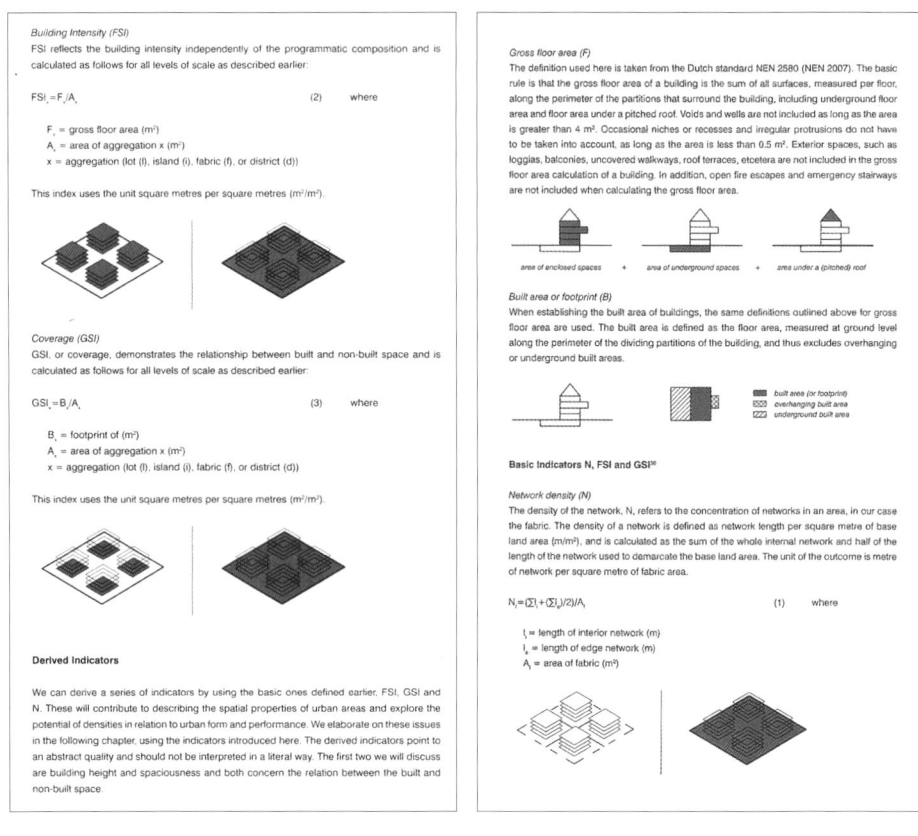

to growing densities. The Vertical Cities Asia competition brief demands a really high density (100,000 inhabitants and 100,000 jobs per square kilometre; around 400 dwellings per hectare). We have seen that this implies at least four times the highest records achieved in the densest cities. Being so dense, all these cities have to deal with difficult questions like traffic congestion, pollution, the lack of air, light or green spaces for their inhabitants, not to mention about participatory city life or social equity.

One should also consider that the one square kilometre district of the Vertical City would have to be connected to several other districts, or to other cities, and this requires a very intense and efficient public transport system.

The largest and densest cities in the world demonstrate their great dependence on public transport, or on the amount people who cycle or walk to their workplace.[12] So reducing the amount of required movements, by increasing telecommuting, mixing commerce and services with housing, and providing a very efficient public transport system becomes absolutely essential, as we have seen in all the proposals presented to the competition.

Architecture alone, without urban considerations, does not guarantee the solution. However, it forms part of the solution. An area intensively occupied with dwellings, services and facilities usually does not allow enough space at the ground floor level for open spaces. Three-dimensional considerations have therefore been taken into account by all the participants in the competition.

Some years ago Kazuyo Sejima argued in her "Metropolitan dwellings study" that high density and the corresponding high buildings did not preclude enjoying a personal open space. She developed different typologies of apartment buildings (with 70 square metre dwellings) that showed

Fig. 19 Spacematrix diagram

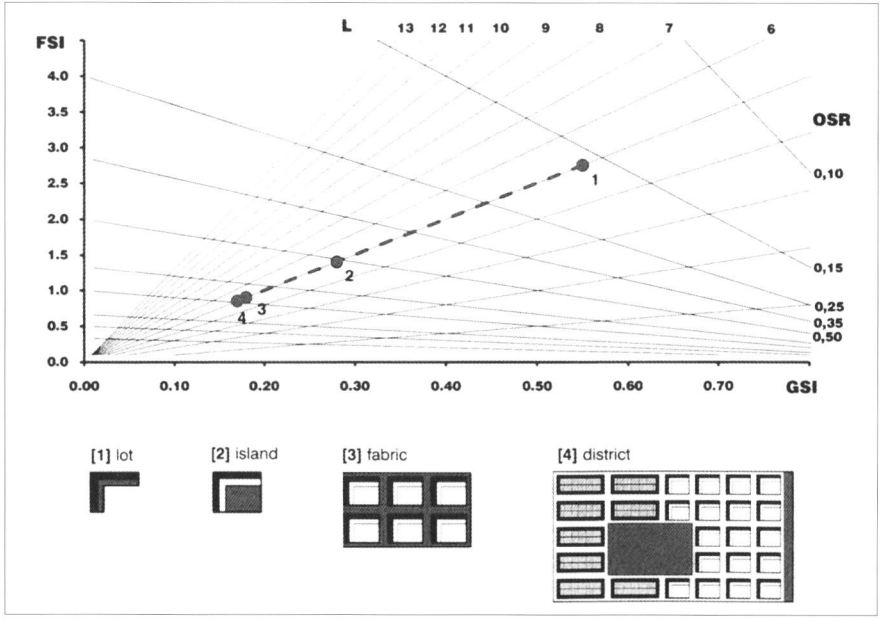

that even with high and narrow buildings that are quite close to one another, it was possible for all the units to obtain sunlight. Terraces of individual units appear like random holes in a flat volume, revealing glimpses of the landscape on the side of the block and reducing its monolithic quality. However, it should be highlighted that Kazuyo Sejima's proposals only achieved a gross density of 120 dwellings per hectare, which is one third of what Vertical Cities requires.

9. Density determines urban form

Scholars have argued that the use of density for anything but statistical purposes is questionable. Also, many professionals and researchers hold the opinion that density and other physical properties are independent of each other.

Having arrived to this point, one should consider the extraordinary rich research of Berghauser-Haupt. "Space, Density and Urban Form" demonstrates that urban density contains valuable information about important spatial propertiesm and has the potential to be effective in developing a method capable of simultaneously articulating quantity and quality (e.g. related to daylight access, parking, privacy and building types).

However, in order to do so, the concept of density has to gain in sophistication and complexity. In this sense, density should be considered a *multivariable* parameter, composed by three main indicators: intensity (FSI), compactness (GSI) and network density (N).[13] To discuss simultaneously these indicators, a three-dimensional diagram, the *Spacematrix*, has been proposed. The y-axis expresses the built intensity of a certain area; the x-axis indicates the compactness of the built environment; while the z-axis represents the network density, which is an indicator of the size of the urban layout. After analysing more than a hundred samples in their research, the outcomes show different regularities. For instance, the variety in profile widths is larger when the network density is lower; the samples with the highest network density mostly have narrow streets and islands that contain low-rise buildings; and wider streets are often accompanied by taller buildings.

The research concludes that by combining building and network densities, the performance of an area, in terms of daylight access, public parking, urbanity and privacy, changes substantially. In short, urban density conditions the performance of an urban fabric.

10. Summary

a Over centuries city builders have searched for the ideal form and dimensions of the city.

b Several recent research projects tried to find a relationship between the measures of urban parameters that ensure more efficient, healthier or even more beautiful cities.

c In our research, although ultimately we could not find the magical dimensions, we discovered some interesting regularities and identified some precise dimensions of street and block that assure better urban scores regarding health, efficiency or even beauty.

d In a broader and more complete interpretation, density really matters and a more sophisticated, multivariable definition of density determines urban form.

e Higher urban densities is an important (but not the only measure) that be required to face the main threats and challenges of our urban societies of the future

f The Vertical Cities Asia competition is seeks to extend these boundaries of the challenge by multiplying by three the densities our most intensive cities, without affecting their quality of life.

g Many students and scholars have been encouraged to "think outside of the box", and I am confident that the competition schemes will be a contribution to future urban planning proposals and decisions.

Notes

1 See Leslie Martin, Lionel March and MarcialEchenique, "Urban space and structures", Cambridge University Press, London (1972) or Meta Berghauser Pont and Per Haupt, "Space, Density and Urban Form". PhD dissertation, Technische Universiteit Delft. Delft (2009).

2 See among Plato writings , "The Republic" or the series of Dialogues.

3 Hippodamus of Miletos proposed some regular city layouts (Hippodamian grid) during the 5th century BC. He seems to be the originator of the idea that a town plan might formally embody and clarify a rational social order.

4 The bastides were usually fortified towns founded in the 13th century in south-west France, where some fine examples still remain. These medieval *new towns* were usually built to a strict grid layout, with equal space allocated to each house and had various functions, including improving security and safety of the residents and promoting trade. A central square often contained a market hall and sheltered arcades around the edges.

5 See mainly Joseph Stübben "Der Städtebau" (1890); Reinhard Baumeister "Stadterweiterungen in technischer, wirtschaftlicher und polizeilicher Hinsicht" (1876) and Rud Eberstadt "Handbuch des Wohnungswesens und der Wohnungsfrage" (1909).

6 Among other main treaties see his report on the first project for the Barcelona town extension (1855); "Teoría de la construcción de ciudades aplicada al proyecto de reforma y ensanche de Barcelona" Theory of city construction as applied to the Barcelona reform and town extension project, (1859); "Teoría general de la vialidad" (General road theory, 1863-67); "Teoría general de la urbanización" General theory of urbanisation, (1867).

7 A "bit" is an information unit that measures the amount of uncertainty that exists in the situation in which one has to choose between two possibilities; for each possible trajectory one bit is added.

8 See Berghauser and Haupt, op cit.

9 Raymond Unwin, "Town planning in practice: an introduction to the art of designing cities and suburbs", T. Fisher Unwin, London (1909).

10 Jane Jacobs, "The Death and Life of Great American Cities", Random House, Inc., New York (1961).

11 23 to Mexico and Guangzhou; 24 to São Paulo; 25 to Beijing and Manila; 32 to Shanghai; 39 to Jakarta, Kinshasa and Delhi; 42 to Karachi and Mumbai; 50 to Dhaka and 58 to Lagos.

12 Public transport covers 24 percent of the total movements towards working places in Shanghai, 55 percent in New York and 78 percent in Mexico. 15 percent of New Yorkers walk or cycle to their workplace, only 1 percent in Mexico, but 67 percent in Shanghai.

13 See Berghauser and Haupt, op cit.

Design Approach for High-Rise and High-Density Living in Tropical Asian Cities

WONG Mun Summ, Richard HASSELL and Alina YEO
WOHA Architects
Singapore

Asia's rapidly growing metropolis demands an alternative strategy on city planning and architecture that addresses the need to live well and sustainably with our climate and urban densities. This paper discusses WOHA's approaches in designing for high-rise, high-density living in tropical and sub-tropical regions. Several main themes that contribute to our key ideologies and design strategies will be identified from our on-going series of built and unbuilt projects. Based on these themes, possible approaches to the Vertical Cities Asia theme of "Fresh Air" will also be discussed.

Multi-Level Zoning & Club Sandwich (Layering) Approach
WOHA's exploration into multilevel zoning involves creative and innovative ways of intensifying land use via a 'club sandwich' approach. This not only results in richness and diversity of cross-programming, but also achieves the triple objectives of minimising the building's footprint, opening up the ground level for activity generators and maximising areas for facilities.

In *Design 2050*, WOHA spearheaded a vertical studio to develop a visionary masterplan for Singapore in the year 2050. The task that the studio posed themselves was to make Singapore safe from rising sea levels while shrinking the ecological footprint of the country to the size of the island. The projects tested new cross-programmed zoning and infrastructure, urban and architectural typologies to address the pressing issues of water, food and energy security. Proposals included residential power plants, multilevel factory / agri-villages, and resort dykes. Four different cross-programmed typologies (Sun City, Bay of Tides, East Coast Parkway, Jurong Plantations), each combining a seawall (the CPR refers to Coastal Protection Ring) with alternative energy harvesting (solar or tidal) and residential, industrial / commercial or leisure use, were explored. As outlined for the studio, hypothetical planning guidelines for all coastal plots of the island were developed, including elements like energy production, water rights, air rights, biodiversity index and ecosystem requirements.

WOHA's 'club sandwich' layering approach was fully demonstrated in our design of the *School of the Arts* (SOTA), Singapore's first specialist high school for the visual and performing arts. The school is unique in that it combines a high-density inner city school with a professional performing arts venue. WOHA's primary design strategy was to create two visually connected horizontal strata, a space for public communication below,

Fig. 1 Visionary Masterplan for Singapore 2050
Fig. 2 Bay of Tides
Fig. 3 Diagram of Agri-villages
Fig. 4 Sketch of Blank Canvas and Backdrop

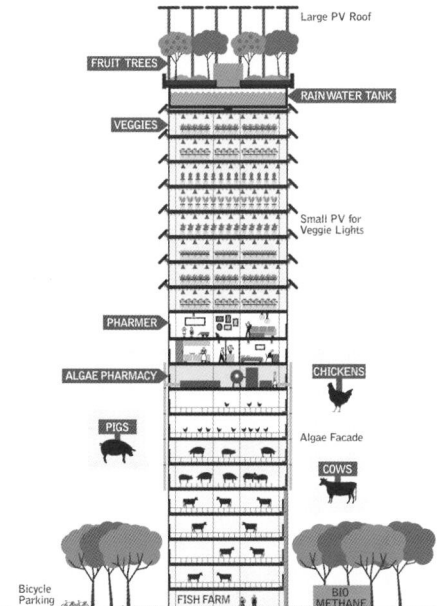

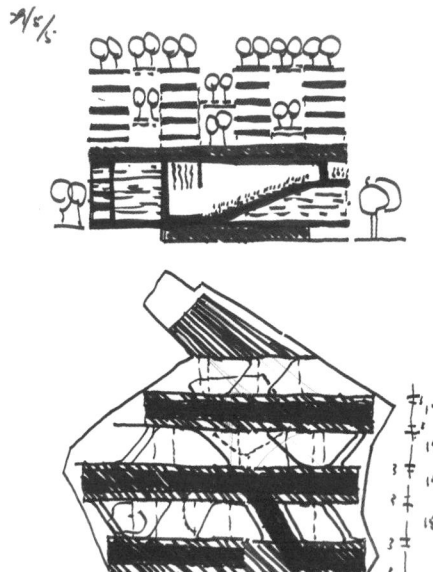

and a space for safe, controlled interaction above. This was achieved by stacking six storeys of academic blocks that we named the 'Blank Canvas', above a pedestal of performance venues that we named the 'Backdrop'. Locating the sports field on the roof top served to create as much recreation space in this dense development as would have been possible on an empty site. This organisational strategy solved the twin objectives of porosity and communication with the public and wider arts community on the one hand, and a secure and safe learning environment on the other.

Multiple Ground Levels

Given the increased stress on the ground level caused by the rapid growth of urban densities, WOHA's approach is to treat the ground plane as a duplicable layer of the city that needs to be replicated at strategic horizons within and between buildings in the sky. This involves the introduction of intermediate levels, comprising social as well as other public and civic functions that serve as multiple ground levels in the sky. The layering arrangement also creates opportunities to achieve dynamic visual links between the blocks/buildings and generates multiple covered tropical outdoor spaces.

WOHA's participation in the *Duxton Plain Singapore Public Housing* competition led to a thorough exploration of high density living. Concepts of 'sky streets' leading to 'sky parks', creating comfortable scaled public spaces in the sky, and a new relationship between the high-rise interior and exterior, were explored. Although unbuilt, the *Duxton Plain* proposal is an important precursor to the following projects.

In designing of *The Met*, a 66-storey high rise residential tower in densely populated Bangkok, WOHA developed a series of sky-gardens and inhabited external spaces as both public and private spaces in the sky. Community areas

Fig. 5   View of SOTA from Bras Basah Road
Fig. 6   Section through SOTA
Fig. 7   View of "Sky Streets" leading to "Sky Parks" from 40th floor
Fig. 8   Sketch showing multiple ground levels

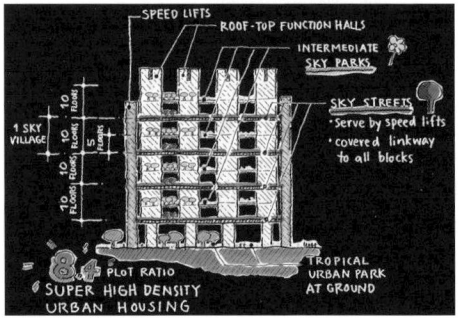

with covered walkways, open-air living areas, sky gardens, barbecue stations, library, fitness corners and recreational areas were created at strategic horizons every 20 storeys, giving all the residents access to high-level views and open-air communal terraces. Private gardens designed with swimming pools and terraces were also incorporated every six storeys, effectively creating miniature garden houses downtown, each with its own little plot in the air throughout the height of the tower.

Eight years after the *Duxton Plain* competition, WOHA had the opportunity to realise our ideas through the Dawson Estate Singapore public housing project that we were commissioned to undertake. In *SkyVille@Dawson*, every apartment in this 960-unit public housing development is designed to belong to an 80-unit "SkyVillage", which shares a common "Village Green". This is a planted common sky terrace every 11 floors, which is overlooked by the lift lobby and circulation spaces leading to each apartment. In this way, every inhabitant crosses a common space when entering or leaving their apartment, and can see the activities in the village green. Activities provided are for study areas, gathering areas, community gardens, play areas and potentially "sheds" for creative and entrepreneurial activities—a high-rise version of the backyard shed.

In SOTA, the academic upper stratum was organised into three long rectangular blocks. These were connected by dynamic visual and physical links, interaction nodes and sky terraces/bridges. WOHA maximised the potential of sky gardens and sky parks, creating a building with numerous tiers of garden decks, shady outdoor play areas and break-out spaces throughout its height, including the roof, which is imagined as a large sky park, complete with a running track bridging over the top of the academic blocks. The section of *SOTA* reveals how the major spaces slip and slide to create a connected series of vertical spaces that are open and airy, yet sheltered from the sun and rain.

Fig. 9   Views of The Met
Fig. 10 28th and 47th Storey Communal Terraces
Fig. 11 9th Storey Swimming Pool
Fig. 12 Section through SkyVille showing Sky Villages
Fig. 13 View from unit overlooking Sky Garden

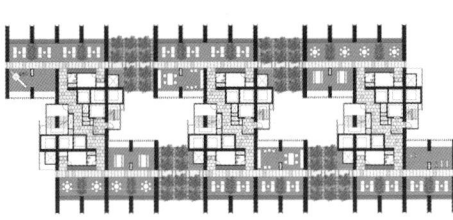

Porous, Permeable and Perforated Buildings

WOHA's key approach is to transform and adapt vernacular and passive responses to climate into the high-rise form and contemporary technolo-

Fig. 14   Dynamic visual links across academic blocks
Fig. 15   View of Roof Terrace
Fig. 16   View of Sky Terrace

gies, with the same aim of creating comfort without the need for mechanical systems. Through perforating the high rise façade with terraces, open spaces and breezeways, natural daylighting and cross ventilation are achieved, making tropical living without air-conditioning possible.

In *1 Moulmein Rise*, a 28-storey, 50-unit residential tower, WOHA developed an innovative "Monsoon Window" façade. The climate of Singapore lends itself to high-rise living that opens up to the environment,

rather than closing it off. However, the risk of torrential rain that is often accompanied by gusty winds is high. WOHA studied vernacular solutions to see if there was potential to adapt them for high-rise projects. The longhouses of Borneo were identified as an interesting precedent for the way they draw air into the space from below. WOHA's contemporary version of the "monsoon window" comprised of a projecting bay window that incorporated a sliding ledge which could be opened during cool weather to allow breezes in but keep the rain out.

The concept of opening up the high-rise, enabling it to breathe within a mega-city, was championed in *The Met*, a building with plot ratio of 10:1, comprising of six towers configured in two staggered rows. This staggered block arrangement and the spaces between them meant that all apartments had access to light and air on all four sides. The perforated configuration also served to carve out breezeways in the interior of the

Fig. 17 View of Moulmein Rise
Fig. 18 Traditional windows of Borneo longhouses
Fig. 19 Interior view of 'monsoon window'
Fig. 20 Illustration of breezeways through staggered block arrangement
Fig. 21 View of opening between blocks

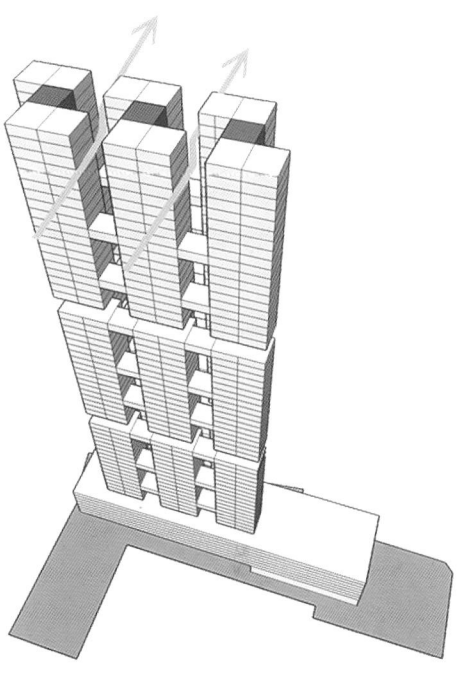

Fig. 22 Designed for cross-ventilation and natural daylighting to every classroom
Fig. 23 Naturally ventilated public concourse
Fig. 24 Cantilevering academic blocks over the urban plaza of SOTA

building, cooling it from inside. Consequently, natural daylight and cross-ventilation is achieved for all apartments, encouraging sustainable tropical living.

In the case of SOTA, the school environment is simple, practical, bright, airy and is designed for maximum flexibility and sustainability. Single-room-thick design allowed cross ventilation to every classroom and the campus to function effectively with or without air-conditioning, and with natural light to all areas. The breezeways in-between the academic blocks were designed for maximum comfort and interaction, allowing students to observe activities happening across the voids, and providing spaces for different sized groups to interact and relax, without leaving the secure environment of the school. The section was designed to catch the breezes and direct them to gathering spaces, while providing shelter from sun and rain. The wind-directing design has proved to be successful and extremely comfortable, with constant cooling breezes even in Singapore's low wind environment.

This concept of permeability was taken further in WOHA's competition entry for the hostel and recreational plot of the *Singapore University of Technology and Design, SUTD* (unbuilt). In this scheme, the student accommodation blocks were developed in response to the sun path and wind patterns of the site. To minimise solar heat gain and maximise natural ventilation, the student hostels were predominantly orientated north-south facing, while all the building ends were orientated to act as natural

Fig. 25 Perspective of elevated accommodation blocks from the sports field
Fig. 26 Aerial view of hostel and laboratory blocks
Fig. 27, 28 Views of "Breeze Canopies" over the "Activity Terrain"

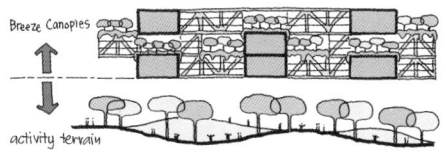

breezeways, funnelling the prevailing winds through the site and under the elevated buildings.

Tropical Community Spaces

WOHA actively seeks to engage buildings in a dialogue with the city and wider community through the liberation of the ground plane for activity generators, creating delightful people spaces designed specifically for the tropics.

In SOTA, extended cantilevers of the academic blocks and the retained large conserved trees create a generous tropical urban plaza that is covered yet breezy. The ground plane is sculpted into a landscape of stairs, platforms and city stages, creating an exciting multi-level space for students and the public to inhabit, offering multiple possibilities for performance and viewing. The public concourse is fully cross-ventilated, lofty and breezy, without any defined boundary fences.

In *SUTD*, the student accommodation, designed as breeze catchers, was envisaged as a wide network of interconnected branches stemming from a series of core circulation trunks, collectively forming a large urban umbrella over the activity terrain of the ground level, providing it with much needed shade and shelter for the tropics. This active combination of wind and shade offered by the "Breeze Canopies", created a delightful, comfortable, tropical environment conducive for student life to sprout and flourish.

Fig. 29-31 SOTA's green façade

Vertical Greenery

WOHA believes that landscape is an important element both from a sustainability point of view and for the end-user's enjoyment. Vegetation is an important part of the material palette for WOHA's high-rise buildings, both internally and externally, thus improving the environmental quality on both the local and city scale.

Part of the design brief of *SOTA* called for opportunities for students and staff to experience and encounter elements of nature given the school's urban setting and its location at what was previously a green field. In response to the brief, WOHA developed a green façade system utilising simple, low-cost technology—deep planters, aluminium expended mesh, and an automatic irrigation system. The green facades act as environmental filters, cutting out glare and dust, keeping the rooms cool, dampening traffic noise, and adding visual interest as these organic facades continue to grow over seasons. The planters are located off walkways, which allow for easy access and maintenance of the plants. The green relief also provides psychological comfort from the harsh urban environment, creating a vertical parkscape that offers pause points of inspiration for staff and students en-route their daily routine.

In *Newton Suites*, a 36-storey residential tower, WOHA achieved 130 percent Green Plot Ratio (counting both horizontal and vertical planted elements) on a dense urban site. Since this achievement at *Newton Suites*, the planning authorities of Singapore have enacted a regulation requiring all new buildings in the central area of Singapore to achieve a green plot ratio of 100 percent over their horizontal surfaces. Landscaping was incorporated from concept level in every possible location—at the ground level, at the carpark podium, at the common lift lobbies, on the vertical walls, and within the private units. The most eye-catching elements are the green walls and the cantilevered gardens. Using a similar green wall system as SOTA, *Newton Suites* features a continuous wall of Thumbergia flowering

Fig. 32–34 Views of Newton Suite's green wall and Sky Gardens

creepers throughout the entire height of the tower. The device succeeds due to the practicality of its implementation, which is located adjacent to an external staircase that enables the planters to be assessed at every level for maintenance, behind the metal mesh. The cantilevered sky gardens are common spaces that project off the lift lobbies at every four storeys. All the lift lobbies are naturally ventilated spaces that overlook these gardens. The gardens incorporate fountains, trees and planting, together with a small bench for sitting. As a trade-off on cost, WOHA convinced the developer that fewer lifts would be tolerable, as waiting time perception is not absolute, but depends instead on the interest of the surroundings. As every lobby overlooks the garden and view, the increase of 20 seconds in waiting time passes without notice.

The landscaping theme has been taken even further in WOHA's design of *ParkRoyal on Pickering* (under construction) that achieves a Green Plot Ratio of 206 percent. Sited along the entire length of Hong Lim Park, on a narrow linear site, the entire façade of the office and hotel building is conceptualized as a vertical extension of the park. A visually striking contoured podium is sculpted to create lofty outdoor plazas, walkways and gardens which flow seamlessly into dramatic interior spaces. The contours conceal raised carparking, melding into lushly planted openings, crevasses, gullies and waterfalls thus creating an attractive urban element. The crisp and streamlined tower blocks harmonize with surrounding high-rise office buildings. They have lofty sky gardens which bring lush greenery to the rooms and internal spaces. Most of the guest room corridors are naturally ventilated and are replete with landscaping and water features creating an alluring resort feeling with natural light and fresh air. Tall overhangs work together with leafy foliage to screen these spaces from the weather and direct sun. The lush greenery is not only visually attractive but also offers environmental relief to its urban built up surroundings. The project demonstrates how architectural design can be

Fig. 35–37 Views of ParkRoyal's lush greenery

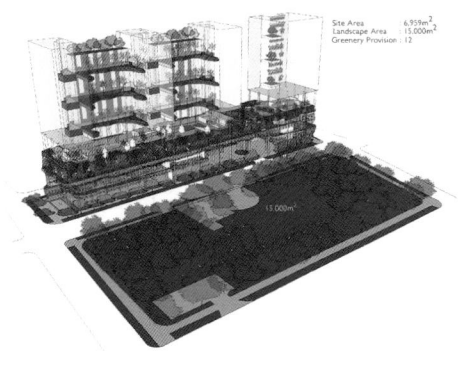

holistic, sustainable and unique, creating a strong product and branding for the developer, an attractive workplace and destination for the traveller, and also a striking and refreshing addition to the city.

Humanistic Approach

Large developments are alienating in many ways. The challenge of high-rise towers is the design for quality of external spaces that emphasizes on the individual in terms of human scale, choice, comfort, while opening up to the climate, community spaces and nature. As tall buildings scale and human scale are vastly different, WOHA constantly investigates the quality of external spaces in high-rise towers.

Duxton Plain, 50-storey buildings inserted into a three storey historic district, particularly surfaced the issue, and was a pivotal building in the firm's oeuvre due to the solutions proposed. The project took the scale of the neighbourhood's fine historic shophouse and four- to five-storey public housing blocks of the 1950s and 60s into the large development. However, when spaces that worked at three storeys, such as the neighbourhood street width, were extruded to 50 storeys, the scale became an inhuman vertical slot, rather than a charming well-proportioned imageable street. To avoid this problem, the vertical slots were divided with horizontal gardens every five floors, creating more stable proportions, which evoke a feeling of comfort, rather than dynamism.

Similarly, *SkyVille* with its intermediate Sky Villages at every 11 storeys takes its proportions and scale from the ubiquitous ten storey housing blocks at Tanglin Halt area, the memory of which is firmly tied to the history of Queenstown. The six storey sky garden divisions of *The Met*, likewise, take its cue from the scale of the postwar Bangkok buildings that surrounds it.

Through empowering owners with individual choices, WOHA also constantly seeks to develop ways in which the individual can be expressed in collective housing. In *1 Moulmein Rise*, WOHA developed a system of climate-modifying façade modules—overhangs, planters, bay windows, sliding windows and sunscreens, which could be rearranged in myriad ways to provide variety. Three different façade designs were developed,

Fig. 38–39 Scale of Duxton Plain, sky gardens every five floors
Fig. 40   Scale of The Met, sky gardens every six floors

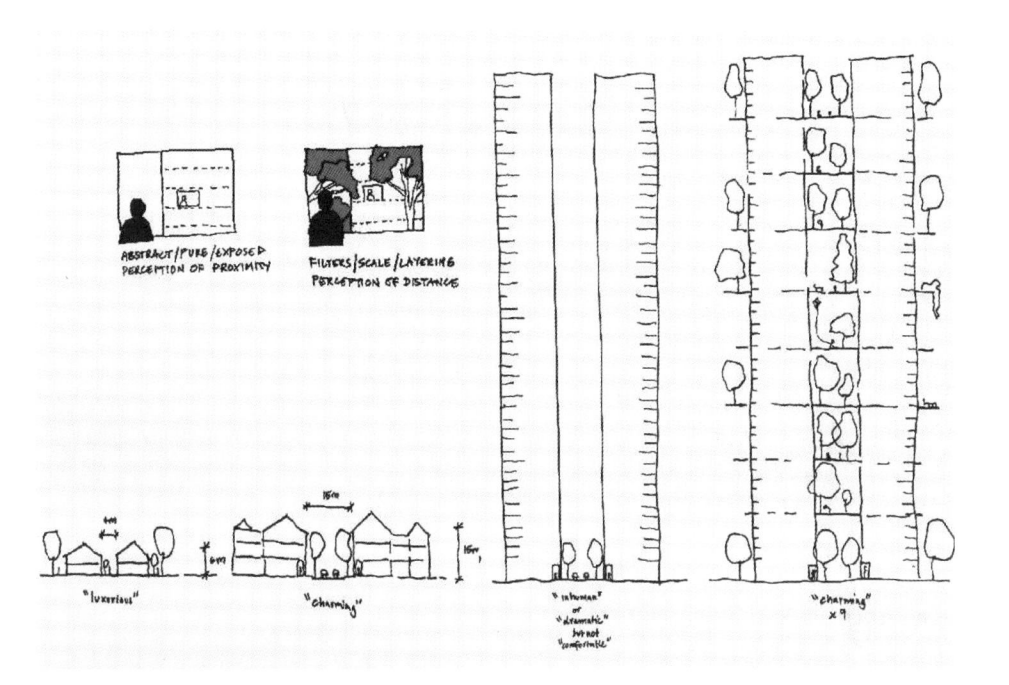

which were then stacked up in a random arrangement. The façade gives the impression of high variation.

In the *Duxton Plain* Public Housing competition, rather than the appearance of variation, the idea was to give individuals real choice in determining their interface with the exterior. WOHA proposed a system of regular façade modules, where buyers could select full height windows, bay windows, storage modules, planters, blank walls—as they saw fit. The idea worked due to the large scale of the project and the small size of the module—each façade component was equivalent to a pixel in an image, and the façade design would in effect be a portrait of the inhabitants and exactly match the population's preferences for openness, privacy and plants.

In *Skyville*, this system was proposed, but was removed due to logistic issues with the sales and tender process. However, another form of individual choice was implemented in the form of floor plans where the buyer has the choice of layouts. This includes a 'flexible unit' where buyers can layout internal walls in a beam free, column free space to suit their lifestyle needs. It is the first time the public housing authority in Singapore has sold such units.

Fig. 41 Proposed façade treatment and Life Cycle unit plans for Duxton Plain
Fig. 42 Façade treatment of Moulmein Rise
Fig. 43 Flexible unit floor plans of SkyVille

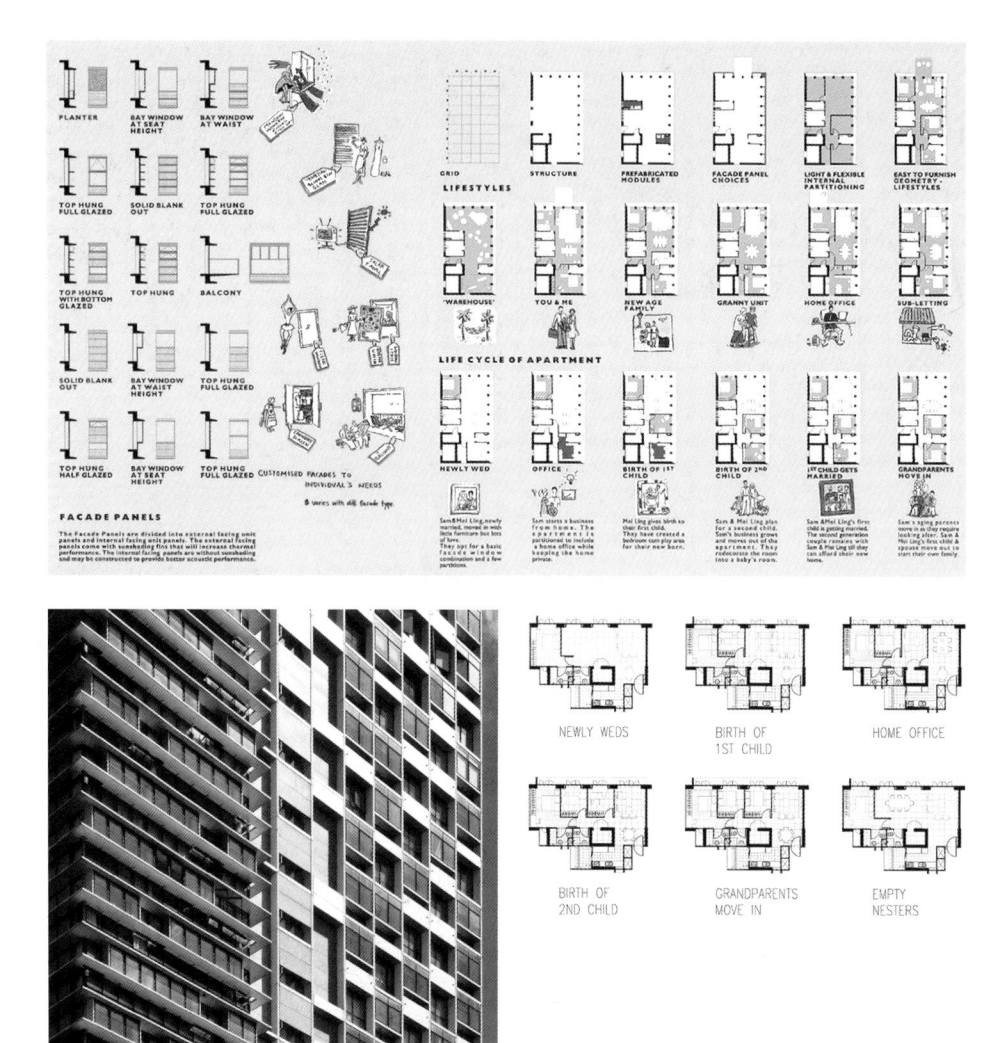

Vertical Cities Asia: Permeable Lattice City

The competition brief of Vertical Cities Asia specified a population density of 100,000 people within a 1 square kilometre (km²) site. Based on this brief, WOHA conducted an exercise in urban densities. Our comparison of the inner city centre densities of Manhattan, Hong Kong and Singapore demonstrated that it would take the equivalent of four stacks of Manhattan City or 4 stacks of Hong Kong central district or nine stacks of Singapore's city centre to achieve a population density of 100,000 people on each 1 km² site. In other words, at the competition brief's urban density, it would take a city footprint of about 15 km² (as compared to 59 km²) to contain Manhattan's 1,585,873 urban population[1], 70 km² (as compared to 275 km²) to contain Hong Kong's 7,030,000 urban population, and 52 km² (as compared to 466 km²) to contain Singapore's 5,115,000 urban population.[2]

1 KM² of MANHATTAN = 26,879 PEOPLE
4 MANHATTANS = 100,000 PEOPLE

MANHATTAN, NEW YORK
15 KM² = 1,585,873 PEOPLE

Taking Dubai's Burj Khalifa, the world's current tallest building that has a project area[3] of 454,249 square metre (m²) as the reference point for high density urban living, we derived that it would require 15 numbers of Burj Khalifas to house 100,000 residents. Since the competition brief's "live" component of the vertical city is specified to make up 50 percent of the total floor space, it is expected that twice this many Burj Khalifas (total 30 nos.) would be needed to meet the "live-work-play" brief of the vertical city. Within the confines of a 1 km² site, this would translate into 3.3 tiers of Burj Khalifas stacked vertically.

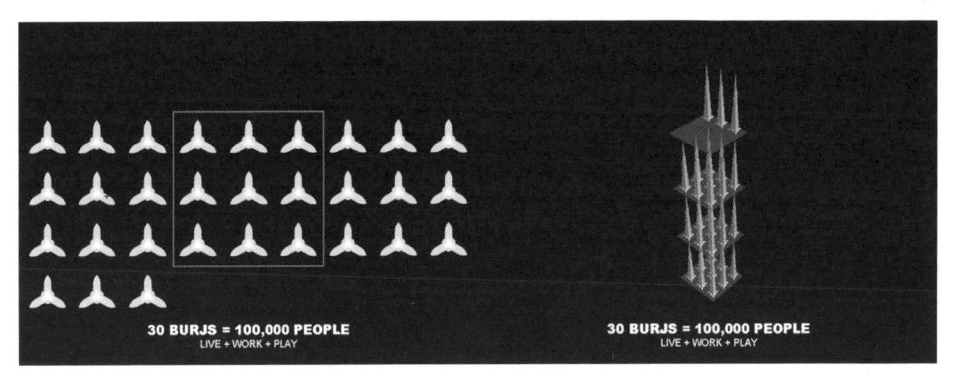

30 BURJS = 100,000 PEOPLE
LIVE + WORK + PLAY

30 BURJS = 100,000 PEOPLE
LIVE + WORK + PLAY

Instead of the sealed glass curtain wall tower typology of skyscrapers that works for temperate and harsh climates, we tested out our tropical high-rise high-density themes based on the model of *The Met* that champions sustainable passive design strategies. With a project area of about 100,000 m² and an estimated personal space of 50 m²/person, *The Met* can accommodate up to about 1,500 residents. A vertical city with a population density of 100,000 would therefore require 67 numbers of *The Met* for its "live" component, and double this quantum (total 134 numbers) for "live-work-play". Within the confines of a 1 km² site, this would translate into three tiers of *The Met* stacked vertically.

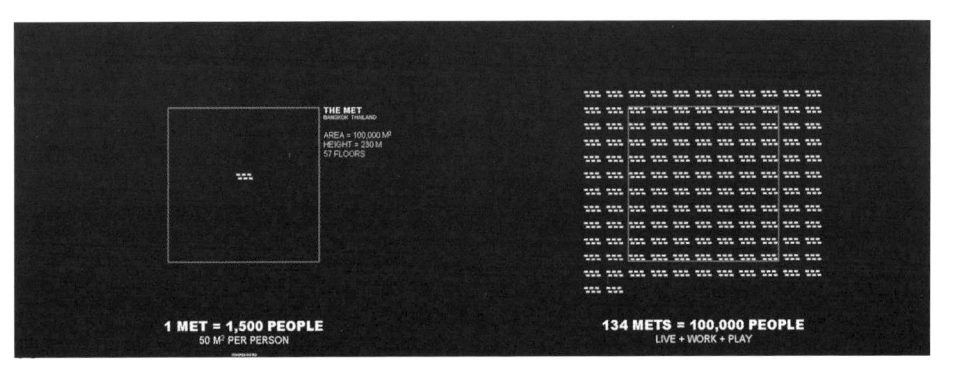

THE MET
BANGKOK, THAILAND
AREA = 100,000 M²
HEIGHT = 230 M
57 FLOORS

1 MET = 1,500 PEOPLE
50 M² PER PERSON

134 METS = 100,000 PEOPLE
LIVE + WORK + PLAY

By devising a one km² city grid with a population density of 111,111 people, we were subsequently able to test this at larger urban scales. Ideologically, we envision a vertical 'Permeable Lattice City' that uses modules of *The Met* as 'City Columns'. These are similarly arranged in a staggered alignment to create a high degree of perforation and porosity resulting in cross-ventilated breezeways at city scale, ensuring fresh air and natural daylighting reaches every part of the inner city. Based on minimal building footprint, these 'City Columns' serve to free up the real ground level for nature reserves, heavy industries, etc, are held together structurally by a network of 'City Conduits' that serve as elevated ground levels, woven socially by layers of "City Community Spaces" and vertically interconnected by multi-cabin lifts and other forms of people mover vertical circulation systems.

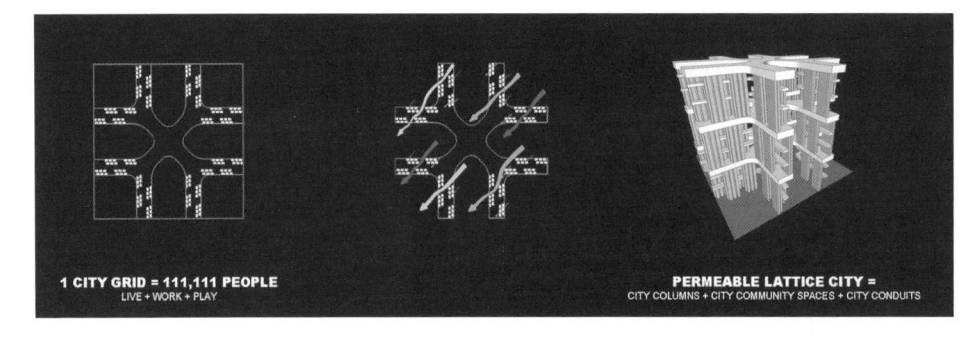

1 CITY GRID = 111,111 PEOPLE
LIVE + WORK + PLAY

PERMEABLE LATTICE CITY =
CITY COLUMNS + CITY COMMUNITY SPACES + CITY CONDUITS

As a basic module, the city grid has the capacity to be extended seamlessly and endlessly in any direction. To test out a population density of one million people, we superimposed nine city grids over Zocalo, the main town square in Mexico City and along South Sathorn Road, the main artery in Bangkok City, to illustrate its impact with the existing city fabric and infrastructure. This was further tested for a city of five million people —a second Singapore—made up of 45 city grids (footprint of 45km²) on Pulau Semakau and its neighbouring islands.

BANGKOK
PERMEABLE LATTICE CITY OF 1 MILLION

Ultimately, this exercise in urban densities suggests that by forming layers of stacked 'live-work-play' communities, introducing multiple elevated ground levels at strategic horizons that relieves the real (existing) ground level, creating openness and porosity between towers that facilitates cross-ventilation of fresh air and natural daylighting, crafting out varying scales of tropical community spaces that encourages social interaction, applying vertical greenery and designing sensitively for human scale, a super dense vertical city can be both highly sustainable and livable, without compromising on the quality of living, if such alternative strategies to city planning and architecture are embraced.

Notes

1 http://en.wikipedia.org/wiki/Manhattan

2 http://en.wikipedia.org/wiki/List_of_urban_areas_by_population

3 http://www.som.com/content.cfm/burj_khalifa

Gridding Manhattan

Alan BALFOUR
Professor and Dean
College of Architecture, Georgia Institute of Technology
Atlanta

The vertical city of the future will result from a combination constraining regulation and economic pressure—architecture, though important, will be a by-product, a secondary effect. The essential structure within which all elements of the vertical city were formed—political, legal, economic and topological—was the conscious creation of a small group of men in New York State in the first decade on the nineteenth century. It was formed as a wholly abstract rational ideal through which to destroy the character and ambitions of a land owning aristocracy, and by which to encourage a culture of open-ended speculation. The success of which continues unabated into the present.

The physical reality of Manhattan emerges from two distinct structures: gridding the island, the climacteric act of the eighteenth century republican enlightenment and, almost in opposition, the creation of Central Park, the greatest work of bourgeois idealism in the nineteenth century. These were products of changing political and social orders as the emerging republic sought to form a new reality.

Manhattan: The Commissioner's Plan
Between 1811 and 1821 a team of men laboured to impose a new order onto the surface of Manhattan Island. Their task took them through the extensive wilderness in the interior of the island and on to the many private estates and farms that had grown along the water's edge for 100 years and more. The task of the team was to drive into the earth 1,549 white marble markers, each 3 feet 3 inches long and 3 inches square, and each separately engraved with the numbers of the intersecting streets and avenues that would cross these points and redefine the city. And when they came upon rock they hammered order into the bare stone with 98 iron bolts, the street numbers forged on to *the meta*l. They were led by a young surveyor, John Randel Junior, who was the author of this most radical of city plans.

Imagine the conceptual force of this act. The colonial city with its late medieval street pattern ran barely a mile north of the fortified southern point of the island.

The ten miles and more of Manhattan Island north of the colonial town was a mixture of forests and rocky ridges, with ancient farms and small settlements along the shoreline. The hills and dales of the interior formed many small valleys whose streams flowed into ponds and extensive marshes. Forcing a marble and iron trace of order across a rural

Fig. 1   New Amsterdam 1680/1700
Fig. 2   New York 1800
Fig. 3   The Manhattan countryside 1820
Fig. 4   A village on Manhattan in the 1830s

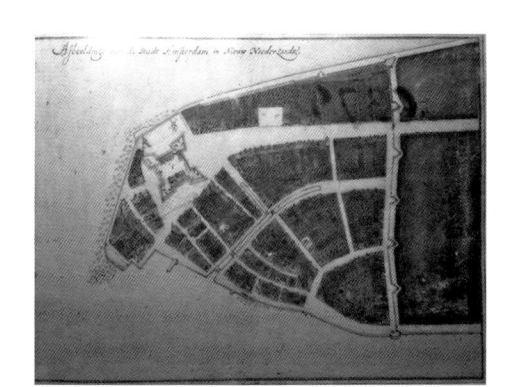

and wild landscape had to be done with axe and scythe, in the face of persistent hostility from landowners, hunters and squatters.

It is too easily forgotten that this ruthless marking of a new order was the product of the modern world's most successful revolution. The signatories of the Declaration of Independence immediately faced the problem of devising the means to achieve social cohesion in the new republic. They were all children of European monarchies, which maintained order from the top down through the structures of rigid class systems, reinforced by standing armies and by a Church that observed the divine right of kings. The new republic had no such structures. It had to invent arrangements that would be driven, with equality, from the bottom up and expected its citizens to take up arms to defend their country and sacrifice private desire for the public good. Such reliance on the moral virtue of their citizens made republican governments fragile. The answer would lie in the application of just and neutral law to all things.

The need to plan for the future of the city was recognized in the first decade of the century with the feverish rise in its expectation of commercial growth. In 1804 the New York Common Council gave instructions that a plan be prepared "for new streets to be laid out and opened". In 1807 the state legislature appointed a streets commission to propose a plan for laying out "streets, roads, public squares of such extent and direction as to them shall seem most conducive to public good". It was to do so in such a manner "as to unite regularity and order with Public convenience and benefit, and in particular to promote the health of the city" by allowing for the 'free and abundant circulation of air'. The recommendations of the Street Commission, which

Fig. 5   The Randel plan 1811

included Gouverneur Morris, major author of the Constitution of the United States and Simeon De Witt, surveyor general of New York State, would have the force of law. In the light of what is to follow, note that 'Public' is an idea of such significance that it must be capitalized; it had replaced the Crown as the ruling authority.

The first task was to carry out an accurate survey of the island. The person chosen to do this, John Randel Junior was still in his early twenties and had been surveyor to General Simeon De Witt. He aimed not only to produce a survey "with an accuracy not exceeded by any work of its kind in America", but also one that blended with Manhattan's topography. He wrote, "I superintended the surveys with a view to ascertain the most eligible grounds for the intended streets and avenues, with reference to the sites least obstructed by rocks, precipices, and steep grades and other obstacles." This suggests he was initially considering a plan, which would sit gently on the rocky landscapes of the island; the results could not have been more different.

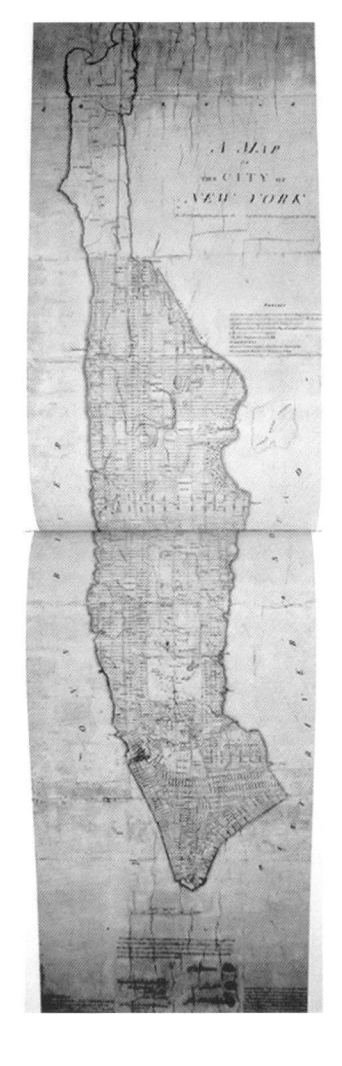

Randel reported regularly to the Commissioners, for whom the form of the plan was a matter of deep concern. The record reflects their discussion as to "whether they should confine themselves to rectilinear and rectangular streets, or whether they should adopt some of these supposed improvements, by circles, or ovals, and stars". Randel's survey was completed in 1810. It provided a scientific mapping of the coastline and a detailed delineation of the topography and water flows of the island. It showed an island essentially unchanged since the Ice Age, a rocky and forested wedge, 4 miles at its widest and 12 miles long. The Commissioners determined, with Randel's advice, that a hard and constant grid would be the appropriate order in which to layout a comprehensive and permanent system of streets on the island. Their reason: "They could not but bear in mind that a city is to be composed principally of the habitations of men, and that straight sided and right angle houses are the most cheap to build and the most convenient to live in." They determined that this future city would consist of 12 north–south avenues, each 100 feet wide and, at intervals of 200 feet, 155 cross streets, each 60 feet wide. The Act that had created the commission made its decision "the final and conclusive law unalterable except by state action". The grid, though vastly disruptive, was accepted without debate. Thus New York City became bounded by 'one grand permanent plan'.

Randel was requested to engrave this sweeping rational order on to the plate of his just completed survey. The resulting drawing, 106 inches by 30 inches, was printed in 1811 and henceforth was known as the 'Commissioners' Plan'. In the months that followed its publication each permutation of the 12 by 155 grid was carefully carved into marble posts and forged into the iron bolts that Randel forced into the land to establish the new order. Forcing this abstract order of reason on to the surface of the island seems a dramatically modern act. Nature mastered without compromise. Man's intellect dominant – projecting on to the island an utterly rational absolute future. The Commissioners' order to stake out the ground with the coordinates is a measure of how firmly they believed that rational order would determine the future, setting the boundaries for freedom within reason. They were not unaware of the force of their proposal. They wrote that the plan provided space enough 'for a greater population than is collected at any spot on this side of China'. Its ruthlessness still shocks. The vast composite structure, which fills the island of Manhattan in the absolute conviction that it was right. It continues to exert its compounding intensity and strangeness on the culture of the city.

At the time of the Commissioners' Plan New York had lost all political power, yet even before the clear emergence of the Industrial Revolution in America the city's leaders believed it capable of powerful commercial growth. The increase in the city's foreign trade after 1790 led one newspaper to predict that New York's population could grow to 700,000 by 1850 and reach three million by the end the nineteenth century. The plan was necessary to control a city that would evolve through commercial enterprise. It was realized that a city based purely on commerce—a new idea—should be formed free from distortions of political, religious or aristocratic power to provide the appropriate field for commercial action. Indeed, Randel was later to write that his plan heightened opportunities for "buying, selling and improving real estate". The Commissioners, though, argued that to have taken the grid beyond 155th Street would have led to speculation beyond reason!

Conceptualization on such a scale has no parallel in the history of cities. In 1803 Joseph Françoise Mangin and Casimer Goerick had developed a plan for the future Manhattan which, unlike the commissioners' plan, proposed clearly distinct densities of grids for the various needs of the emerging city—health, recreation, commerce, and community—but the commissioners would have none of this. Like the proposed Erie Canal, which become the greatest engineering project from the first half of the nineteenth century, and created the wealth that drove the development on the city, the planning of Manhattan was seen as an 'internal improvement' that gloried in the supremacy of technique over topography. The same rational determination that drove the building of the canal was present in the grid, the same men and the same revolutionary spirit.

Because the city had lost political influence the plan made no attempt to anticipate future centres of power. In the new republic neither gods nor kings would command any special place. For the first time a city was conceived as a de-centred and univalent field of enterprise. The only power in its future would be commerce. The plan, however, did have two specific designations of use. One plot of land high on the west side was, in enlightened fashion, 'concentrated for the purpose of science'. And the largest clear area in the grid, just north of Greenwich Village, was designated The Parade. This was a nation still under constant military threat from Britain.

In *Gotham*, Edwin G Burrows and Mike Wallace argue that the grid established Republican as well as realtor values in its refusal to privilege particular places or parcels. All plots were equal under the commissioners' regime and the network of parcels and perpendiculars provided a Democratic alternative to the royalist avenues of Baroque European cities. The shift from naming streets to numbering them, beyond promoting efficiency also embodied a lexicographical levelling; no longer would families of rank and fortune memorialize themselves in the cityscape.

The plan asserted republican order over lingering Tory tendencies among the old families, and the royalist landscapes along the river's edge. It forced equality not only by the discipline of the grid, but by the small size of the lots. It was the pressure of ambition on the small lots that forced Manhattan into the sky. The plan was a new beginning.

The configuration of Manhattan Island allowed for a plan that was wholly internal to itself; there were no major roads crossing it and no favoured link to any of the surrounding lands. The attempt to remove the only major historic route north through the island, now named Broadway, failed: usage proved more powerful than the law, but only in this one case. With the increasing pace of street openings Broadway alone resisted submersion beneath the gridiron, and continues to this day to give complexity and texture to the monotonous walls of the grid.

The gridiron has lost none of its control on the reality and on the political, social and economic forces that led to its adoption. These remain embedded in its continual evolution. Place yourself in the minds of those commissioners advocating in public a plan without charm, without centre, without bias. In this, and consciously so, it is the antithesis of the European city. The European city reinforcing and flattering the powers of Church and Crown structured to demonstrate hierarchies of power; structured to resist change. The new American city ordered to allow continual change in a structure of constant order, a neutral field for the public pursuit of commercial enterprise; structured to constrain all ambition in a frame of reason. The neutrality, the lack of emotion is almost painful. This city will be a tough place.

Randel engraved the final Commissioners' Plan in 1821. It is beautifully drawn with faint echoes of Piranesi. It depicts three superimposed

Fig. 6   Randel's final plan 1821

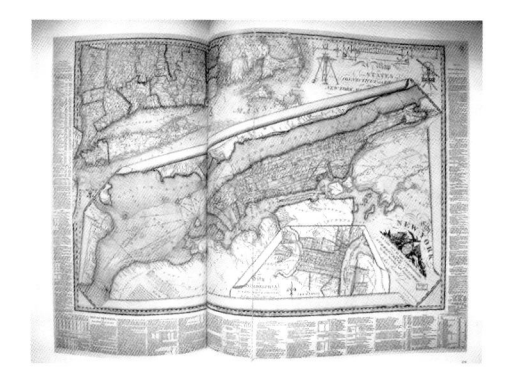

maps. At the top it is a small map of New York State, across the centre is the great grid plan and across the bottom, in a *trompe l'oeil* effect suggesting an unrolled drawing dropped below the main work, is a small plan of Philadelphia which was laid out by William Penn in 1683. Randel in offering this venerable plan as evidence of the historical use of the grid could have been attempting to diffuse criticism. But more than that he was presenting the new Manhattan as a direct descendant of Penn's noble plan for Philadelphia.

The plan has never ceased to be attacked. Influential Classics Professor at Columbia, Clark Moore, wrote in 1824 that, "the great principle which governs these plans is, to reduce the surface of the earth as nearly as possible to dead level. The natural inequities of the ground are destroyed, and the existing watercourses disregarded. These are men— who would have cut down the Seven Hills of Rome". He resented the plan because of its impact on his extensive property in Manhattan but subsequently and successfully developed his land within the rules of the grid, to become the area that is now Chelsea. Edgar Allan Poe complained that the grand plan limited the picturesque development of the city because "streets were already mapped through areas that may have different potential." Poe was much concerned with the plan's levelling effect on the society. "The great uniformity in the breadth and circumstances of the streets" failed to produce a variety "which is necessary for the adequate habitations of classes, differing extremely in opulence, but must be found united in the population of a great city." The overly democratic or neutral character of the grid was a persistent concern. Burrows and Wallace quote citizen William Duer who complained that the commissioners, "had swung the scythe of equality across the island replacing the country estates of the privileged classes with block after democratic block, no one necessarily better than any other, each equally exposed to the ebb and flow of the market."

The architectural historian Vincent Scully wrote in recent decades that the 'implacable gridiron' created a frame to support the American tendency towards private luxury and public squalor. John Reps, the most passionate recorder of the American city, wrote that, "the fact that the gridiron served as a model for later cities was a disaster whose consequences have barely been mitigated by recent city planners". Lewis Mumford, the wise defender of social democracy, wrote that Randel "with a T-square and a triangle—the municipal engineer, without the slightest training as either an architect or a sociologist could "plan" a metropolis". He summed it up as "civic folly". Given the plan's radical egalitarianism, this is a very bourgeois view from such an old lefty.

The grid would provide the frame within which this new democ-

Fig. 7   The new city emerges, Manhattan 1859

racy would advance, a neutral field that would protect, but not interfere with, individual rights. The grid would unify ambition within a frame of reason. It would manifest public order. It would bind all ambitions and anxieties and oppositions into a coherent whole. The grid would be both the least and the most public interference with private enterprise. The grid would be in the exact sense the public realm. Such a political concept suggests a desire either for unity or intellectual dictatorship. As the result of a tactic designed to produce uniformity of opportunity, New York has become a city of factions or fiefdoms, each centre of power playing out a highly idiosyncratic game exaggerated by the constraint of the grid.

The Commissioners' Plan was directly paralleled by the national plans that not only determined the boundaries of states but also laid the virtual reality of a grid over thousands of miles of undeveloped heartland, which it subdivided to structure the commercial, educational and civic order of community. Even now, as can be seen from the air over the Midwest, this desire for order marks lines for miles across the cornfields, and most roads are on the Cartesian grid.

With Randel's marble stakes as a guide the geometric pattern of streets was slowly engraved on the land. There was ample compensation for landowners whose property was being brought within city order. They were free to develop their land but only within the constraints of the grid. An observer wrote in the 1830s that none of Manhattan's ancient hills, dales, swamps, springs, streams, palms, forests and meadows would be permitted to interrupt the fearful symmetry of the grid. The Common Council, entrusted with establishing the new order, was empowered to demolish and remove any streets that stood in the path of the gridiron. Thus the Bowery village laid out in 1779 on a true north-south grid was slowly removed as Third Avenue cut through the city.

The rule of law did not last long and, predictably in a great commercial city, the development of land became an increasingly competitive. It was driven by the rapid growth of road and rail links east through the independent cities of Brooklyn and Queens on to Long Island and north into the Bronx. Gradually, the unity that was demanded by the grid faded as the public realm became the commercial realm. This was a gradual shift and, as it evolved, the need to give significance to an American idea of society became more emblematic.

Fig. 8　The grid moves up the island Manhattan 1870
Fig. 9　Speculation in the 1870s
Fig. 10　Broadway in the 1880s

Fifty years after embedding the grid into the soil of Manhattan the city forced into it a new element: Central Park. Central Park is a miracle that gains its grandeur from being both a complement, and an opposition, to the grid. Its natural-seeming landscapes are made glorious within an intense and rigid frame. Although the essential difference between grid and park is a product, in some measure, of the random forces of history, it is a beautiful reflection of both a shift in the politics of order and in *the met*aphysics of the Western cultural imagination: eighteenth century reason, cold and disciplined, ensuring order through the force of law; nineteenth century civic society trusting in human nature and sensibility to maintain social harmony—the park would bring out the best in people and can be seen as the most sympathetic stage on which to enhance the natural harmony of society. Both aspects seem present in Thomas Paine's pamphlet Common Sense (1776), while government promotes our happiness only "negatively by restraining our vices, society promotes our happiness positively by uniting our affections". Grid as government and the park as society are exquisitely thesis and antithesis: one could not have been created without the other.

The first important public expression of a major inadequacy in the Commissioners' Plan came in editorials by William Cullen Bryant in the New York Evening Post. Although the matter had been long in his thoughts it was first publicly expressed in July 1844: "If the public authority who spend so much of our money in laying out the city would do what is in their power, they might give our vast population an extensive pleasure ground for shade and recreation." The commissioners had admitted that their plan made little provision for public space: "It may be a matter of surprise that so few vacant spaces had been left [open in the plan] and those so small, for the benefit of fresh air and consequent preservation of health." The note continued: "Certainly, if New York had been situated alongside a small stream, such as the Seine or Thames," it might have needed more ample public space". "But those large arms of the sea which embrace Manhattan Island render its situation, in

Fig. 11 Crystal Palace, Sydenham, Joseph Paxton 1854

regard to health and pleasure, as well as to the convenience of commerce, peculiarly felicitous." Not so, thought Bryant.

The leaders of mid-nineteenth century New York culture were deeply impressed by the parks of Europe, particularly those in London. Bryant used the Evening Post persistently to promote the need for a great public park and landscape architect Andrew Jackson Downing took up the cause in his magazine The Horticulturist. The effect of the lobbying in the press was such that in 1850 both candidates for mayor were strongly in support of creating a city park. In April 1851 newly elected Mayor Kingsland presented to the city council a clear and strong concept.

> *Such a park, well laid out, would become a favored resort of all classes ...There are thousands who pass the day of rest among the idle and dissolute in porter houses, or places more objectionable, who would rejoice in being enabled to breathe the pure air in such a place, while the ride or drive through its avenues, free from the noise, dust and confusion, inseparable from all thoroughfares, would hold out strong inducements for the affluent to make it a place of resort.*

It is a statement with a healthy spirit of egalitarianism. Downing, too, encouraged an egalitarian vision for the park. The New York Times, however, was not so sure. It loathed the notion of giving the very poor, the Boweryites free access:

> *As long as we are governed by the Five Points [the poorest, roughest part of the city], our best attempts to elegance and grace will bear some resemblance to jewels in the snouts of swine. Rather the park should never be made at all if it is to become the resort of rapscallions.*

Locating the park would take several years and much political and legal wrangling. The major competition was between a site on the East River and the central site where the park now lies. All the debates took place against a background of the city growing more rapidly, and with more prosperity, than anyone could have predicted. The strongest opposition came from those who saw such a use of land as limiting the open field of enterprise that the grid provided. In November 1853 the State Supreme Court appointed commissioners to take the land in the central part of the island, much of it rocky ridges above marshes and woodland. The competition to prepare designs for the park was announced in October 1857.

Frederick Law Olmsted had been a farmer and a journalist. The journal recording his travels through the South conveys a dread of slavery and foresees troubles ahead. During a journey through England he found great pleasure in the new parks being created by Sir Joseph Paxton: his report of a visit to Birkenhead Park near Liverpool delights in the mixing of the classes dashing for shelter from the rain. It was Paxton who conceived of the Crystal Palace for the Great Exhibition in London in 1851, and it was Paxton's example that led Olmsted to become America's great landscape architect and artist of civic life. However, although Olmsted overshadows all the others who contributed to making Central Park, it was formed as much by the forces of history and circumstance as by any one imagination. The formative influence on the design was the thorough mapping of the topography and watershed by Lieutenant Egbert Viele who was appointed engineer in chief for the new park in 1854. Olmsted was appointed park superintendent in 1857, just before the competition was announced. Olmsted later claimed that he had no intention of entering the competition until invited to partner with the English architect Calvert Vaux. And the power of the design came much more from Vaux than from Olmstead, but Olmstead had the power of the pen.

In his writings Olmsted conveys the sense of statesmanship and grandeur of vision that he embodied in the park:

> *The whole island of New York would, but for such a reservation, before many years be occupied by buildings and paved streets; that millions upon millions of men were to live their lives upon this island, millions to go out from it – and that all – would assuredly suffer – from influences engendered by these conditions. The time will come when New York will be built-up, when all the grading and filling will be done, when the picturesquely varied rock formations of the island will have been converted into the foundations for rows of monotonous straight streets, and piles of erect buildings. There will be no suggestion left of its present varied surface, with the single exception of a few acres contained in the park.*

At a time when the street grid had barely reached the middle of the island, Olmsted saw clearly in his mind's eye the city that would arise around the great park. In a letter to William Robertson in 1872 he wrote, "I wish to present to you that it was designed as a park to be situated at the precise central [point] of the city of two million …There is every reason to believe that the park will [one day] be enclosed by the compact town the borders of which were a mile away when it was laid out." He foresaw a time when an artificial wall would surround the park, as high he wrote, "as the Great Wall of China". Here he gives us a glimpse into his imagination.

He states clearly in his report to the park commissioners that his park would be "an antithesis of objects of vision to those of the streets and houses" of the grid-bound city. The many picturesque moments offered in the shifting landscapes of the park—these objects of vision— were drawn mainly from the English landscapes of the eighteenth and

Fig. 12   Central Park 1868
Fig. 13   Bird's eye view of Central Park 1859, John Bachman

nineteenth centuries, the landscapes of Capability Brown and Joseph Paxton. There is a distinct similarity between the splendid balloonist's view of Central Park and a similar view of the Crystal Palace at Sydenham in London: both landscapes are filled with different events animated by a profusion of movement.

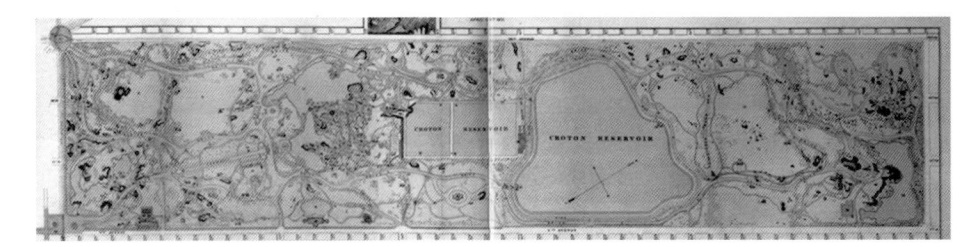

Looking at the plans of a European city it is easy to recognize the centres of power. They present a palimpsest of shifting layers of order as culture moves from the power of the Church to the power of the king, then to merchants and then industry. Then come marked changes in the organic texture of the city as its population expands, dramatizing the distance between wealth and poverty. City form and fabric is the direct residue of the political, economic and social project. Manhattan from the air shows none of the conflicts and power plays reflected in the European city. It is marked by one dominant opposition—park and grid—an exquisite juxtaposition in *the meta*physics of reality. The grid, formed to govern freedom within reason, frames a great park designed to be a natural enhancement of social harmony. In the park the spiritual has primacy over the material and the expedient. In the grid the streets are continually reformed in expediency and speculation. Yet the juxtaposition is filled with paradox: the naturalness of the park is achieved by the absolute control and manipulation of nature. It is the city that represents nature's more basic forces in the survival of the fittest: God in reason versus the illusion of God in nature.

There is a more profound political dimension in the contrast between these realities, between the mercantile republicanism at the turn of the nineteenth century and the conservatism at the mid-century. The park is European, a bourgeois infection that reflects a weakening of the egalitarianism of the republic. An attempt at creating a crucible of social harmony, the park in ways served to dramatize difference. In effect, although offering highly intricate events and vistas and the much-celebrated separation of traffic, the Greensward plan was distinctly unfriendly to the working classes. As the authors of Gotham

Fig. 14 Central Park 1880s
Fig. 15 Seneca village in the 1870s
Fig. 16 Manhattan 1876
Fig. 17 Central Park

point out, recreations like dances and picnics were forbidden, as were the rituals of working-class Republican political culture; military displays were banned, along with civic processions and public oratory. Instead the tree-lined mall was reserved for genteel activity: promenades and polite, but not political, exchange, the middle class in its carriages and the working class on foot.

The creation of Central Park disrupted some of the poor of the city more directly. Over 1,600 residents in shantytowns in the area were displaced including Irish farmers and German gardeners. Seneca village, a black settlement at Eighth Avenue and 82nd Street, which had three churches and a school, was levelled.

However, well into its second century the park is the great public forum of the city, fostering social harmony within a more complex society than would have been conceivable in the nineteenth century.

By 1850 rational idealism had been replaced by a belief in the power of social harmony. By 1890 the spirit of egalitarianism was being eroded by harsh competition, and by 1920 the city's growth was merely another manifestation of laissez-faire speculation, shaped increasingly by the demands of the automobile. But neither could undo these two realities formed from eighteenth century reason and nineteenth century sentiment.

Note

This is an edited version of an essay from Alan Balfour's NEW YORK, World City, published by Wiley Academy, London (2001)

The Vertical Reconstruction of Living Space

WANG Shu
Chief Architect, Amateur Architecture Studio
Professor and Dean, School of Architecture, China Academy of Art
Hangzhou, China

Introduction
In Asia, particularly in China, the original structure of cities is changing in general. Such change happens simultaneously where there are large amounts of urban development. The process of the change and disintegration of the city structure, the way of life and the architecture language is a subject that contemporary architecture is facing right now, whether we desire it or not. It is interesting that the various possibilities from different times and directions can exist at the same time. With a large, growing population and the serious shortness of urban land, it is inevitable that the living spaces develop vertically. Simple functional effectiveness and the illusion of modernity have led to an alienated way of living that calls out for architecture to return to an authentic city life and local environment. The vital problem then, is to think about the contemporary high-rise building, especially residential building in urban China as the reconstruction of a localized living world.

China is experiencing a rapid development as if we were being transported by a time machine. Thirty years ago, I described the lifestyle of "pursuing 'nature' to fit nature". The values, construction methods and the architecture system continue to exist even today. However, over these thirty years, we have experienced what the western world had experienced over two centuries. Today, the traditional landscape-architecture system that once dominated the whole country has almost disappeared completely, and what remains can be no longer described as a system.

Beijing, Shanghai and Guangzhou are the Chinese metropolises that have populations of over twenty million inhabitants and are known internationally. Their rapid urban development seems to represent the changes happening in urban China, with high-rises everywhere. However, other than these three cities, there are more than 120 other Chinese cities with a population more than one million. The changes taking place in these cities represent the depth and breadth of the changes in urban China; and the pursuit of the high-rise is the symbol of the changes. This pursuit reflects the pressure of a large population, the shortage of land, the desire of humans to change their way of life, the craze for the capital accumulation brought by the high-rises, the blind eagerness for the symbols of modernity and fear of being left behind by the changes.

Fig. 1 Bird's-eye view of Hangzhou city, c. 1950s.
Fig. 2 Traditional high-density "horizontal life"
Fig. 3 Painting of Wuxie Mountain. Artist: Chen Hongshou. Ming Dynasty.

Hangzhou

Hangzhou, where the Amateur Architecture Studio is located, is representative of the changing Chinese city. As the city has a special position within the Chinese urban cultural tradition, the changes of the past thirty years in Hangzhou are symbolic. Two centuries ago, Shanghai was merely a fishing settlement with only a few thousand people, but a thousand years ago, Hangzhou was the capital of China with a population of more than one million. This was the era when Hangzhou was at the peak in painting (especially *Shanshui* painting), poetry, scientific inventories, and economic system. Another element that gave Hangzhou much fame around China is its landscape urban structure that is related with *Shanshui* painting concept of combining urban elements and natural landscapes, particularly the well-known West Lake, situated between the city and the surrounding hills. This "landscape first" urban structure concept was widely influential in China over the last millennium. It kept the balance between natural beauty and man-made objects, and ensured that the concentration of landscape restricted the enlargement of urban area. This restriction was a self-conscious one, and Hangzhou became a high density city enclosed within a defined region. People brought natural objects they liked into the high density buildings. Within narrow courtyards, elegant gardens inspired by *shanshui* paintings were constructed with imagination, and these were called "*shanshui* inside cities". The West Lake that occupies half of the city was not simply a forest and water landscape, but was overlaid with an artificial pathway system and structured as a large-scale *shanshui* painting. Hangzhou was so influential that the Forbidden City in Beijing also applied the pattern. The emperor of the Qing Dynasty actually built a miniature Hangzhou within the Summer Palace compound. Many cities in China, with aspirations to be like Hangzhou have a lake named "West Lake".

Viewed from the map, the urban structure, area and population of Hangzhou did not change very much from a thousand years ago until the 1950s. Between 1950 and 1980, there were slight changes with the urban area enlarged one time and the population increased to about 1.2

million. However from 1980 until now, the population in the downtown of the city increased to four million and the urban area enlarged ten times. This was not simply urban enlargement. In fact, no matter whether it was the old city or the new developments, the original pattern of high-density courtyard buildings and the street systems were completely destroyed, with the new high-rises colonizing the entire city.

Four Questions
The changes that occurred in Hangzhou are representative of the changes that are happening in urban China. In this regard, I think that there are four questions that current Chinese cities cannot avoid. The first one is that if landscape, architecture and the city formed an inseparable unit in traditional nationally-dominant landscape architecture, and if we feel that the breakdown of this system is detrimental, should we not need to re-evaluate the traditional system? This landscape architecture system, belittled for about one century, has a close relationship with nature that represents higher ethics and values than the architecture that we are familiar with now. Such an architecture system that pursues value of nature is different from that of the Plato-Pythagoras value system. If we are brave enough to admit this, we should rebuild our cities with modern editions of these values in the new reality.

Secondly, urbanization in China has brought about changes far more than the extent of the research in traditional city, architecture and landscape have attempted to analyze. It is hard to imagine that rapid urban changes are affecting not only cities, but also villages. In order to construct a new highway system, myriads of mountains that were once depicted and painted by ancient literates and amateur artists have been ruined by explosives. Dam building has destroyed water-borne traffic and caused water villages to lose their special nature. Cities are now covered by polluted air as the road system continues to expand every month. Every city is expanding, and consumes more and more land. It is becoming harder to separate urban areas from the surrounding natural environment. In the summer, when the temperature rises, air conditioners are switched on, and every city faces insufficient electric power. The land-destroying architecture cannot be sustained because of the coming crisis in resource and ecology.

Thirdly, up to thirty years ago, almost all cities in China retained the ecology-city style with high residential densities. Over the last three decades, there was huge population pressure with twenty million people flowing to cities every year, and there was also the collapse of community relations in new residential areas. Economic growth also lead to great demand for residential and commercial land, leading to the rapid and massive building of high rises in the big cities, which in turn led to traffic congestion. All these are factors in the collapse and dissimilation between urban society and traditional balance between the natural and urban environments. The result is that the city geography changed totally, and urban life tended to become a completely artificial entity, unreal and illusive. Of

Figs. 4–5 Initial sketches for Ningbo Tengtou Pavilion (Urban Best Practices Area at Shanghai Expo 2010)

course, the traditional landscape-architecture system could not adapt to such a change immediately. What we need is to rebuild a modern system, capable to rebuilding living area in a real and intimate sense.

Fourthly, traditional China had established a fast-fitting construction system with earth, timber and other natural materials that are easily used in construction and restoration. In the process of restoration, the materials are recycled and re-used. Another characteristic of this construction method is the 'shallow base' which prevents and reduces the harmful destruction of the land. Since construction is based on space requirements, the building can grow in any scale. The use of local materials also led to widespread diversity. The pursuit of "nature" does not only reflect in the craft of structural design but also in the adaptation and adjustment to the natural geography. This method even turns real nature into a constructed element in establishing the living site. Humans fabricate all kinds of natural topography according to the interpretation of 'nature'. In this system, the literates establish the rules while the craftsmen are in charge of the constructional aspects. Ideally, the two groups cooperate together, but the reality in China today is that the designers and architects receive western-style education and the buildings are built with in-situ concrete, especially in the construction of high-rises. Such a system will finally lead to the end of the pursuit of 'nature'.

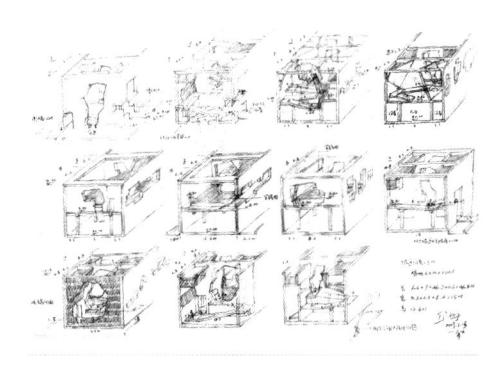

Rebuilding Contemporary Local Chinese Architecture

Over the last decade, the Amateur Architecture Studio has developed an innovative and site specific experimental methodology. This methodology, combined with parallel research on contemporary urban and rural architecture, begins with small-scale architectural experiments, which are implemented into specific metropolitan public spaces and high-rise residential dwellings. These experiments will ultimately be carried out on an urban scale, over an entire city. The Studio seeks answers to questions such as how to locally reconstruct the unique urban fabric in Chinese cities where the original Chinese building ideology that is interdependent with the natural landscape to contemporary conditions in China; how to cope with large scale demolition and reconstruction in Chinese cities; and how to reinterpret the tradition of local design by introducing a way to recycle buildings. In a consistent series of projects such as the Xiangshan campus of the China

Figs. 6–8 Vertical Courtyard Apartment in Hangzhou. Completed 2007.

Academy of Art, Amateur Architecture Studio has attempted to propagate a concept of "Rebuilding Contemporary Local Chinese Architecture".

The design of high-rises is complex, but the design of high-rise residential buildings is undoubtedly the most difficult. It has become fashionable to copy the patterns from Hong Kong or Singapore, but these patterns are not related to the local original urban structure, dwelling pattern, community and life styles of the Chinese city. It is arguable that the construction of any high-rise dwellings means the destruction of the corresponding urban structure. Under the pressure of construction cost and of maximising the amount of usable space, it is difficult for architects to attempt new solutions. This is the reason why there are so few Chinese architects that seek to be innovative and undertake research into the design of high-rise dwellings. Yet this is a critical issue since high-rise dwellings building under construction in most of the hundred plus Chinese cities with over one million inhabitants.

In 2001, the Amateur Architecture Studio was commissioned by a Hangzhou real estate company to design a high-rise residential complex. Before the commission, I discussed with the client for two years. The site is located in the east entrance of Hangzhou, adjacent to the approach to the bridge over the river. This important location required a good design here, but the disadvantage of the noise from the bridge was inevitable. The shape of the site was irregular, which made it impossible to place more than a single row of buildings. Since the client required 120,000 square metre (m²) of constructed space, it meant the height of the buildings would have to be around 100 metres. The distance between the buildings would also be short, and the building depth would have to be at least 15 metres. In Hangzhou, people are used to natural ventilation and sunlight from the south. Normally, the depth of the building is less than 12 metres, so 15 metres would not be well received.

To me, whether these problems were solved depended on whether there was creative concept. The real difficulty was that I was faced with a blank site. There was no urban structure and no unique cultural reference as the adjacent residential communities were the same as any other urban outskirt community in China. So I proposed a scheme of 'Vertical Housing', a unit with two floors, eaves in the front and back. The height of the balconies varies from two to four metres, which would be fine for trees less than 6 metres high. In fact, the six building towers were laid with 200 double-height courtyards. The different plants in each courtyard were recognizable from the ground and at the same time block the noise of the traffic. Every two floors had a 10m^2 public yard that functions as a neighbourhood space. On the ground level, I designed for high-density commercial buildings to form the street system of the city. The nature of the design was an attempt to maintain the local traditional urban texture characteristics by making the two-floor high-density traditional street blocks vertical. People would feel that they lived in a two-storey house at any height in the building. There were eaves, trees, grass and flowers. This also provided two scales for the building: one was recognizable at a distance from the city, with buildings were constituted two-level courtyard boxes ('city scale'). The other was from the inside of the courtyard boxes, appropriate for recognition at closer distance ('neighbourhood scale').

The main structures were concrete, but the exterior walls of every courtyard were covered with traditional blue bricks. As for the building density and distance, I didn't think they were an issue. I always believed that good city atmosphere needed sufficient density. At the end, the amount of constructed area was slightly over 130,000m^2. The design was finally accepted because we applied an active attitude and turned the disadvantages into opportunities of research. Acceptance of the design approach is reflected in the 90 percent occupation of the project.

However, the part of the design that was not realized reveals some problems: the ground level high-density commercial buildings that would have formed the urban connections system was omitted as the real estate company didn't consider it was necessary for the street space to do anything, nor was it required by the urban planning authorities. I had also planned for the residential block and the original street to be open to each other. The real estate developer was afraid this could cause security problems. So boundary walls were constructed and security guards were employed. From these details, we may see how problems of the city arose and how the original city lifestyle collapsed.

There were also other problems that relate to the quality of life: the design of buildings provided tree planting space, but whether the residents planted trees was left up to them. I observed that, initially, few residents planted trees, but gradually more and more of them did. The buildings also provided possibilities for additional construction. After the residents moved in, many glass houses appeared on the courtyards of the balcony, adding much individuality to the buildings.

Multitasking Spatial Infrastructures: Slender Urbanism and Mobility Models

Marisa YIU
Assistant Professor
School of Architecture, Chinese University of Hong Kong

Towards a Multitasking Infrastructure

Multitasking is used to keep all of a computer's resources at work as much of the time as possible. It is controlled by the operating system, which loads programs into the computer for processing and oversees their execution until they are finished. Thus, Multitasking involves overlapping and interleaving the execution of several programs. This is often achieved by capitalizing on the difference between a computer's rapid processing capacity and the slower rates of its input/output devices.[1]

In extending this framework of multitasking conceptually, this paper examines, Hong Kong as a spatial laboratory for 'Vertical Cities Asia' and how its infrastructure-led development stitches together thriving urban communities. These communities demonstrate how their relationship to mass transit development has created formally and informally diversity, and demographic pluralism for Hong Kong's population. If a city is based on efficiency, convenience, mixing and clustering of human capital[2] to generate vitality and social sustainability, then what can multitasking accomplish in an urban sense? As architects and planners, how do we propose vertical structures that utilizes minimal resources, embraces community life, programmatic mixing with mass interconnectivity? Traditionally, efficiency and planning is measured in architecture and urban planning through planimetric terms; however, can we rethink efficiency through a sectional strategy both in architectural space to three-dimensional networks that accounts for user's behaviours and culture? Design and planning is no longer a two- or three-dimensional physical exercise but a *4D-plus* (four-dimensional-plus)[3] proposition: where social aspects, people's interactions and behaviours, programmatic processes allow a cross-cultural understanding on the shaping of cities and vice versa.

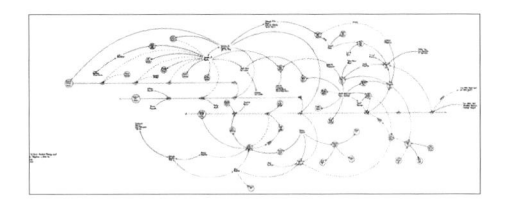

Opposite page
Fig. 1   Drawing by Mark Lombardi

This page
Figs. 2–4 Photographs by Michael Wolf, Hong Kong

Hong Kong as a 'Spatial Laboratory' of Density and Verticality

In looking at Hong Kong as a spatial laboratory and a 'model' city of experimental verticality, Hong Kong's geographic position and complex histories (from a British colony to a Special Administrative Region of China), we can pose provocative questions. With case scenarios (and fragments of the city) in this paper, I will illustrate the powerful relationship between private and public partnerships, the role of capital infrastructure and charitable organizations, the strategic development of multi modal networks, the corporate versus the grassroots, and the function of public spaces. These contemporary and contested conditions generate a productive analysis on the ecological infrastructure of mobility and community. In *Splintering Urbanism*, Michael Peter Smith has argued, all urban places are now "*translocalities* with multifaceted and multi-scaled links and connections elsewhere. There is a need to expand the study of transnational urbanism to encompass the scope of transnational processes, as well as to focus future urban research on the local and translocal specificities of various transnational socio-spatial practices".[4] Through the lens of selected Hong Kong case organizations and *translocalities*, I demonstrate how efficient transportation networks challenge the notion of a 'street' and its compact vertical spaces that maximize potentialities for a diverse range of people. Hong Kong's Mass Transit Railway (MTR) intermodal transportation co-exists with multiple programmes to offer valuable time-based interactions, and organizations like the Hong Kong Jockey Club Charities Trust give light to the increasing public and private social activities. These are key agents in the shaping of the Hong Kong social and community life: that have created a synergized infrastructural-led development to form a series of corporatized spaces that negotiate local identity, cultural sensibilities and economic ingenuity within the urban fabric and communities.

With the MTR's high speed efficiency, it has facilitated Hong Kong peoples' connectivity expeditiously from home to work, to school, and to leisure and entertainment areas. Due in part to the tight spatial dimensions of the domesticated environment and dwelling units, the MTR's fast and reliable people mover is the highly desirable transportation for the majority of population to connect to others spaces of convenience. The eighty stations today, "with about 1,800 railcars in eight major de-

Figs. 5–7 Various Hong Kong transport networks.

pots, and 68 light rail stops with 120 trolleys in one depot"[5] within Hong Kong has introduced multiplier effects of cross-programming. According to Mr. CY Leung's research[6] (Convener of the Executive Council of Hong Kong), 85 percent of apartments in Hong Kong are less than 56 square metre (m²). From the 2008 Housing Authority and Rating and Valuation Department statistics, Leung notes; 6.8 percent of the population live in flats 60 to 69.9m², 5 percent live in apartments between 70 to 99m², and a surprising small percentage, 3.1 percent, live in apartments 100m² or larger. However, the extremes are questionable: where luxury apartments are on one end and the current disenfranchised population of cage dwellers reside on the other end of the spectrum. These are the urban slum dwellers, the underprivileged group who live in dire conditions, in cages of only 1.7m² (can rent for HK$ 167 a month). Social workers estimate at least 100,000 people live in inadequate housing, a category that includes cubicle, cage, rooftop and partitioned dwellings.[7] Most recent luxury apartments such as 'The Arch', a 65-storey residential development (above the Kowloon airport express station) have monthly rents that range from HK$ 38,000 to $55,000, and sale prices from HK$ 10,000,000 to 53,000,000 for apartments of 77.1 to 117.1m² saleable area. Recently, Mr Vernon Martin, an appraiser, noted in a government auction of land that, 'Two sites sold at an average price of HK$ 1,309.9 psm (per square metre). Completed homes are expected to sell for an average price of over HK$ 2,895.8 psm.' With this backdrop of information, the majority of Hong Kong population is typically squeezed into smaller apartments relative to other parts of the world. Thus, many spend time out of their domestic environments in public and shared spaces. With hyper-frequent two-minute waiting interval times per train, large populations can travel en masse to other sites of convenience: shopping malls, airports, transport hubs and destinations of work and public spaces with extreme fluidity.

As Hong Kong[8] has progressed, the rapid infrastructural development has created an advanced, dynamic and liveable society with a current population of 7,003,700[9] Hong Kong is known as one of the most densely populated areas in the world. The small portion of flat land avail-

Fig. 8 Research and Mapping of relationship between housing and MTR networks.
Fig. 9 Photo of 'Pencil tower'

able for construction in Hong Kong is only 220 square kilmometres (km²) (out of the entire land area of 1,104km²), which has led to a hyper-concentrated high-rise environment. However, due to land lease arrangements and development control plans, Hong Kong conserves three-quarters of the territory as country parks or natural landscapes. According to Carol Willis in a 2008 symposium entitled, Vertical Cities: Hong Kong | New York, she notes, 'the cumulative built area of Hong Kong is only 259km². Its seven million citizens live at an average density of 18,1299 per km², the average density of Manhattan is also likewise 70,000. This means that all of the population of Hong Kong on the island or in distant transit base *New Towns* live at the density of Manhattan. Today Hong Kong has surpassed New York City in terms of number of high rises'.[10]

Hong Kong has an urban density of 29,400 people per km²; with some development areas as high as 54,305 people per km² (such as Kwun Tong district). With some comparison, we can witness Hong Kong's incredible density of inhabitants measured against other cities[11] from the participants in the Vertical Cities Asia conference:

Table. 1 Density comparison between cities represented by participating universities in the Vertical Cities Asia symposium.

City	Region and Year of Statistics	Area (km²)	Population	Population Density (per km²)
Hong Kong	City (2009)	1104	7,003,700	6,480
	Note: areas like Kwun Tong district have the highest, with 53,110 persons /km². The most densely populated district among the 18 District Council districts of Hong Kong.			
	Central and Western District (2006)	12.55	250,000	20,200
Shanghai	City (2008)	6,340	13,910,000	2,194
Amsterdam	City (2010)	219	780,152	3562
Delft	City (2010)	24.08	96,760	4,031
Tokyo	City (2010)	2188	13,162,000	6,015
	Tokyo-Shinjuku (2011)	18.23	319,624	17,532
	Note: closely compared to Central or Wan Chai in the role of infrastructure and mixed use.			
Singapore	City (2011)	710.2	3,771,700	5310
	Marina Bay (2011)	3.6	TBD	TBD
Berkeley, California	City (2010)	45.833	112,580	2456

Vertical and Horizontal Transformations: Slender Typologies, Pencil Towers, Mass Housing, Vertical Factories, Interconnected Urban Alleys and Public Living Rooms.

Hong Kong's land scarcity and expensive living conditions has given rise to typologies that represent the pragmatics of governance and the socio-economic development of survival; however, most of these functional and practical typologies have disappeared and given way to newer developments or new functions. We witness not only the dominating landscape of public housing projects[12] by the Government to house the increasing population in Hong Kong since the 1950s, but also Pencil Tower structures. This Pencil Tower typology has no specific definition; however, these dot part of the older areas of Hong Kong. These plots are owned by private developers who need to build and maximize profits on small pieces of land. The smallest consist of one apartment per floor, with a usable floor area as little as 16m², which is then replicated for another thirty storeys. The load-bearing structure is typically reinforced concrete and the floor plan takes up the maximum allowed by the building codes for the specific plot. There is no set definition for a Pencil Tower; however, 'one definition could be the relationship of the usable floor area of one floor to the height of the building. This would be an aspect ratio. Utilizing this to define the pencil tower yields a border value of about 1.00. That means that any tower that has a ratio of height (in metres) divided by usable floor area (in m²) that is equal or greater than one, is a pencil tower'.[13] Another phenomenon, and

Fig. 10   'Hong Kong panorama'

building typology in Hong Kong that is worth noting are the government subsidized flatted factories of the 1960s. These flatted factories allowed units for small manufacturers to rent inexpensively and sited close to the urban areas with ease access to labour and transportation.[14] Besides the government factories there are also privately developed vertical factories from the 1980s onwards (located mostly in the older industrial areas of Kwun Tong, Kwai Chung, Wong Chuk Hang and Chai Wan areas). These utilitarian buildings represent the pragmatics of older building typologies of Hong Kong and warrant fascinating social, urban and economic considerations of their typological development and future transformative power in their technical, physical and social implications for an urban fabric.

With such tightness, Hong Kong inhabitants have demonstrated creativity in home, work and public spaces with ingenuity. In acknowledging space as a constraint yet as a normative condition, Hong Kong people treat public space and the public realm as private space: as urban living rooms. As witnessed by Michael Wolf's contemporary photographs, he captures and explores the individual improvisations and adaptations of this lack of private domesticity. He states:

> *Private acts happen in public places: laundry, even vegetables are dried on fences surrounding the housing estates, house plants are raised in back alleys, shoes are jammed under outside water pipes because there is no space inside for them, washed gloves are hug to dry on barbed wire. If there is no more space inside, something must go out: mops, shovels, pots and pans are hung on hooks on the walls outside of apartments. In order to survive in this dense environment, one must be able to adapt. In comparison to the ordered and well-planned European cities, Hong Kong is almost like a plant – it grows organically, making space for itself wherever possible. The face of a newly built public housing estate is a blank slate – several years later its facade reflects the improvisational talents of its inhabitants.*[15]

Not only are back alleys exploited, large and small public spaces are interwoven on ground level, while rooftops and large shopping malls activate the notion of a three-dimensional vertical public ground. The 'ground', the 'street' is elevated, submerged and inverted. This understanding and need of flexible public spaces are important spatial prerequisites in building contemporary cities of vertical density.

Driven by its physical constraints, socio-economic factors, market forces and government policies, affordability of residential living is extremely challenging. More recently the major tension of market demand and supply is due in part to the monopolies of the large real-estate developers in Hong Kong and also by a new demographic of home owners. Increasingly, Mainland Chinese investors' are finding ways to secure their wealth in the Hong Kong property market, generating an overheated market.

> 'Home prices in Hong Kong have risen about 45 percent since the end of 2008 due to record low interest rates, tight supply and interest from the mainland. Chinese buyers are estimated to have bought more than a third of upmarket properties sold in the first half of this year, compared with a fifth last year and 15 percent in 2008. Under a programme launched in 2003, investors have been able to gain residency in Hong Kong by investing HK$ 6.5m (US$ 840,000) in real estate, equities or other assets. Residency attracts interest from overseas investors given the city's low income tax rate and, especially for mainland Chinese, access to quality public medical services and schools.'[16]

This has resulted in an overheated property market, and pressures in the lopsided provision of the much needed affordable housing.

Urban Communities and Programmatic Interconnectivity
In Hong Kong, the relationship between 'hard' infrastructure and 'soft' community is layered, differentiated and continually emerging with captivating time-based negotiations and urban processes. When the Mass Transit Railway (MTR) was inaugurated in 1979, the transportation was built with three goals in mind: to react to the fast population growth and build-up of connections to housing in the *New Towns*, and to elevate the traffic congestion of Hong Kong. The Colony outline plan as well as the Mass Transit Study attributed the cause of urban traffic congestion in 1960s to growth of private vehicles. MTR was the solution after the government planned meticulous studies, in the late 1960s.

MTR was originally a government-owned statutory corporation (Mass Transit Provisional Authority) tasked with overseeing the rapid transit network's initial construction and operation. With huge passenger carrier capacity, the MTR singlehandedily reduced the amount of road usage and altered the transport patterns over the years. Hong Kong's British Government authorized the construction of the MTR construction in 1972, and the first line opened in Kowloon in 1979. Over time, the MTR system was progressively extended: beneath Victoria Harbour to Hong Kong Island in 1980, to Tsuen Wan in 1982, adding a second underwater tunnel in 1984, completing Hong Kong Island's mainline in 1985. These four urban lines (30 route miles) formed MTR's core network until 1998 when the relatively longer (21-mile) suburban line to Hong Kong Airport and Tung Chung (Lantau Island) was added, costing US$10.6 billion. MTR was partially privatized in 2000 when Hong Kong Special Administrative Region's (HKSAR) government sold 23 percent of MTR shares to private investors.'[17] Today MTR has grown and represents a highly networked globalized interconnected multitasking infrastructure that connects to buildings, commercial zones, airports and Chinese cities across the border, just to the north of

Fig. 11   Location of 1 km² studies.

Hong Kong. MTR represents a circulatory switching conglomerate with multiple ventures with global capital, corporations and the government. However, MTR's 'hard' planning and infrastructure has benefitted many sub-communities to create informal soft flexible infrastructures and urban economies.

MTR's *4D-plus* networks give rise to urban communities that enliven the vitality of city life: economically and socially. As Edward Glaeser argues, much-needed 'face to face' interaction[18] and human clusters benefit human capital as producers and consumers for any creative economy and innovation. What is interesting is the local to global connectivity in a space and time continuum that the MTR can provide for this human capital and speedy exchange. As the Hong Kong became more sophisticated and dense, the relationship of 'urban community' and 'infrastructure' has proven more intricate and dynamic. This illustrates the adaptations and integration of the use of efficient networks. I have mapped and selected the relationships of five micro communities and scenarios of current research, each representing various stages in Hong Kong's development. They are selected for their high density, their activities and streetscape dynamics: Mong Kok, North Point, Wanchai, Causeway Bay and Hung Hom. A one km² zone placed around these dense areas focuses on the MTR transit nodes and 'Hubs'.[19] These studies share very peculiar relationships between space, network mobility, Chinese contemporary culture and programmes. In daily observations, photography and mapping techniques, interviewing and analysis we observe how the urban dense cores allows for a variety of needs which give rise to multitasking community infrastructures that benefit users and consumers.

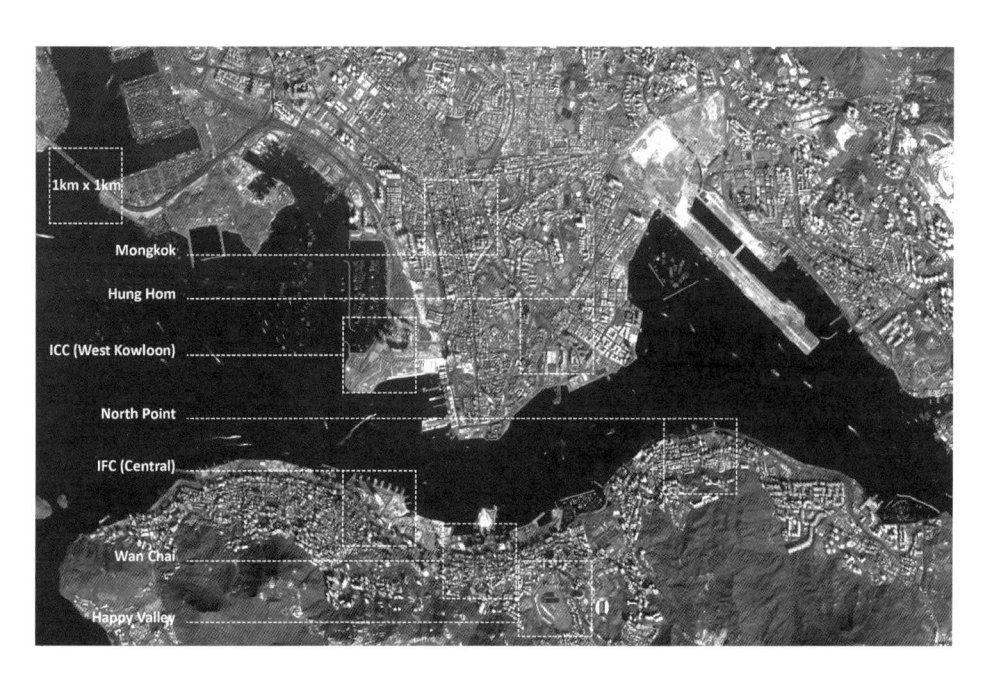

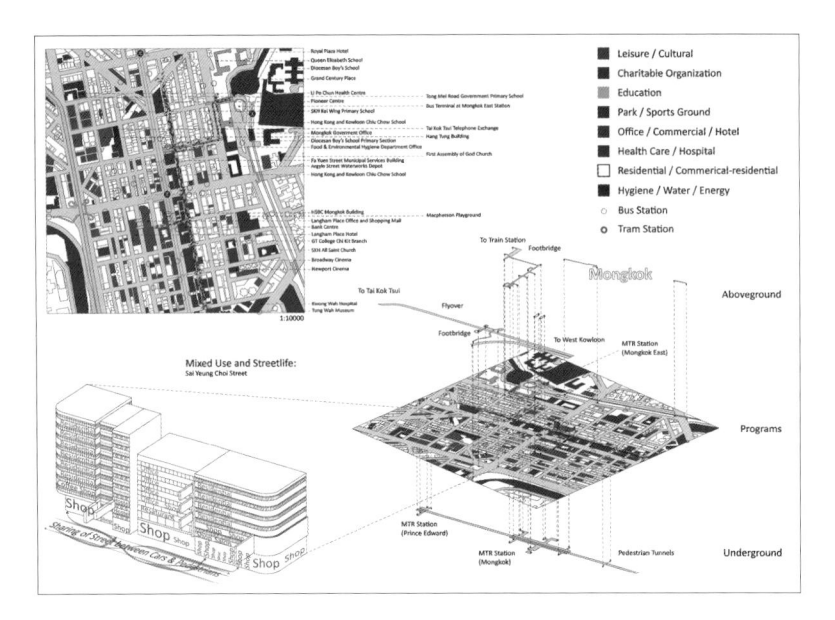

Fig. 12 Mong Kok analysis
Fig. 13 Wan Chai analysis

4d+plus scenarios: *The One km² Hong Kong Case Scenarios*

a *Mong Kok Streets.* Mong Kok's one km² zone contains an interplay with commerce and street life present programmatic time-based shifts. The MTR has generated a connected public space, where open space and a pedestrianized commerce has produced a consumer's paradise overlaid as shopping streets and leisure zones within a tight dense area. With a small amount of playgrounds and pocket gardens along the urban fabric this zone connects to both the East Rail line and Tsuen Wan line with convenience.

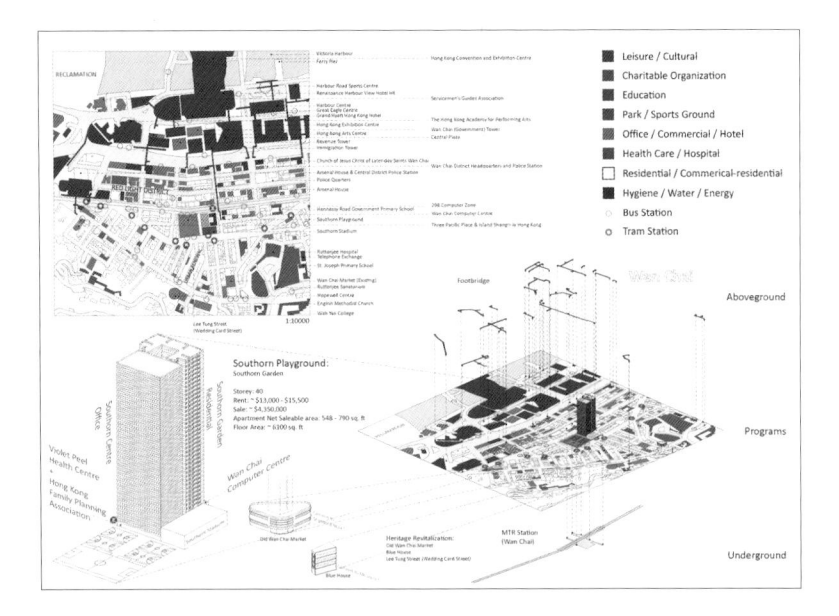

b *Wanchai's Elevated Connections.* The Southern playground area near MTR area demonstrates tight commercial programmes and diversity of usages. This site connects to business areas on the waterfront, the red light district, computing centres, tram lines through the most intricate series of pedestrian walkways and multi levels spaces. Further south, small heritage revitalization and tower building projects are underway. Open spaces allow transit economies to

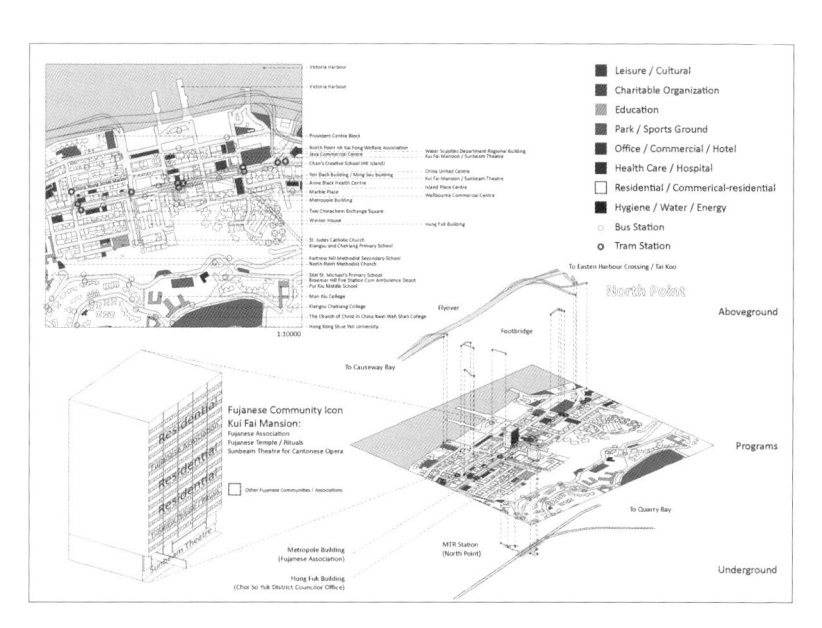

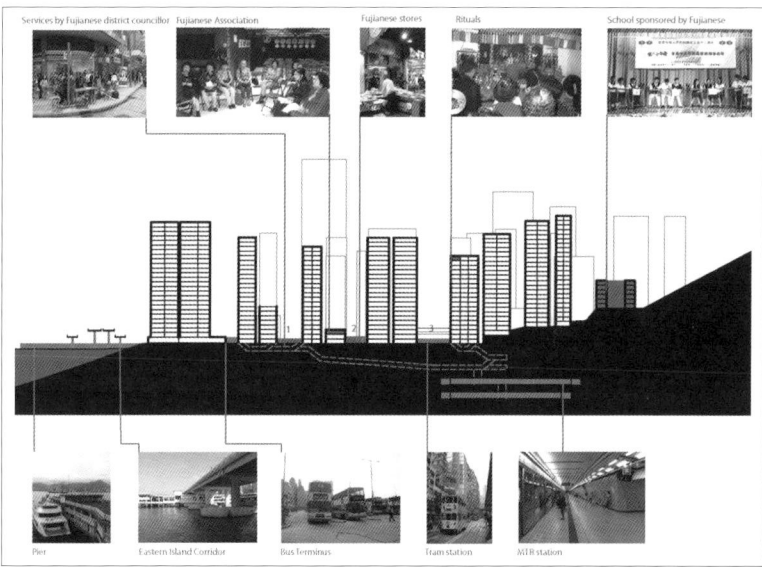

Fig. 14   North Point analysis
Fig. 15   North Point sectional analysis

produce efficiencies in buying and selling. Wanchai station also connects to various transport modes, and showcases a rich history of its topography and land reclamation.

c *North Point's Urban Resistance.* Driven by a unique overlay of transportation and localized qualities from the trams and minibus network and MTR, the wet and dry market economies dominate with local urban vibrancy; however, local district councillors and strong neighbourhood representation have dominated and resisted major new developments. This group and the areas have activated and resisted progressive urban development due to its history as a leftist enclave. It houses the largest Fujinese community of immigrants. Buildings are highly layered, complex with history and contemporary mixing of programmes that have existed with infrastructure yet with an understanding that patterns of resistance to restore and celebrate localized identities as needed in vertical city environment such as Hong Kong.

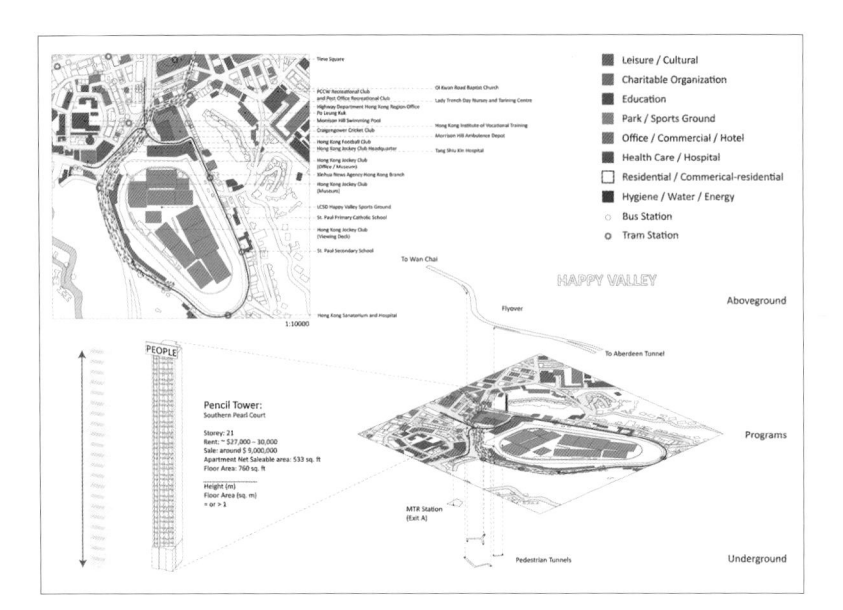

Fig. 16   Happy Valley analysis
Fig. 17   Happy Valley

d   *Causeway Bay And Happy Valley.* A hyper-energetic area with various regional Asian influences of commerce and department stores. Japanese stores like SOGO are situated directly above the MTR. This area has the highest number of Japanese restaurants, 'sky bars', multi-programmed mixed-use vertical shopping buildings, vertical blood donation centres to hair salons. It is within a short walking distance to the famous Jockey Club racecourse in Happy Valley. This area showcases a *hyper* model of physical, spatial and conceptual model of non-profit and profit making enterprises. This connects to social enterprises and the support network for health institutions and hospitals. This highly dense environment takes solace with the large swath of open space in Happy Valley, where every Wednesday the entire neighbourhood transforms into a visual spectacle of gambling and horseracing. This open and public space leisure ground coalesce overlapping conditions for various needs. The track was rebuilt in 1995, and became a world-class horse racing facility. Several football, hockey and rugby fields are encircled by the horseracing track.

e   *Hung Hom's Cultural Traditions.* The MTR-owned property above the station, *the Met*ropolis (a consortium with Vigour Ltd, jointly owned by Cheung Kong Holdings Ltd and Hutchinson Whampoa Ltd) demonstrates the variety of service apartments, office towers, roof gardens and hotels, on top of a major transit terminus. Surrounding it, the built fabric has various scales of small street alleys to larger open areas of the Polytechnic University, to large buildings of belonging to funeral parlours in this area. A variety of uses dominate the urban alleyways such as temporary worship areas. Hung Hom station is

Fig. 18   Hung Hom analysis
Fig. 19   Hung Hom

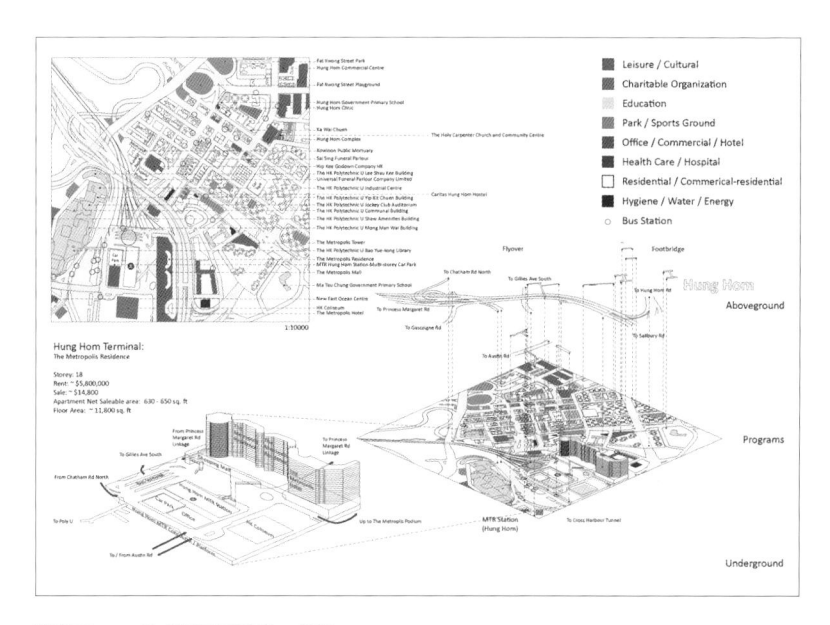

one of the oldest train stops due to the history of the Kowloon Canton Railway (KCR) that was developed prior to the MTR.[20] Hong Kong built its railway, the KCR, between 1906 and 1910 (Kowloon to Lo Wu station), but railway development was not a priority until the 1970s. In 1973, KCR underwent a modernization programme involving the laying of double tracks and electrification. The terminus at Hung Hom was constructed between 1974 and 1975, and by 1983 all electrification was complete. Before the electrification in 1983, there were only four cross-boundary immigration counters at Lo Wu. Following electrification, the counters increased to 22 and a five-storey joint-inspection station at the Lo Wu control point began operation in 1985. In December 2004 and April 2005, the automated passenger clearance system and automated vehicle clearances were introduced respectively. According to Ho Pui Yin's research, from 'January to June 2007, an average of 259,800 travellers a day passed through Lo Wu control point, representing a 2.26 percent growth over same period in 2006. Approximately 92 million travellers passed through in 2006, a large increase from the 7.95 million travellers in 1982. Another major transformation for networked development was when MTR leased KCR's network for 50 years in 2007, effectively merging subway and commuter rail into a system of five suburban lines (covering a total of 117.5 km). Today, MTR commuter rail continues to handle long-distance trains from Beijing and Shanghai.

Multitasking: Architectural Artefacts and Social Entrepreneurship
As clearly demonstrated by these case study areas, the MTR station hubs have created dynamic streetscapes with vibrant local economies and cultural sensibilities which also function vertically, as they are stacked and packed in section as well. However, what are the limits and consequences of this? Through detailed observation is it possible to introduce new ecological and sustainability strategies, intermediary interventions that are de-

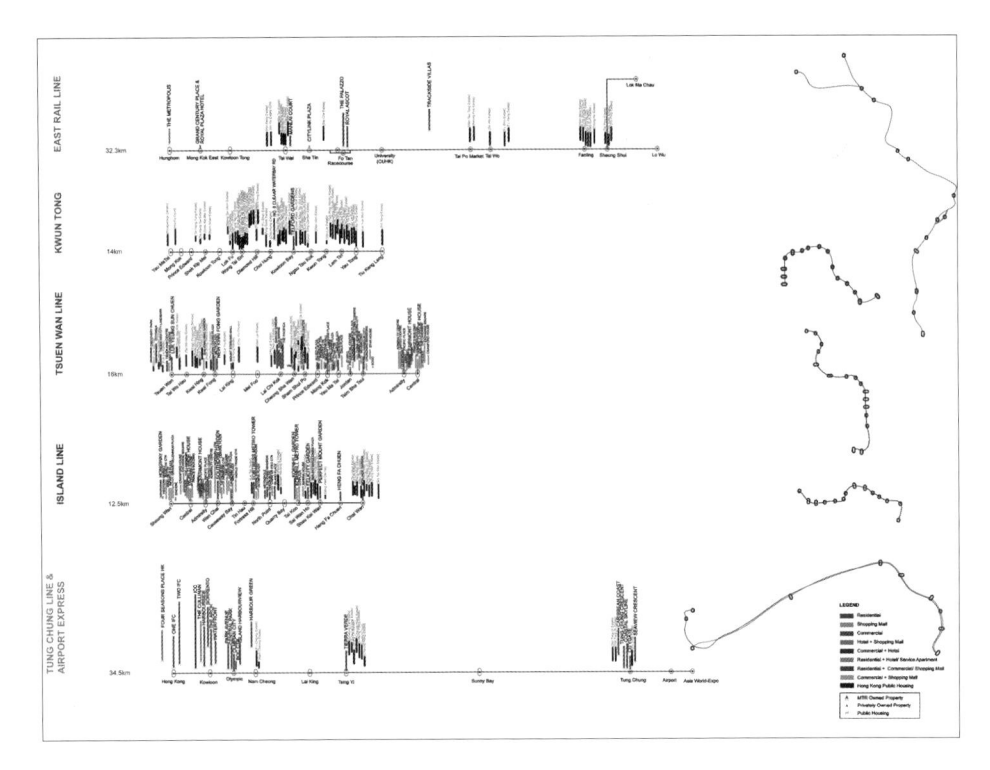

Fig. 20   MTR property and Speed network analysis diagram

signed and created to further improve on this human connectivity? Since property development is integral to the MTR's long-term revenue strategy and its 25 stations are embedded into large housing, shopping, and entertainment complexes owned or managed by MTR, the total 70,000 residential units and 1.4 million m² of commercial real estate can have a huge impact on the urban and living environment. In addition, MTR owns 12 major shopping centres, five office buildings, and the 88-storey International Finance Centre (additionally, MTR awards development packages to third parties in exchange for a share of profits).[21] With this intensity, architectural artefacts and interventions are needed to help further innovate and highlight grassroots ingenuity that has found opportunities within the logic of the mass transit networks. These highlight the potential tribulations and solutions to such rapid connectivity.

Observations and strategies for interventions:

a   In various MTR stations, the hyper connectivity also relies on transferring to other transportation intermodal networks. The bus networks and government planning policies currently has designed intricate and clever urban guidelines such as the 'saw tooth peripheral' system—where buses, mini buses enter and leave swiftly—with high capacity and efficiently. However, it still creates stagnant air pollution problems. So how can future air quality design strategies be integrated for the many dense transit areas, such as micro air-condition ventilated booths during waiting? As Hong Kong has dense urban fabric and a high level of on-grade traffic, people are constantly competing for *Fresh Air*.

b   The Octopus card is a contact-less smart card application used as an integral part of everyday life in Hong Kong. Launched in 1997, the Octopus fare collection system is an innovative system eliminating the need for commuters to find exact change. It also allowed all

Fig. 21   Hung Hom Station directory maps

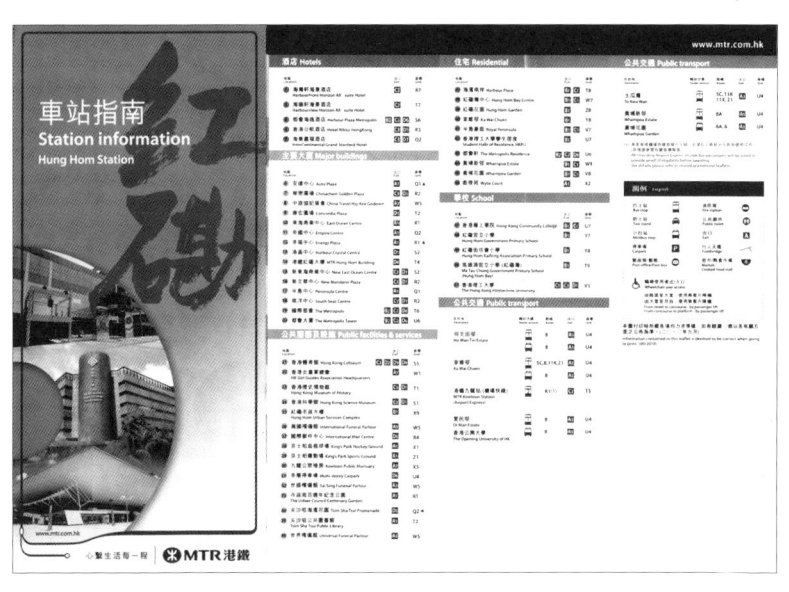

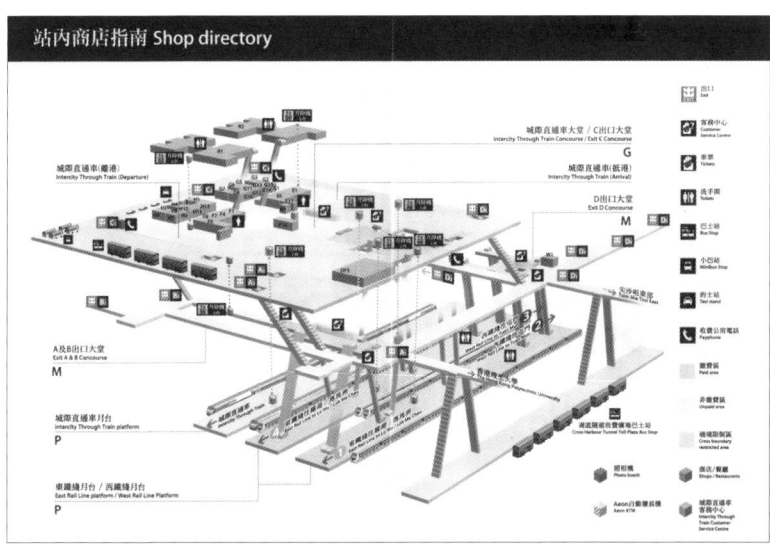

to travel across multiple public transport modes using a single card and creates a portable fast-tracked system that needs no advanced ticket buying. This reduces much of the travelling time. However, the Octopus card also creates interesting potential problems for people who 'exploit' the MTR network for business. A phenomenon of interest in the last few years (now greatly reduced due to new restrictions) are a large number of nimble businesses that use the MTR network to deliver goods, such as informal courier services who work 'without leaving the network'. Now there are corporate by-laws that state 150 minutes as the maximum time allowed in the transport system without extra costs being incurred. If surpassed, a person will be directly penalized and the octopus card will be immediately traced. Still, though various social enterprises, small 'grey market'[22] businesses and informal economies are on the rise: laundry services, courier feeders, and even vegetable farming delivery services utilize mobile manual human transporters. These offer more direct and efficient from of deliveries and services.

c Various charities and social development organizations, such as the St James Settlement, offer free haircuts for the elderly. Perhaps this could be brought into the stations with ease? The MTR has also introduced concessionary travel fees for elderlies on certain days (HK$ 2 maximum fare on any MTR journey taken on Wednesdays and public holidays) and has witnessed an encouraging increased of elders travelling to and from destinations. This could improve their health whilst providing spaces for them to connect with others.

d As witnessed in another case study, a woman began using urban alleyways as storage holding units for waste collected for recycling. She had accumulated a lot of wealth in this industry as recycling collections that has no formal structure in tight urban spaces for collection. Can these systems be introduced and programmatically tied in with the larger waste recycling industries? Could mobile compost stations be strategically plugged in to also benefit both waste and farming programmes?

e There are ingenious micro farming industries, vegetable market economies that could use the network to transport efficiently its goods and deliveries.

These small-scale observations perhaps can lead to further beneficial ways of tapping into the infrastructure to benefit the more mobile and transitory economies of Hong Kong. This can lead to a creative and innovative way for socially sustainable concepts to be intricately intertwine with the city's inner workings. Perhaps this economy of the *temporary* within the interstitial space of the city provides a new perspective for urban manufacturing at larger scales.

Towards a Vertical Cities Asia
The understanding of these intersections demonstrates a need for a new generation of multitasking infrastructural led development for 'Vertical Cities Asia' (VCA), from the viewpoint of the user to benefit social and community life of a city. This needs to work with the agenda of sustainability, not only on countering urban sprawl (Norman Foster's technological skyscraper innovations like the Tokyo project), nostalgic and prescriptive methods (New Urbanism's theory), the importance of the selection of materials (William McDonough's Cradle to Cradle theory), learning and creating interconnectivity from natural systems (Ken Yeang's bioclimatic systems) or advocating for the use of 'renewal energies' (Thomas Herzog) but also from people-centric behaviours. How can we take advantage of human interactions and the aesthetics of exchange as a potential? How can we give a social dimension to architecture and urbanism by performing more with communities' interactions and behaviours, rather than designing with a prescriptive planning imposition in mind? Occupants' activities and the human interfacing with the built form have not been the major

focus in the discourse of sustainability. This is still in its infancy.

To create a vibrant, vital, vertical city there is much more analysis needed to avoid strict zoning and loose definitions of mixed-used development models. The term 'mixed use' is often an urban development phenomenon and does not take into account the buildings within the mixed-use development. Terms such as 'the 24-hour city' invoke frenzied around the clock entertainment and socializing; but this is a superficial development objective. 'Similarly, town centre vitality is sometimes equated with a highly compact life cycle, where all needs—living space, work space, shopping, and entertainment and so on—are all in immediate proximity, characterized by some recent inner city loft-style live and work apartment developments'.[23] Hong Kong proves that physical living vertical complexes can thrive, so long as reliable transport networks are available to connect the living density to spaces of conveniences. Spatial proximity and living 'mixed use' is not the only case for the majority of Hong Kong, where the desires for living, entertainment areas, and public spaces are fluidly connected but not required to be in the same building or same neighbourhood. The MTR and local intermodal transportation are the connectors.

For a Multitasking spatial infrastructure for VCA, the following are some assumptions, propositions and research for further inquiry:

1 Efficiency is needed. Connectivity is a must. Mass mobility in a city supports dense vertical cities. Therefore the networked systems of a vertical residential building (can exploit more above and underground by excavation). This must integrate stronger with horizontal connectivity.

2 In rapid developments, small architectural and urban interventions in a city fabric must be created to accommodate transitional zones (such as stacked system interchanges). Well-ventilated chambers can create healthier zones for highly urbanized cities like Hong Kong. These transit spaces can perform no longer as singular functions but are seen to maximize multitasking functions.

3 Pedestrianized public spaces and 'streetscapes' are needed. They have no specific scale but can also be appropriated by people. They are the collective urban living rooms and elevated public spaces. These must have flexible and event based usages.

4 Chinese-Asian culture has tolerated compact living. Normative 'inter-generational' living, where an increasing healthy ageing population, small families are the basis of design for residential units.

5 Rising consumption patterns, and leisure activities and infrastructure is part of cultural and community life. Corporatized infrastructure can give life to local people.

Fig. 22   Hong Kong Networked Mobility models

6   Must support sustainable communities, encourage urban grey economies and social enterprises. Local entrepreneurship gives livelihood to benefit the community itself to generate new local based economies and tourism branding networks.

7   If the future is to embrace a demographic that is more singular in lifestyle (young urban, upwardly mobile, smaller families, to an ever-ageing healthier group and more individualized living), then how do we proactively design with this is mind?

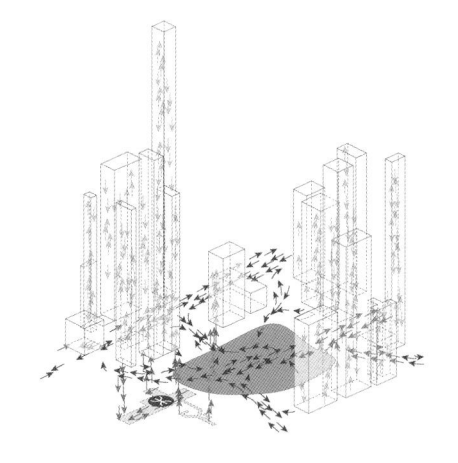

8   Active spaces, urban breathing voids, programmatic events must work with mass Asian cultural needs. As such development models of residential, mixed commercial zones of work and play must retain a balanced context that allows large voids and nature zones. These can provide equilibrium for urban density and urban biodiversity.

9   Relationship of the public and private ownership is critical to produce a Vertical Cities Asia model, such as the MTR or Charities trust. Organizations are linked and overlaid to mutually benefit multiple urban economies and innovation.

10   'Slender Urbanism' typologies both horizontally and vertically can be developed further to advocate for a flexible, and dynamic continuum, packed programmatically in section.

Network Mobility Models

> *The experience of the city is increasingly subject to the flows and interchange generated by the increased circulation of people, vehicles, and information. The rhythm of these flows, which changes the character and function of space over time, has come to have no less significance to the experience of the city than the height of its buildings, the width of its streets, and the disposition of its monuments. The traffic of people, vehicles, and information are also the environment and material of the city. (Alex Wall, 1996, 159).*[24]

With globalizing conditions such as the distribution of new technologies, multi nodal transportations, simultaneous 'just-in-time' post-fordist production, global brand franchises of 'infrastructural consumerism'[25], customization techniques, logistics systems and corporate networks, these highly networked capital flows must integrate and intersect with localized Asian traditions and sensibilities. How do these networks intersect with a Chinese community life, legacies and cultural traditions? A metropolis, a city, its architecture, geography and landscape can no longer be planned nor designed as static and independent entities; but as dynamic highly networked systems. Connectivity and hybridization of programmes and functions are imminent. With the rise of regional bi-cities (Hong Kong-Shenzhen; or future developments such as the Macau-Zhuhai-Hong Kong as inter-dependent urbanism examples) or tri-partite global cities[26] phenomenon of New York, London and Hong Kong as linked financial capitals) or 'tiered' Chinese cities that connect to regions such as the greater Pearl River Delta. Contemporary Asian cities are facing incredible rates of transformation and urbanization. With current discourse and debates relating to future cities, architectural urban landscapes, such as the latest edited volume entitled *Ecological Urbanism* (by Mohsen Mostafavi with Gareth Doherty) where they call for an 'imaginative and practical method for addressing existing as well as new cities'.[27] These are frameworks of theory and practice that currently examine commonalities for a much-needed new inquiry into the sustainability of the city, requiring 'new ethics and aesthetics' of the urban for planning the future cities. A need to embrace complexities of urbanism has to come out of design and urban 'processes' that are dynamic, and not on objective and prescriptive design principles. As a city's infrastructural networks and flows propel new forms of research and practice; cities ultimately all face the challenge to compete and better utilize their resources, to better formulate unique identities of global cultures and local identities, to improve the quality of life for its citizens, and to elevate sustainability awareness as a common goal. How vertical cities and the social development of citizens interweave for the benefit of all extends out of an ecological infrastructure that allows for multitasking solutions in highly interconnected ways.

Notes

1. Definition from Encyclopedia Britannica
2. Notes from Glaeser, Edward L. Triumph of the City: How Our Greatest Invention Makes Us Richer, Smarter, Greener, Healthier, And Happier. New York: Penguin Press (2011); and his writings: "Great cities are not static—they constantly change, and they take the world along with them. When New York and Chicago and Paris experienced great spurts of creativity and growth, they reshaped themselves to provide new structures that could house new talent and new ideas. Cities can't force change with new buildings—as the Rust Belt's experience clearly shows. But if change is already happening, new building can speed the process along. Yet many of the world's old and new cities have increasingly arrayed rules that prevent construction that would accommodate higher densities. Sometimes these rules have a good justification, such as preserving truly important works of architecture. Sometimes, they are mindless NIMBYism or a misguided attempt at stopping urban growth. In all cases, restricting construction ties cities to their past and limits the possibilities for their future. If cities can't build up, then they will build out. If building in a city is frozen, then growth will happen somewhere else." Glaeser, Edward L. How Skyscrapers Can Save the City, March 2011, Atlantic magazine
3. Notes: In reference to earlier built projects featured in Bullivant, Lucy (ed.) 4dsocial : Interactive Design Environments. Bognor Regis, West Sussex: Wiley (2007). (Our installations from design office ESKYIU that dealt with networks of labour for sites in Chinatown NYC factory and cultural production).
4. Michael Peter Smith believes that "future urban research ought to focus considerable attention on comparatively analysing diverse cases of transnational network formation and translocality construction". Reference from Graham, Stephen and Marvin, Simon. *Splintering Urbanism* : Networked Infrastructures, Technological Mobilities And The Urban Condition London ; New York : Routledge (2007), pp 35.
5. Reddy, A.V., Lu, A., & Wang, T. (2010). Subway Productivity, Profitability, and Performance A Tale of Five Cities. Transportation Research Record, Vol. 2143, pp. 48-58; and from MTR statistics and reports.
6. Presentation by Mr C. Y. Leung from Housing – The Market and Public Policy, BRE Advanced Lecture Series, Department of Building and Real Estate, Hong Kong Polytechnic University, March 2nd 2010
7. Thomas, Lisa (2009) As Recession Eases, No Escape for Hong Kong's Cage Dwellers, www.time.com/time/world/article/0,8599,1917897,00.html#ixzz1R1LN4R7F (accessed 8/21/2009)
8. Hong Kong became a colony of the British Empire after the First Opium War (1839–42) and was originally made up of just the island of Hong Kong. The colony's boundaries slowly extended in stages to encompass the Kowloon Peninsula and the New Territories by 1898. It was occupied by Japan during the Pacific War, after which the British resumed control until 1997, when the PRC acquired sovereignty. Hong Kong is now a Special Administrative Region (SAR) of China. Under British rule, Hong Kong was known for its laissez faire economics, minimum government intervention under the ethos of positive non-interventionism. This greatly influenced the current culture of Hong Kong, often described as 'East meets West'. Today, under the principle of 'one country, two systems', Hong Kong has a different political system from mainland China.

Hong Kong's independent judiciary functions under the common law framework. Hong Kong's unique geographic location, its Kowloon peninsula, its outlying islands surrounded by the waterfront and a deep bay harbour, has created much of the port and trade exchanges since its founding. As a former colony, Hong Kong's manufacturing base was built on its strategic location and elite networks. Today, most of the manufacturing and businesses have all moved north to southern China, or even further inland. Hong Kong today is predominantly a large financial service hub with a focus on tourism and services trade.

9   www.gov.hk/en/about/abouthk/factsheets

10 Carol Willis' statement from the Vertical Cities: Hong Kong–New York symposium; and, Wong, Kam-Sing "Designing for High-Density Living" in Ng, Edward (ed) Designing high-density cities for social and environmental sustainability. London; Sterling, VA : Earthscan (2010).

11 In the 1950s: Mark 1/11 (H-blocks, 6-storeys high, 60-72 units per level, single rooms with partitions, communal toilets, 11.5 sqm per family); Mark III (8-storeys, 32 units per level, central corridor access, public toilets, power supply for each unit, 14-21 sqm for a family of 4-6); In the 1960s: Mark V (15-storeys, 58 units per level, lift access per every third floor, private balconies with toilet, water and supply for individual units, 14-27 sqm for a family of 4-8); In the 1970s: Slab Blocks; Twin towers (with central voids, 20-23 storeys, 34 units per level, single loaded corridor, lift to each floor, private balcony, kitchen and toilet, cross ventilation, 36 to 44 sqm for a family of 4 to 8); H-Block; In the 1980s Linear Blocks; Trident I and II (Trident I is a tower block, 3 arms from a central lift core, 34-storeys, 26 units per level, central corridor access; 6 lifts with access to each floor, cross ventilation, a/c, 28 sqm for a family 3-4); In the 1990s: Harmony; Concord (Harmony: 16-18 units per level, prefab standard design, various units of different sizes, ac, electricity cut off, emergency generator, CCTV system, 17 sqm for a 1-person unit; 34 sq m for a 1-bedroom unit, 43 sq m: 2-bedroom unit, and 52 sqm for a 3-bedroom unit. Information reference to diagram from Hong Kong, Abitare 450. Milano: Editrice (2005), pp 129; and Y.M. Yeung and Timothy K.Y. Wong (eds.) Fifty Years of Public Housing in Hong Kong : A Golden Jubilee Review and Appraisal. Hong Kong : The Chinese University Press for the Hong Kong Housing Authority, Hong Kong Institute of Asia-Pacific Studies (2003)

12 Information on earlier research conducted by Prof. Dr. Chris H. Luebkeman with students from the Chinese University of Hong Kong, www.darkwing.uoregon.edu/~struct/courseware/hk1/hk1_pencil/pencil.html

13 These began the export-led industries and manufacturing for HK in its rise to industrialization from Castells, Manuel. The Rise of the Network Society. Cambridge, Mass: Blackwell Publishers, (1996) pp. 203-204.

14 Wolf, Michael. Hong Kong: front door/back door. London: Thames & Hudson (2004).

15 Lau, Justine, "Hong Kong to limit property investment immigration", Financial Times, 13 October 2010

16 Notes extracted from Reddy, A.V., Lu, A., & Wang, T. Subway Productivity, Profitability, and Performance A Tale of Five Cities. Transportation Research Record, Vol. 2143 (2010) and He, Peiran. Ways to Urbanisation: Post-war Road Development in Hong Kong. Hong

Kong: Hong Kong University Press (2008). Chapter 4, Construction of Mass Transit Systems, pp. 150

17 Notes from the introduction to 'Our Urban Species' in Glaeser, Edward L. (2011) ibid. He states that "Cities, the dense agglomerations have been engines of innovation since Plato and Socrates. The great prosperity of contemporary London, Tokyo etc. comes from their ability to produce new thinking."

18 From the Glossary of *Splintering Urbanism* (2007). The authors state: "Nodes are the dominant nodes that articulate and connect the flows of major infrastructure systems".

19 He, Peiran. Ways to Urbanisation: Post-war Road Development in Hong Kong, Hong Kong: Hong Kong University Press (2008) Chapter 6: The Electrification of the KCR.

20 "Hong Kong's subways are profitable because of high asset productivity, resulting from a strategic 'prudent commercial' design for high utilization and traffic density, a land-grant financing framework, more commercial freedoms, lower overhead costs and asset replacement needs." (from Subway Productivity, Profitability, and Performance: A Tale of Five Cities).

21 Grey (or gray) markets are also known as parallel markets. It is the trade of a commodity through distribution channels which, while legal, are unofficial, unauthorized, or unintended by the original manufacturer. The term 'grey economy', however, refers to workers being paid under the table, without paying income taxes or contributing to such public services as Social Security and Medicare. It is sometimes referred to as the 'underground' or 'hidden' economy. Unlike black market goods, grey market goods are legal. However, they are sold outside normal distribution channels by companies which may have no relationship with the producer of the goods. Frequently this form of parallel import occurs when the price of an item is significantly higher in one country than another. This situation commonly occurs with electronic equipment such as cameras. Entrepreneurs buy the product where it is available cheaply, often at retail but sometimes at wholesale, and import it legally to the target market. They then sell it at a price high enough to provide a profit but under the normal market price. International efforts to promote free trade, including reduced tariffs and harmonized national standards, facilitate this form of arbitrage whenever manufacturers attempt to preserve highly disparate pricing. Because of the nature of grey markets, it is difficult or impossible to track the precise numbers of grey market sales. Grey market goods are often new, but some grey market goods are used goods. A market in used goods is sometimes nicknamed a Green Market (Wikipedia definition).

22 Urban Land Institute (ed.), Mixed Use Development handbook. Washington: ULI (1987) and Mixed Use Development, Practice and Potential by Department for Communities and Local Government. www.communities.gov.uk/documents/planningandbuilding/pdf/156291.pdf (accessed 6/21/11).

23 Wall, A., 'Flow and interchange: mobility as a quality of urbanism'. In Architecture in cities: Present and future, Barcelona: XIX Congress of the International Union of Architects (1996), pp 158-66.

24 A strategy for supporting competition, branding, diverse pricing and segmented marketing of a wide range of infrastructure products and services within markets which are more or less regulated (from *Splintering Urbanism*)

25 The phenomenon of nylonkong as referenced to Elliott, Michael (2008) A Tale Of Three Cities, www.time.com/time/magazine/article/0,9171,1704398,00.html (accessed 1/17/2008)

26 Mostafavi, Mohsen and Doherty, Gareth (eds). Ecological Urbanism. Baden, Switzerland: Lars Müller (2010)

Lessons from High-Intensity, Mixed-Use Urbanism in Singapore's CBD

Waikeen NG
Associate Professor
School of Design & Environment
National University of Singapore

Introduction

This paper traces the origins of the concepts of high-intensity mixed-used urbanism as it has evolved in post-independence Singapore. The focus is on a heterogeneous group of built examples of high-density mixed-used developments within, or in close proximity, to the Central Business District (CBD). Some of the developments date back to nearly 40 years, and this generational duration make it ideal to compare them against original intentions as well as with the newer examples. These first urban development projects of the 1960s set the tone for other seminal developments to advance the ideas of high-density urbanism through the 1970s and 1980s. The diversity of the case studies and their urban/street level vibrancy (or lack thereof) provides glimpses of a future that didn't materialize. The most recent developments reveal insights into the ways that this form of urbanism might further evolve.

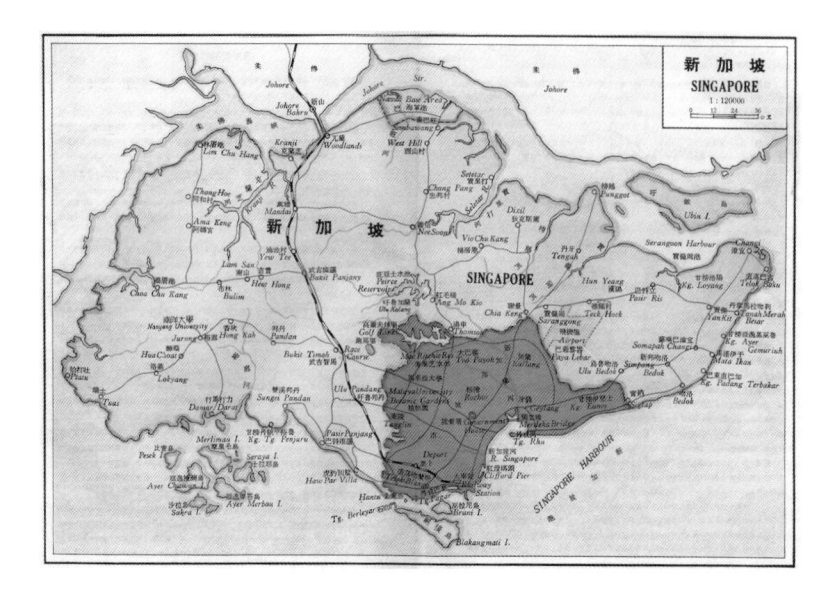

Opposite page
Fig. 1 Map of Singapore in the 1950s

This page
Fig. 2 Aerial view of Tiong Bahru
Fig. 3 Urban Renewal Precincts, 1966

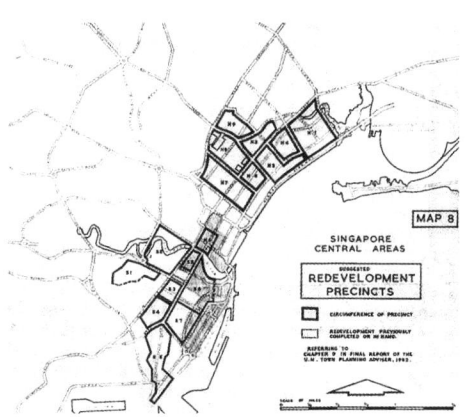

Origins of Urban Renewal

When the Singapore Improvement Trust (SIT) completed the 1958 Master Plan, Singapore was at the cusp of a significant change. The People's Action Party (PAP) would win the 1959 General Elections and would lead the island-state to full independence and set in motion its dramatic urban transformation. The 1958 Master Plan preserves what we might consider today the quaint notion of an urban-rural division in Singapore: the administrative limits of the City of Singapore, which covered about 90 square kilometres (km^2), about 15 percent of the land area at that time. In 1958, there were 1.5 million people living on the island, of which 75 percent (about 1.1 million) lived within the municipal limits. This meant that the population density in the historical areas of Singapore were well in excess of 12,000 people per km^2. The overcrowded living conditions, further aggravated by the post-WWII baby boom, were certainly not the type of "high intensity urbanism" or "multiple intensive land use" being promoted today.

To their credit, the British colonial administration was certainly aware of the problem. The SIT had been set up in 1927 to meet the housing needs of a growing population. The jewel in SIT's crown was the modest Tiong Bahru Housing Estate, based on Garden City ideals imported from Britain. When first completed, the layout of the Estate and the architecture would have appeared to be universe away from the congested conditions of Chinatown. As elegant an urban solution as Tiong Bahru was notwithstanding, SIT vastly underestimated the scale of the challenge and population growth, and managed to build only 23,000 units over 32 years. Consequently in 1960, a year after PAP's electoral victory, SIT was replaced by the Housing Development Board (HDB). The fledgling HDB was an organisation on a mission, and one of the highest priorities was the urban renewal of the Central Areas. Eventually, HDB had to focus on its core objective, which was housing, and the burgeoning urban redevelopment and renewal responsibilities for the entire island were assigned to a separate authority, the Urban Redevelopment Authority (URA), in 1974.

In the early 1960s, Singapore requested for, and received, technical advice on town planning from the UN. Professor Erik Lorange led the study on urban renewal, and one of the major recommendations of the study

Fig. 4 Beach Road Apartments
Fig. 5 Golden Mile Complex
Fig. 6 Precinct North 1 in the 1970s
Fig. 7 Precinct South 1 in the 1970s

was the identification of 17 precincts[1] in the Central Area for urban renewal. The government accepted the recommendations and incorporated them in the 1966 Urban Renewal Programme. The highest priorities were the precincts located at the edges: Precinct North 1 (at the mouth of the Rochor River) and Precinct South 1 (Havelock/Chin Swee Road, with the area around Outram Prison added subsequently). Earlier efforts at urban renewal had been piecemeal (two blocks of rental flats along Cantonment Road completed in 1963, for instance) or necessitated by the Bukit Ho Swee fire in June 1961. The 1966 Programme was the first concerted effort by the new government to undertake a deliberate re-making of the urban fabric. Consequently, the redevelopment of Precinct North 1 and Precinct South 1 introduced the high-intensity urban development typologies and experimentation in Singapore for the next two decades, and to an extent, to the present day.

The Tower/Podium and the Mega-structure

Precinct North 1 was completed in 1969, and comprised six 16-storey blocks of public housing. Although the appearance of the Beach Road Flats has been altered slightly during the recent Upgrading Programme, but the original planning principle is clear: 14 stories of apartments above a two-storey commercial (mainly local retail) podium, with an overall plot ratio of about 3.0.

There were also private developments within the precinct. The most significant architecturally is the Golden Mile Complex, completed in 1973. This stand-alone, self-contained "mega-structure" containing residential, commercial and retail uses has canonical status as one of Asia's first built examples of the Japanese Metabolist ideals, envisioning a new type of high-intensity mixed-use urbanism and marking the end of a proposed "Golden Mile" that extended northwards from the Singapore River/Civic District.

Fig. 8 Outram Park nearing completion in 1968
Fig. 9 Pearl Bank Apartments

Precinct South 1 was developed at the same time, and following a similar typology of a tower/podium residential complex and a stand-alone mix-use mega-structure. Their relative scale of Golden Mile Complex and Pearl Bank vis-à-vis public housing is best appreciated from the aerial views.

The public housing at Outram Park (completed in 1967, demolished in 2002) was more extensive of the two precincts, although it maintained the same plot ratio of 3.0. Here, the residential component comprised twelve HDB apartment blocks (with over 1600 units), while the more extensive two-storey podium had more mixed-uses uses as both local and national retail as well as professional offices and a bus terminal along Outram Road. When the adjacent 38-storey Pearl Bank Complex was completed in 1976, it achieved a list of superlatives: tallest residential building; largest number of units in a single block; highest density for a private development. The plot ratio, at 6.95, is more than double that of the Outram Park apartments. Like the Golden Mile Complex, this iconic circular development was also influenced by Metabolist and Corbusian ideals.

In addition to its 272 split-level luxury apartments, there was a "Sky Park" on the 27th level (that included a ballroom and function room) and a crèche on top of the parking structure. During its heyday in the 1970s, the Pearl Bank Complex and the Outram Park developments was a dense and lively combination of public-housing, commercial, high-end housing and transport links—the very model of a high-density, high-intensity mixed-use vertical precinct.

What the pilot urban renewal projects in Precincts North 1 and South 1 achieved was to set out the architectural and planning typologies for high-density/high intensity developments in the Central Business District (CDB) of Singapore—the tower/podium and the mega-structure—that was to prevail fairly unchanged for the next two decades. In the next sections, we will review some of the significant projects of these two typologies.

Tower-Podium Complexes

The Tower/Podium typology of residential 'slab' blocks on a two- to five-storey commercial or retail podium was only implemented within the Central Areas of Singapore. Although the growing population was gradually being housed in *New Towns* outside of the Central Area, and at lower densities that did not require such a typology even in the Town Centre areas, there was still a demand for a number of these high-density, high-intensity developments within the Central Areas. A typical example is Tanjong Pagar Plaza, completed in 1977 by the HDB, comprising 924 apartments in five

Figs. 10–11 Tanjong Pagar Plaza
Figs. 12–13 Chinatown Complex

blocks that vary in length and height from 15- to 22-storeys. The five blocks sit on both a two-storey commercial and local retail podium with a series of open courtyards, as well as a parking structure which provide a direct access to the apartment. It is also linked to a market/food centre. This project, which has a plot ratio 3.87, is an early refinement of the typology, with fairly intense urban activity in the podium levels that contrast with the relatively underused podium roof level. The contrast between two realms is a recurring characteristic of this typology.

Completed only in 1981, the Chinatown (or Kreta Ayer) Complex is one of the last examples of the tower/podium typology. A compact development by the HDB comprising two 21-storey residential blocks and a five-storey podium, it is one of the most urban places in Singapore with multiple intensive land uses: basement car park, semi-basement wet market, street-level community spaces and local retail, food centre and roof-top communal/sports facilities, not to mention the covered links to adjacent residential apartments and cultural facilities. The Complex, particularly its street level spaces, is the focus of much urban activity and has become the authentic heart of 'new' Chinatown (the 'old' Chinatown having become gentrified and touristy).

The buildings of the Tower/Podium typology as exemplified by these two examples continue to be vibrant and lively urban spaces. Since many of the built projects date from the 1970s, there are many senior citizens among the residents citizens. There is however, a growing group of young professionals, many of whom are internationals, who rent individual rooms or share apartments. The on-going evolution of these building complexes as they adapt to the changing demographics and urban environment will be a rich topic for further research.

Figs. 14–15 People's Park Complex – today and in the 1970s

Stand-Alone Mega-Structures

The second of the two typologies for high-density/high intensity developments in the Central Business District (CDB) of Singapore is the stand-alone/self-contained mega-structure. Typically, this typology is a mixed-use development undertaken by the private sector, on a site that the URA has acquired, amalgamated then made available under the Government Land Sale programme. Without the facilitating role of the URA, this typology would not have been possible, or at the very least, as widespread. One inevitable consequence of facilitating this typology is that substantial areas of 'fine grain' urban fabric were permanently altered.

People's Park Complex is one of Singapore's (and indeed Asia's) architecturally significant modernist buildings. Completed in 1973, the building is intellectually indebted to *the Met*abolists as well as Le Corbusier's *Unité d'Habitation*. The site was originally a public park (hence, "people's park") that was later occupied by an outdoor market. Since the site is located at the foot of Pearl's Hill, the market was known as Pearl's Market, which continues to be the Chinese name for the complex. On the strategic one-hectare site in the middle of the densely-populated Chinatown area of Singapore, and already a successful marketplace, the People's Park Complex was designed to be a high-dense, highly intensive "instant city", a vertical precinct comprising a 25-storey residential slab block of 280 apartments with Corbusian "streets in the air" and a five-storey podium, designed around a large (and originally, naturally ventilated) atrium space. This "city room" around which the different layers of spaces flowed, was a highly influential innovation.

With a plot ratio of 7.5, the Complex housed office and retail spaces, hosted exhibitions, and there was even a wax museum at one point in time. The circulation spaces, especially at the first floor, mimic an actual city with intimate connections to adjacent uses and even across New Bridge Road. The Complex and the surrounding streets surpass even Chinatown Complex for the levels of urban activities. After nearly four decades, the residential and communal roof top areas appear a little worse for wear, but the commercial and retail areas remain as busy as ever. In fact, with the construction of the Mass Rapid Transit (MRT) station immedi-

Figs. 16–17 International Plaza – exterior and internal atrium from 37th floor
Figs. 18–19 Raffles City – Aerial view in 2011 and atrium with original sky bridge in 1986

ately adjacent, and the somewhat tacky Chinatown Garden Bridge across New Bridge Road, the Complex is busier than ever, with an urban intensity that matches the busiest areas of even Kowloon, Hong Kong.

International Plaza has the distinction of having one of the highest plot ratios in Singapore. Built on a URA Land Sale site as an version of Chicago's Hancock Tower, a self-sufficient building containing all that is needed for urban living: a seven-storey podium containing shops and restaurants and car parking, 25 floors of offices, a medical centre and health club (including a pool) on the 36th floor, and 182 apartments and penthouses from the 37th to 50th floors. To encourage the experimental attempt to integrate what was a "new" urban work-live balance, URA allowed an increase in the built-up area, so the effective plot ratio was a whopping 19.7.

The building was completed in 1976 and has since undergone some minor upgrading to the podium facades and internal layouts. Unlike People's Park Complex, which is spatially more nuanced with layers and deliberate plays with the ambiguity inside-outside/public-private, International Plaza is clearly the more conventional development, at least at the podium level, where the desire to maximise rents have led to small shops along narrow, cramped corridors.

The final project in this brief review is what is probably the best, most fully-developed example of the stand-alone mega-structures: Raffles City. The development was completed in 1986 and comprises a four-storey podium and four towers of various heights up to 73-storeys podium. It is a masterly development of a single urban block on what was the site of Raffles Institution, one of Singapore's oldest schools.

The Raffles City development was

Figs. 20–21 The Pinnable@Duxton
Figs. 22–23 Clementi Mall and Clementi Town Centre

envisioned as a "city within a city" with an office tower, two five-star hotels, convention centre and retail. Unlike the other examples, it was designed from the beginning with connections to the City Hall MRT station (a major interchange station) and a future underground mall as well. It can be argued that Raffles City learnt from, and incorporated the most pertinent elements from its precedents: variation in block heights (Tanjong Pagar Plaza), the "city room" concept (from People' Park Complex), multiple intensive land uses, etc.

Towards 'Vertical Precincts': New Approaches Since 2001

With Raffles City, the stand-alone megastructure typology reached a high point, and it is difficult to find another urban development project after it that advances the concepts of high-density urbanism. Instead of advancing or remaining in stasis, I suggest that what has taken place since 1986 has most been a regression. For example, the lively street urbanism of Toa Payoh or Bukit Merah Town Centres (early 1970s) has morphed into the air-conditioned sterility of Tampines Regional Centre (early 1990s), a static collection of stand-alone office buildings and shopping malls.

A new impetus occurred in 2001 with the international architectural design competition for the redevelopment of *Duxton Plain*. The competition was for the redevelopment of a 2.5ha site in the Central Area where two of the earliest high-rise (10-storey) blocks were first constructed in 1961. The brief called for 50-storey residential towers. While this is not a mixed-use development, the significance of the competition is the breaking of the glass ceiling in terms of building height and residential density. It was also significant in that it would be

Figs. 24–25 Dim Sum ... or Poon Choi?

the first major public housing project in the CDB in over two decades.

The competition drew over 200 entries from around the world. The winning entry, by a local architectural practice, comprised seven blocks arranged in the shape of a hook, and featured sky bridges at the 26th and 50th storey. The 26th storey sky bridge is accessible only by residents, and includes a running track. The 50th storey sky bridge is however open to the public (for a small fee). The landscaping and community facilities at the ground level are of also of a very high design quality, and the plot ratio that was achieved was 9.1. Both the winning and runner-up schemes generated and tested out new planning and design ideas that would make ultra-high-rise living feasible, attractive and sustainable. The project, which came to be called Pinnacle@Duxton was completed by HDB in 2009, eight years after the competition. With 1848 apartments, the Pinnacle@Duxton is a welcome residential addition to the CBD. The high demand for the apartments is a bellwether for reversing the dearth of residential options in the area.

The second recently-completed project that signals a new approach in the planning and design of high-density, high-intensity 'vertical precincts' is Clementi Mall, which was completed in 2011. Clementi Mall is the redevelopment of one end of the existing Clementi Town Centre. The Town Centre was constructed in the early 1980s as an open street with low-rise housing with local retail. At either end was a cinema, or there were supermarkets, a medical centre, a food centre and market. The new complex is a dramatic intensification of density and use. It comprises two 40-storey blocks of public housing (380 apartments) that partially sits on a eight-storey podium comprising retail spaces, four levels of car parking (two basement), the bus interchange and even a much-needed and appreciated community library on the fifth storey. The building is directly connected to the Clementi MRT station, ensuring a seamless modal interchange, channelling people to the bus interchange as well as into the other parts of the Town Centre.

While I would hesitate to suggest that Clementi Mall represents a reinvention of the HDB Town Centre, the building is certainly a hybrid of the two typologies: it is part mega-structure, part tower/podium. It is also part enclosed mall (as in Tampines Regional Centre) and yet conserves the open-air mall of the existing Clementi Town Centre.

Vertical, Volumetric ... or both?
At the end of *The Making of Hong Kong: From the Vertical to Volumetric* (Routledge, 2011), the authors[2] almost playfully summarize the two concept using two well-known Chinese cooking dishes: "*dim sum*" and "*poon choi*". Just as individual *dim sum* dishes are served in separate bamboo baskets and conserve their individual flavours, so too vertical segregation of uses that is common in most burgeoning cities. The flavours of *poon choi* on the other hand intermingle with one another, and likewise volumetric spaces.

    I suggest that there is a case for both approaches: On one hand, the *dim sum* approach is needed (indeed desired) by residents who will have an option to escape to precious privacy away from the urban intensity at the street level. On the other hand, and certainly at the street or near-street levels, the *poon choi* approach is essential to achieve the messy, rowdy, lively urbanism so evident at Chinatown Complex and People's Park Complex (and looks like Clementi Mall would also achieve).

    One of the critiques of vertical cities is the apparent inefficiencies of residents having to travel down to the street level before they can access another building. A tall building is also not simply a horizontal street made vertical. The tower/podium typology (Tanjong Pagar Plaza etc) was a partial solution in the provision of a 'thin' two-storey interconnecting podium. By increasing and overlapping uses and activities of the stand-alone mega-structures, it is possible to create a much 'thicker' urban layer (Chinatown Plaza, Raffles City, Clementi Mall) that facilitates more connections at different levels. The way forward then perhaps is a hybrid solution: part tower/podium, part mega-structure; part vertical, part volumetric. The urban experience of our horizontal cities is both complex and varied; our vertical ones should aspire to the same.

Notes
1   Thankfully, only a few of the 17 districts were "renewed". They comprise a large part of the existing Conservation Areas, and Singapore would have lost a tremendous part of its built heritage if the programme had been fully implemented.
2   Barrie Shelton, Justyna Karakiewicz and Thomas Kvan.

ONE City

Matthias HOLLWICH
Lecturer, Department of Architecture, University of Pennsylvania School of Design, Philadelphia
Co-Founder Hollwich Kushner, New York City

Cities are becoming the primary settlement for the majority of people, it was estimated that in 2008 half of the world's population was living in cities, and by 2050 it could be more than 70 percent. The idea that a networked, internet-driven society will populate remote areas has been proven unsubstantial. People move to cities mostly for economic opportunities, but when does that trend stop? Will it stop at the moment when everybody is living in a city? Or will that go even further, to the point where everybody is living in ONE city?

If that is the case, and we take the density of the competition brief as a basis, then this will create a city for 1.3 billion people, which will occupy 13,000 square kilometres; a city spanning 115 by 115 kilometres—a high density city filling the Beijing Metro area. Looking into such an extreme scenario, it becomes apparent that the city structures of today are not fit for the future and that they have to be radically rethought. Not just in regards to traffic, loss of farmland, environmental pollution, financing, land use, public transportation, and ownership—but even more so in regards to quality of life.

Making cities work and thinking about the city as a machine for living is the wrong approach; we have to look at the city as a place for the fulfilment of individual dreams, lifestyles, and desires—especially for the people who are forced to move into them. Cities need to offer its inhabitants qualitative relationships: connections to nature, culture and tradition, socializing environments, and identity. When cities put lifestyle first, new and previously unseen qualities for humanity will unfold within hyper-urban societies.

Today's cities seem to sprawl endlessly. The distance goods, services and people travel is now measured in hours or kilometres rather than meters. The megacity is possible, and smaller versions are already being built. These cities are designed from a perspective that is both architectural and engineered, but rarely based on the experiential quality of the people who will fill them.

Cities should be a place for people to fulfil their needs, wants and desires; an experiential environment to stimulate both physically and psychologically. Cities must be rich with variety; urban, in tune with nature, personal, social. Lifestyle design is a necessity, not a trend; the need for a realignment of how we consume and build over and around nature is obvi-

Fig. 1   China
Fig. 2   Chinese cities

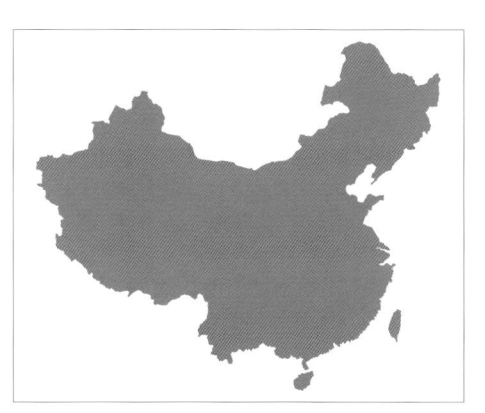

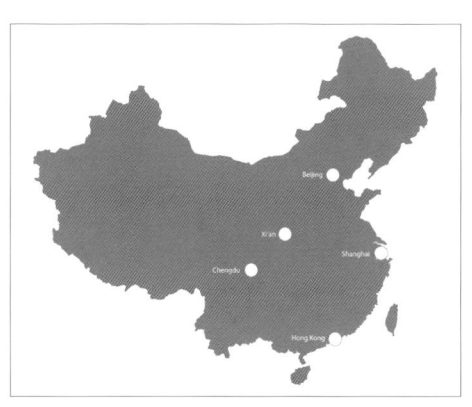

ous. Future cities must emphasize multiple scales; the individual experience is the master plan.

Taking a look back at what may soon be the future, we find many avant-garde explorations that reconsidered urbanity both massive in scale and departure from the norm. The highly rational work of Hilberseimer, the gently floating cities of Yona Freidman, the technical fantasies of Archigram, the highly opportunistic sketches from Rem Koolhaas' City of the Captive Globe, the bold yet strikingly pure imagery of Superstudio; city design needs an enriched senses of imagination, scale, nature, experience and humanity.

The two prototypes developed by our team of students at the University of Pennsylvania School of Design focused on the relationship between city and nature: revolution, the city over nature, and evolution, nature over the city.

"Hover" is a revolutionary idea; an inversion of the traditional city. The city is dense, a compact layered web of urbanity hovering over nature with people and nature on top of everything. The proposal lets air flow freely around and throughout the city, letting nature flourish under its thin, porous canopy. A city of 100,000 will necessarily be enormously expensive. We focus on reducing the real cost of the environmental impact caused by construction, and maximizing the value gained by expanding nature and urbanity simultaneously.

"Park City" is an evolutionary idea; designed for the inhabitants experience first, the commercial developer interests second. The proposal is a communal scenographic environment; a city draped in a green blanket and shaped to perform spatially and environmentally, not individual shapes and unrelated forms. The highly regular street and structural plan grid is manipulated in section to produce a new topographic interior whose peak performs spatially, scenographically, and environmentally. A hybrid model of typical city and topographic feature enriches individual opportunities to experience the diversity of spaces and environments.

We must take cities to the extreme, and develop symbiotic relationships between massive scales of humanity, urbanity and nature. Rather than cultural sterility in favour of mechanic performance or hermetic biospheres, we propose open nature, vast wild and cultivated ecospheres, broad and diverse. We cannot build more vague suburban horizontality or automobile 'strip' environments first observed in Las Vegas. Cities need to be more in tune with nature and man, a return to cities in nature and nature in cities. The city must be a form serving the community and not corporate iconographic intentions.

The pressing issues of today demand radical new city designs, they are urgently needed and must happen. Pursuing them will become the responsibility of upcoming generations.

"Hover" is a revolution, a radical rethinking of every city. "Park City" is an evolution, a hyper-natural maturation of today's city typology. Both offer a new prototype of urbanism, and exhibit the potential of the designers and cities of the future shaped from the creative minds and hands of our emerging talents from the University of Pennsylvania.

Fig. 3 Chinese cities expansion
Fig. 4 Beijing expansion
Fig. 5 The ONE city

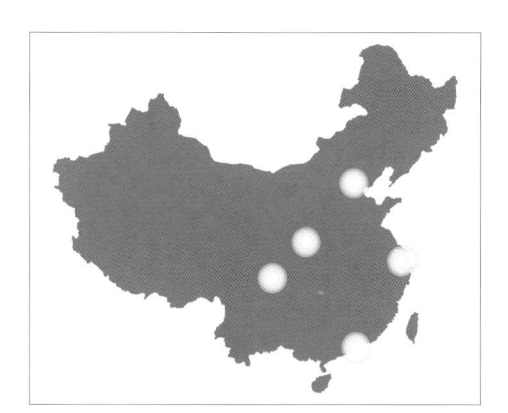

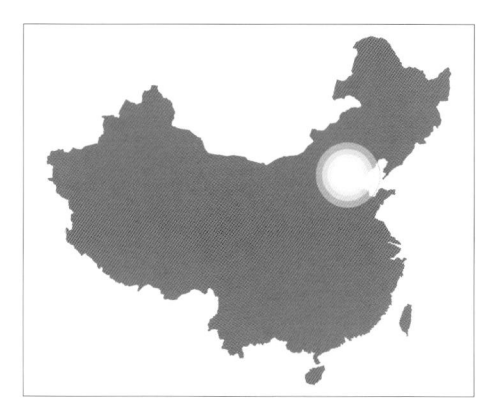

Key Issues in the Design Approach of Megastructures

YAO Dong (Lecturer) and HUANG Yiru (Professor and Vice Dean)
College of Architecture and Urban Planning (CAUP)
Tongji University, Shanghai

Land Shortage
With the rapid urbanization over the last three decades, China is leaping forward from an agriculture country to an industrial one. If we maintain this rate of urbanization, statistics suggest that by 2020, 50 percent of Chinese will reside within urban areas; and this figure will rise to 75 percent by 2050. Along with the increasing demand of urbanization and development, the nation is facing a land crisis—lacking not only developable land, but also arable land. Senior government officials have pointed out that, "from the aspect of investment and inputs, our urbanization which is overwhelmingly relying on the land, is not sustainable. Some cities use their land very extensively; while others extend their construction plan without any consideration. Between 1999 and 2007, when the urban built-up areas increased by 7.2 percent, but they housed only an additional four percent of the new immigrants to the urban areas. With this urban development patterns and the built quantity expected in 2020, China will need another 90 percent of built up land to fulfil the 2050 goal of urbanization rates of 75 percent."[1] [Fig.1]

Opposite page
Fig. 1 New Developing Zone in China share the extensive land usage

This page
Fig. 2 Le Corbusier's 1930 plan for Algiers (Perspective)

Obviously, the shortage of land resources has become a major constraining factor in China's urban development, overshadowing most other building factors. To solve the land crisis, high-rise high-density models have become the norm in many big cities. The situation worsens when the land value rises way above the construction cost. This phenomenon occurs not only in China but also in many other Asian cities with that have increasing populations and urban densities. It appears that 'vertical cities' is the only option open to us.

Since skyscrapers are already a very developed iconic typology, we would like to explore the megastructure as another prototype for our future cities and the key issues in the design approach.

Revolutionary Idea
In traditional language, the term "Megastructure" is used to indicate buildings and constructions with extreme scale comparing to its counterparts, such as the Pyramids in ancient Egypt, the Great Wall of China, and so on. Fumihiko Maki is the first person to reinterpret it into the vocabulary of architecture. As one of the core member of the vanguard group "Metabolists", then having taught both in Harvard and Washington University in St Louis, Maki gave the first architectural definition of the Megastructure in his book "Investigations in Collective Form".[2] From his view point, there are three prototypes of collective urban forms: compositional form, mega-structure and group form. He defined a Megastructure as "a large frame in which all the functions of a city or part of a city are housed" that has been "made possible by present day technology."[3]

Along with the development of construction technology such as high-rise building and the long truss beam, the fantasy of utopian cities became close to reality in the early twentieth century. However, the first Megastructure plan as a real carrier of the human inhabitant only emerged after the First World War, by one of the major founder of modern architecture and modern planning—Le Corbusier. His 1931 proposal "Project A, Fort l'Emepereur" is a super long housing highway bridge complex. [**Fig. 2**] Because of its seemingly unlimited structure length and infill of the individual housing, this proposal is regarded as the real beginning of the Megastructure. Although Le Corbusier never used the word, his innovative idea did affect almost all Megastructure design that followed.

Fig. 3   Constant's 1960 plan of "New Babylon"(1960)
Fig. 4   Yona Friedman's 2007 aerial city plan for Shanghai

As an unprecedented urban form, Megastructure concepts stirred the passion of many architects and artists, especially in the era after World War II. Having survived the war, many European countries and also Japan faced the task of relief construction and urbanization. Many people became homeless even though a huge amount of housing was built, and large areas of arable land were converted into built up areas. This is a similar situation faced by many newly developing Asian cities today.

During this period, many plans were invented/designed: some of these became popular and were even discussed by ordinary people and remained influential even in twenty-first century. This include: "New Babylon" by the Dutch artist Constant Nieuwenhuys [**Fig. 3**]; "Spatial City" by the Jewish-French architect Yona Friedman [**Fig. 4**]; the "1960 Plan for Tokyo" by the Japanese architect Kenzo Tange [**Fig. 5**]; and the "Plug-In City" by the British vanguard group "Archigram" [**Fig. 6**]. Unlike the four Utopian designs above, the American architect Paolo Soleri and his followers was able to implement his design. Although the desert town of Arcosanti [**Fig. 7**] remain in the early phase after several decades of work, Soleri learned a lot from the implementation and developed a new theory called "Archology" and its model building type as the "Hyperstructure". In his theory, buildings in three-dimensions will replace the traditional two-dimensional cities and will achieve ecology, where human and environment can reach their true harmony.

Over several generations, the Megastructure has been realised in many places: "MM21" in Yokohama Bay and Crystal Island in Moscow have become national landmarks and draw even more attention worldwide. Amazed by such Megastructures (and the potential profits), many Chinese developers have set their sights on building Megastructure cities in the coming years. For instance, Vantone, a Beijing-based property developer, has commissioned a set of conceptual plans of 'vertical cities' that it has exhibited around the world.

Reinstalled Functions

Given the shortage of land and the excessive property prices on one hand, and the advances in contemporary constructional technologies, not to mention the financial support of real estate tycoons, it appears that the

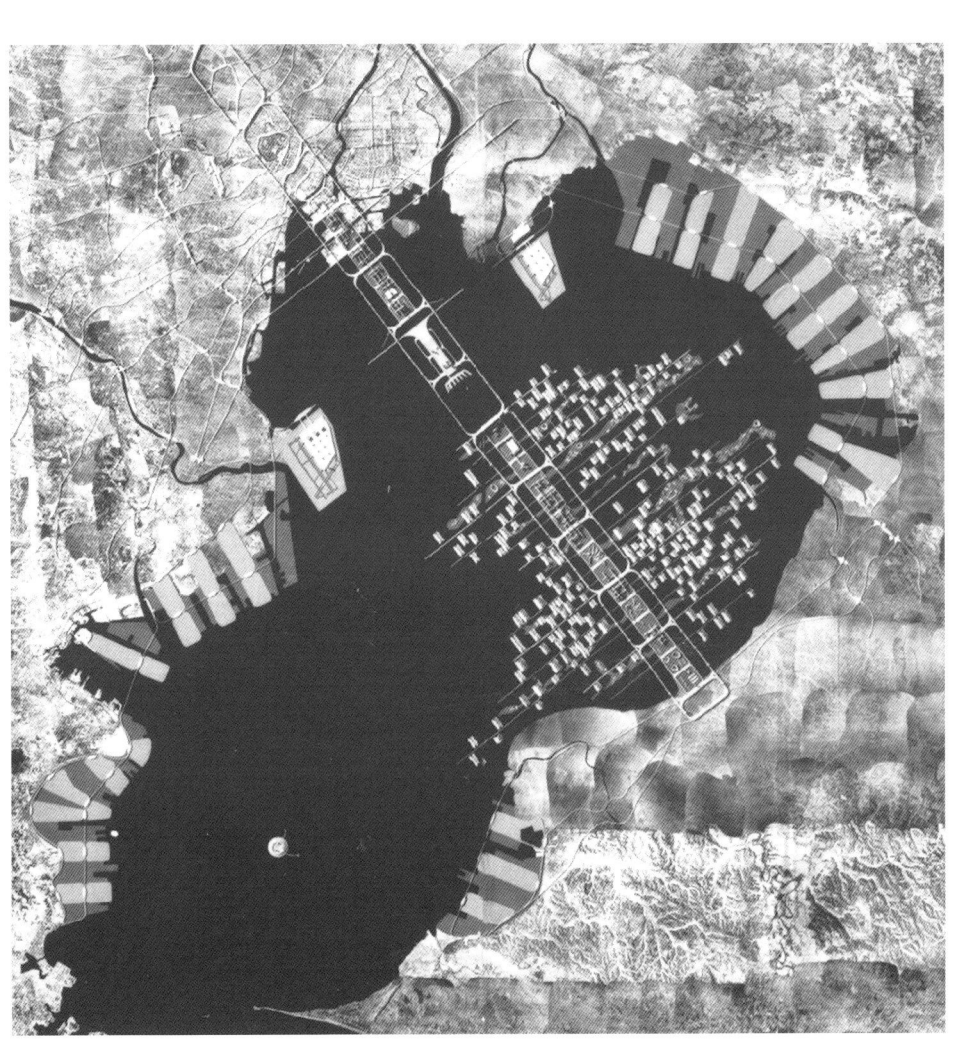

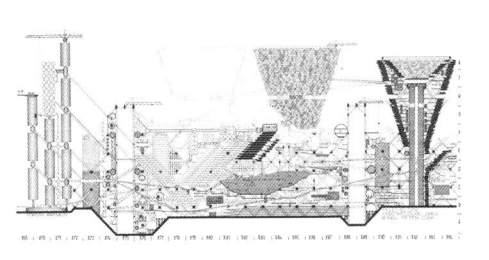

Fig. 5   Kenzo Tange's 1960 Plan for Tokyo
Fig. 6   Archigram's 1964 plan of "Plug-in city"
Fig. 7   Paolo Soleri's plan of eco-city Arcosanti

major obstacles facing the realisation of a megastructure city have been overcome. However, there are still many questions that remain before such a project can be made possible. One of the most critical questions is how to reinstall the functions of a normal, ordinary in a vertical manner.

According to Maki, a Megastructure city can contain an extremely high population density on a small piece of land, and provide all or part of the functions of an ordinary city. Defined in this way, we observe that two types of very high density developments already exist. Both types have a very high-rise building on top of a multilevel podium complex that houses a number of city functions, the major difference between the two is about the geography of the podium. In the Hong Kong model, most of the podium is above the ground; whereas the Yokohama model extends its podium deep into the underground. The two types show a little difference, for example, the street scale in the Hong Kong model is narrower. Both vertical models can be considered amplifications of traditional high rise towers. This is the "birthday cake" typology with a system of vertical lifts and horizontal transportation at the ground level. Consequently, all movement lead to the ground level, which will never escape from the situation of overcrowding. As the key issue that high density cities receive the most criticism, the potential resolution of the overcrowded ground level is a possibility with the megastructure city.

It is common knowledge that most activities in urban living have different destinations; some are linked with the outside, while others are not. Seen this way, all city activities can be grouped as internal or external and the two groups often do not intersect. Merging the two abruptly not only causes the deterioration of the ground level density and traffic congestion, but also involves a great waste of the time of the people undertaking the activities. For instance, family members who live in different but adjacent towers must head to the ground level in order to meet each other because it is the only way possible. What if we add another system aside from the elevators connecting the ground? Furthermore, if the megastructure city is big enough, we can place all activities with less outside connection to another level in the air, then what we will not only reduce the ground traffic but the interruption those functions experience in ordinary models. As a result, both categories of functions will become more efficient.

In summary, all functions of Megastructure city can be placed into two or more levels with only one of them at the ground level. The ground level system emphasizes the strong connection to the outside world will compose of underground garages, pedestrian walkways, elevated highways, other public transportation and logistics. This system ensures that the Megastructure city remains in contact with the outside world of not only human civilization but also nature as well. To maximize the blend of Megastructure and the natural environment, the footprint of the ground level will be minimized. [Fig. 8]

Social Connection
Another system, above the ground level, will emphasize the linkages between the inhabitants as well as the independence of the Megastructure. The "sky system" may contain many stories that house various city functions that serve the inhabitant, such as the City Hall, schools, offices and shopping centres etc.; all of which need fresh air.

Hovering above the ground, the roof top of the "sky system" could become another outdoor space where social connections can occur as they do in traditional cities. Other than for emergency uses by ambulances or fire engines, the roof top or "sky deck" is reserved for all pedestrian activities, and welcomes those who love the organic lifestyle we enjoyed before the industry age. The "sky deck" also functions as a refuge area during emergencies. After arriving to the "sky deck" by elevators or escalators, residents can reach most of the city functions on foot. Horizontal

Fig. 8   Multileveled stages in megastructure leave little footprint and lead to a more efficient city

linkages will be reintroduced to become the major traffic carrier which avoids the prevailing "elevator-holic" vertical cities.

To avoid the segregation of functional city, every community in the Megastructure city will house various functions that serve its residents. Small offices, convenience stores, clinics and kindergartens can be reached within short distances. The new lifestyle of 'Small Office Home Office' (SOHO) and internet-based businesses make possible the reduction of long distance commuting for everyday life. People in the Megastructure city will be able to lead a more ecological life by means through all of the above.

Although there are many advantages listed above; there remains a question mark about social life in the Megastructure city. It is not clear how much time is required for the inhabitants to get used to the new geography; how they can find their way in the new city form; how to identify their social status with the new urban context; and how to adapt their living arrangements in the megastructure as they age.

Sustainability of the Megastructure

Eighty years has passed since Le Corbusier designed his Utopian "Project A, Fort l'Emepereur". Although the Megastructure city has been reinterpreted by a number of design vanguards, none of them has been fully built. It is frustrating that no one can determine if the idea can survive in reality. In our view, in addition to the technical or financial obstacles, the sustainability of the Megastructure city is another issue we have to consider.

Can the Megastructure city adapt to time, like ordinary cities do over the course of human history? Like all created objects, a city has a lifespan. All cities will disappear, some because of war, some because of natural disasters and the rest because they could not provide for their citizens any more. In the era of high technology, we are capable to build artificial environments that combat climate change, but can we make the Megastructure city that can adjust itself when its inhabitants change?

In the history of the Megastructure city, some schemes (especially those from *the Met*abolists) were designed to be adjustable; some of them were designed to be movable, like those from Archigram; some of them were designed with up-to-date renewable energy technologies. Unfortunately, none of them have been proved to be true. Kisho Kurokawa's Nakagin Building, the miniature metabolist building, never adds or detaches any unit. Ron Herron's Walking City only witnessed its creator moving like other urban nomad. It has also been pointed out that

Dickson Despommier's Vertical Farms will cost more energy than it proposes to save.[4]

It is time to establish a new strategy for sustainable Mega-structure cities; otherwise this idea will only remain on the bookshelf of science fiction novels. The Megastructure city does not have to be self-sufficient, but it must be able to adjust itself. To achieve this goal, we believe that an on-site precast construction and installation industry must be integrated into the Megastructure ecology. This industry will and must become one of the mainstay industries in the Megastructure city. It can reduce energy expenditure from transportation and productive pollution from the very beginning; it can employ the inhabitants through the lifespan of the city; it can recycle and provide units and parts to meet the changing demand of the megastructure and its civilians.

Conclusion
In the 1970s, when housing was no longer the major social concern, the Megastructure concept lost it novelty and became purely an architectural interest. Theorist Reyner Banham wrote in his masterpiece, Megastructure, that "since no architect who considers himself worthy of his craft can bear to stand by and see his design destroyed, especially grand designs on the scale of city, the Megastructure proved to be a self-cancelling concept."[5]

In the new millennium, similar to the situation that developed countries faced in the 1950s, the cities in the developing Asian countries face an even more critical shortage of land and housing resources as well as very high urban densities. With technical and financial support, as well as the critical study on the function reinstallation, social reconnection and sustainability, we are looking forward to see the Megastructure city become another possibility other than the forest of skyscrapers.

Notes

1 Shouxin Li, 2003. Mr. Li, Shouxin is the director of the planning department of the National Development and Reform Committee. The viewpoint is quoted from the report listed behind. Wang, Jiang. Chinese urbanization rate will overpass 50 percent in "the Twelfth-Five Plan"(王优玲、江国成. "十二五"期间我国城镇化水平预计超过50%)[N/OL]. Beijing: Xinhua Net, http://news.xinhuanet.com/fortune/2010-03/29/content_13268575.htm

2 Maki, F. Investigations in the Collective Forms. St Louis: Washington University, (1964).

3 Ibid.

4 The Economist. Vertical Farm: Does it really stack up [N/OL]. http://www.economist.com/node/17647627

5 Banham, R. Megastructure: Urban Futures of the Recent Past. New York: Harper & Row, (1976).

Urban Breeding Grounds in Chinese Greenfields

Kees CHRISTIAANSE
Chair of Architecture & Urban Design, ETH Zurich
Founding Partner KCAP Architects & Planners, Rotterdam/Zurich/Shanghai

Introduction

Europe is currently experiencing an "urban Renaissance" as a result of the changing spatial demands of the economy. The economy has become more service-oriented, more flexible, variable in scale, more customized and subject to continuous cycles of redefinition. As a consequence, a more diverse and flexible "urban" environment enabling manifold modes of physical interaction between people is becoming indispensable to accompany the inherent social and cultural transformation.

For example, in the current transformation of south-eastern central Rotterdam [**Fig. 1**], we can observe a radical difference in dealing with building typologies, programmes and public space in relation to the recent past. Different building typologies in various architectural styles are realized, but the buildings always have bases, allowing flexible use, whereas programmes in the upper parts vary from social housing to upgrade lofts, offices and hybrids in-between. As one can see in the perspective of the market area [**Fig. 2**] the buildings behave not unlike the medieval Laurens church: they neither form pure solitary objects, nor solid perimeter blocks. This hybrid quality finds its counterpart in the character of public space, which oscillates between a street that is cut out of the urban mass and a square on which the buildings stand like chess pieces. Thus a dynamic dialogue between buildings, programs and the public space network, reinforced by the market stalls, is established.

As families and other household-types are increasingly embedded in multiple social networks, the demand for flexible and mixed-use quarters, with

Opposite page
Fig. 1　South-Eastern Central Rotterdam. The red tower is KCAP's Red Apple in the Wineharbour quarter
Fig. 2　Weekly market in eastern central Rotterdam. Background buildings by KCAP, MVRDV, CIE and Hans Kollhoff.

This page
Fig. 3　Townhouses in Rotterdam-South by KCAP.
Fig. 4　Valerius Street Amsterdam, c. 1935.
Fig. 5　Architecture Forum Zürich in Kreis 4 Quarter with exhibition of ETH-Studio research.

amenities that range from child-care and 24-hour shopping facilities to web-based production or high-grade public transport, is increasing.

The town-house, a flexible reinterpretation of the traditional one [**Fig. 3**], usually has a double ground-floor or souterrain/bel-étage, in which either a whole house, a house with home-office or practice, a double maisonette or four senior-apartments can be accommodated. The transitional zone between the public and private invites owners to use it as a front garden, bicycle-storage or a show-case for their products. Sometimes courtyards house larger studio- or workshop-spaces, where middle-sized production and manufacturing may take place.

Europe's urban centres and nineteenth century neighbourhoods formed the early stage for this process and have been able to accommodate this urban renaissance. Their main features are: identity, multi-directional street patterns, varying plot-sizes and flexible typologies. With their socially diverse history, they constitute "urban breeding grounds" that have proven to play a substantial role in support of economic vitality, social integration and cultural production between its diverse communities.

The Valerius Street in the Amsterdam Old-South quarter, where I was born in 1953 [**Fig. 4**], used to be a mixed street dominated by middle-class households, but also contained lower and upper class people. Dairy shops, vegetable markets, bicycle workshops as well as small manufacturing marked the street corners. Today the area is the victim of Jane Jacobs' "Self-Destruction of Diversity". As a 'breeding ground' it was so successful, that a strong gentrification wave created an expensive street, where the shops and studios have been exchanged for gourmet restaurants, finance and law consultants and art galleries for the establishment. This process can be seen in many cities and although the process produces a degree of segregation and disparity, it must be considered as a form of urban renewal and of adding value. Gentrification is hard to stop, but can be steered.

The "Kreis 4" quarter in Zürich [**Fig. 5**] is still in an earlier stage of development. Diverse social groups, from poor overseas immigrants, young architects and prostitutes to yuppie-bankers and older indigenous residents still flock the streets that are lined with a diversity of shops, cafés, galler-

Fig. 6 Bird's-eye view of Lloyd's Quarter Rotterdam.
Fig. 7 Temporary gardens on unbuilt plots at Müllerpier, Lloyd's Quarter.
Figs. 8–9 Oostelijke Handelskade Amsterdam, mixed use project with existing warehouses, KCAP.

ies and workshops. Neighbourhoods like these are subject to intensive research into their internal mechanisms, in order to find policy recommendations and design guidelines that are able to 'coach' their unique qualities. The picture shows the exhibition of our ETH-studio work in the showcase of the Architecture Forum in an old shop.

These qualities have also inspired the successive wave of urban renewal in industrial and harbour sites, where these principles have been successfully translated. It triggered a change in paradigm in urban design, as we can see in the docklands of Amsterdam, Rotterdam and Hamburg.

Whereas the early waterfront sites in Amsterdam, Rotterdam and London were developed as pure mono-functional housing estates, projects like the Lloyd's Quarter [**Figs. 6 & 7**] in Rotterdam already experimented with various degrees of income groups, different typologies and re-use of existing industrial buildings as offices, lofts or film- and theatre-studios.

In the OostelijkeHandelskade project in Amsterdam [**Figs. 8 & 9**] the logical luxury-only programme for a prime site was abandoned in favour of a mixed palette of social housing and loft-studios next to expensive penthouses and up-market offices, while the ground floor was occupied by restaurant "15", a franchise by Jamie Oliver, where ex-delinquent youths work as waiters and kitchen-helps to reintegrate into society. The new architecture, with rusty specks in the facades reminding its nautical history, and the restored warehouses hold each other in a geometric embracement, creating bold public spaces— 'the city as loft'—that invite the users to occupy them with their activities.

The urban renaissance even has an impact on greenfield development, which became less mono-functional and centralized in its transport and amenity concepts. Although greenfield planning continues, peripheral areas in Europe are clearly in crisis and gradually replaced by the revitali-

Fig. 10   Bijlmermeer Quarter, Amsterdam, 1960s.
Fig. 11   Bijlmermeer, aerial photo of transformation.
Fig. 12   Bijlmermeer, new street-oriented development, KCAP.
Fig. 13   Red Apple, Wine Harbour Rotterdam, KCAP.

zation of brownstone sites or even demolished and replaced by new mixed developments.

An interesting example is the Bijlmermeer quarter in Amsterdam, a 1960s mono-functional social housing neighbourhood [Fig. 10]. During a long time it was the biggest housing estate in the Netherlands, fully designed according to modernist urbanism with elevated highways and functional segregation. Although in terms of building standard and quality this project can match many Chinese mass-housing projects, the increase in crime and deprivation as a result of social and racial problems, urged the City of Amsterdam to take the bold decision to demolish the whole quarter and replace it by low-rise, middle density housing, mixed with other functions [Fig. 11]. The dykes with elevated highways were removed and replaced by grade-level avenues along which mixed-use projects with commerce in the base were projected [Fig. 12].

Within the city, brownstone sites were re-developed, providing the "urban Renaissance" with relevant typologies [Fig. 13]. This trend of intensification and slow-growth raises hope for the re-establishment of a European cultural landscape balanced between city and nature. The conditions are favourable, considering the limited footprint of the average European city and the fact that approximately 500 cities, with an average of 150,000 residents, form a network with a maze width of about 100 kilometres.

Except for a few large agglomerations, like Paris or London, European cities are still fairly compact with road- and rail-network and high-speed train-tracks under construction [Fig. 14].

In Asia, especially in China, the situation is the opposite. The mayor cities are much larger and much farther apart, and undergo an enormous growth. Here, approximately 500 cities of at least three million people form a network with a maze width of 750 kilometres. Their fragmented footprint rapidly expands into the landscape. Large mono-functional com-

Fig. 14 Satelite image Western Europe.
Fig. 15 Satelite image Asia.
Fig. 16 Google Earth of Chengdu, 45km height.
Fig. 17 Google Earth of Randstad Holland, 45km height.
Fig. 18 Mass housing near Suzhou Creek, Shanghai.
Fig. 19 Gentrification in Julu street, Shanghai.
Figs. 20–21 Tian Zi Fang, Shanghai.

pounds with centralized services are constructed [**Fig. 15**].

A striking difference show two Google-Earth pictures, taken from the same height, one from Chengdu [**Fig. 16**], showing a centralized city fanning out across the countryside, the other from the Randstad Holland [**Fig. 17**], including Amsterdam, Rotterdam, The Hague and Utrecht, a decentralized, low-rise metropolis with vast green areas in between.

Figs. 22 Tian Zi Fang, Shanghai.
Figs. 23 KCAP office, Shaan Xi Road, Jingan, Shanghai.

Remarkably the two areas contain more or less comparable population figures.

On the one hand, this is understandable, as it is comparable to the post-war reconstruction period in Europe, when large scale suburbs with mass-housing and centralized amenities were rapidly constructed in order to meet the demand for housing as a result of the baby-boom.

However, after a violent development boom with mass-housing along Suzhou Creek [Fig. 18] the authorities acknowledged that development should be regulated.

Although the cultural backgrounds between Europe and Asia, and hence the concept of urbanity, are quite different, in several areas of Shanghai and Beijing, one can observe similar urban renewal and qualification processes as in Europe, where old urban typologies or industrial sites have been transformed in vibrant urban places. Here we can also observe the relationship between typology and economic development: artist studios, fashion workshops, architecture and engineering firms and restaurants are set up in brownstone buildings with flexible ground floors opening to the street. [Fig. 19]

In the Tianzifang neighbourhood one can, like in Amsterdam-South also already observe the "self-destruction of diversity", where an old workers quarter now is turned into a vibrant tourist zone with souvenir shops, boutiques and Italian restaurants lining the ground floor of the brick buildings [Figs. 20 & 21]. Around the neighbourhood new typologies of low-rise high-density brick apartments show the added value of the area and the emergence of interesting new typologies based on traditional references [Fig. 22]. It is no irony, that our KCAP-office is housed in such an area, where the Dutch ministry of culture has rented a collective building for Dutch design firms to promote themselves in China [Fig. 23].

Another example is from the Shenzhen 'villages' where density and ground floor activation have gone hand in hand and produced vibrant types of urbanity. In terms of social sustainability, these examples also show that 'care' for the environment is triggered by some urban typologies and not by others.

Shenzhen's urban regeneration areas of Sungang and Qingshuihe [Figs. 24, 25 & 26] have become outdated since the warehouse facilities cannot meet contemporary needs anymore. Despite the vanishing importance as a logistics centre, rich urban life has settled itself at its fringes and gradually infiltrates the area. For the urban regeneration of the site, KCAP did not propose a fixed regeneration masterplan, as is common practice in China, but an open framework and a development strategy.

Figs. 24–26 Shenzhen Creative Gateway, KCAP.

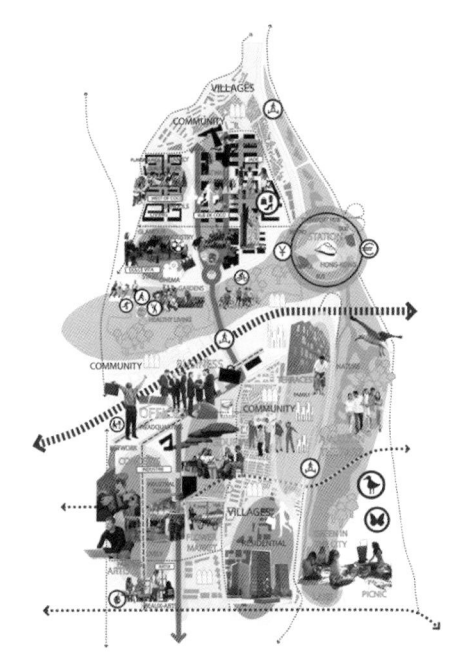

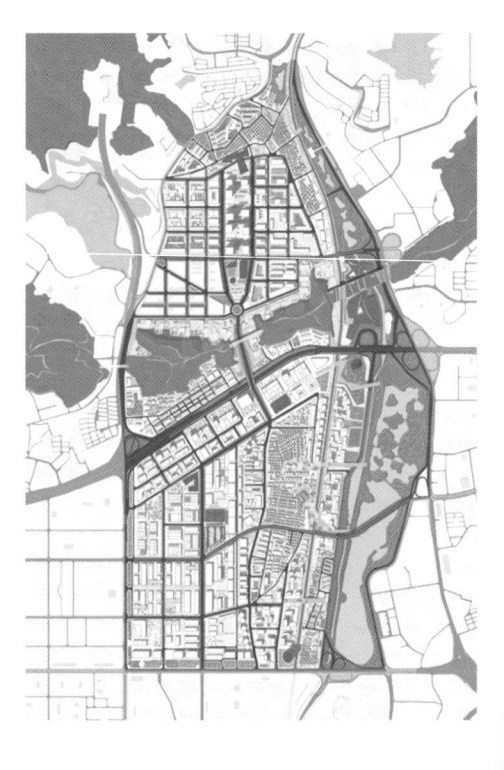

This approach is based on the acceptance of the current urban condition as a starting point. Instead of grand projects, the design introduces a series of measures and projects to be integrated in the existing fabric, respecting the qualities of the site. The framework will continue the urban history of Shenzhen as the result of pragmatism rather than beaux arts design. Based on detailed typological studies, the plan defines zones of different scale and transformation potential. In a separate study, new programs have been defined, that are based on the existing fine grain of economic networks but bring them to a higher economic profile. Next to design, creation, management and sale of fashion, the focus will lie on industrial and furniture design as well as media and film industry. This economic profile will be complemented by high quality housing and a chain of public buildings. In its positioning the area will not only play an important role as the extension of Luohu district centre, but also as a creative gateway to and from Hong Kong.

As the current urbanization tsunami in a long-term perspective may cause massive problems in the field of economic flexibility, social sustainability and mobility, a process-oriented, open-ended urbanism based on integrated urban development with a combination of residential, production, service-infrastructure and public transport is urgently needed.

Meanwhile, KCAP designed three large greenfield developments, Green Town in Beijing [**Fig. 27**], Trinity in Shenyang [**Fig. 28**] and Keqiao Urban Ballet in Shaoxing [**Fig. 29**], in which the pressure to build high-density mono-functional housing is translated into an attempt to create more differentiated neighbourhoods. Although they are not idle, they definitely mark a step towards

Fig. 27 Greentown, Beijing, KCAP.
Fig. 28 Trinity, Shenyang, KCAP.
Fig. 29 Keqiao Urban Ballet, Shaoxing, KCAP.

a more conscious dealing with large scale greenfield development.

Green Town is located in a green district for the Chinese middle classes, outside the fifth orbital road in the southeastern part of Beijing at a distance of about 15 kilometres from the centre. Its programme consists of 3.500 residential units and a community centre. Like in the townhouses in Rotterdam, the residential blocks are preferably oriented on the ground level with as many entrances as possible. Ground floor units can be used in a flexible way. Uniformity in materials and the repetitive use of private outdoor spaces contribute to the area's cohesion. The community centre, which is traditionally an essential component of Chinese residential areas, contains a swimming pool, a restaurant, bars, an internet café, a sports and a dance hall, sauna, day care facilities, a library and two tennis courts on the roof. The ground floor is completely transparent. The shopping area is deliberately placed on the edge of the neighbourhood, enabling residents of adjacent quarters to use these facilities and softening the effect of gatedness in the area.

The Trinity site is integrated in an overarching masterplan for the entire left bank of Shenyang, envisioning the development of an eight-kilometre 'linear city' running parallel with the river. Like Shanghai and Rotterdam, Shenyang 'jumps' over the river establishing urban life and multiple centres on both sides of the river. The river Hun will transform from being an edge into a 'green' centre. The masterplan is based strategically on the proximity and relation of the area to the river and on being a self-supporting neighbourhood. The plan defines three centres and two landscape axes. It maximises the outward orientation of the commercial and business facilities. Consequently, apartment towers are placed on a base where commercial functions are housed and a considerable amount of town-houses with flexible grade-level counteracts the apartment towers. Within this main frame, an archipelago of districts, each of which with its own sub-centre, are the founding principles of the urban concept.

"Keqiao Urban Ballet" [**Fig. 29**] presents KCAP's masterplan for a 45-hectare site in Shaoxing. The area, which is currently occupied by redundant textile industry and residences, will be redeveloped for residential use with community functions, sport and commercial facilities in a landscaped setting of waterland and parks.

Keqiao is the major development area of Zhejiang province, occupying a strategic location between Shaoxing, a city of three million inhabitants, and Hangzhou, close to Xiaoshan airport and along the highway to larger local cities and further to Shanghai. With its unique landscape of lakes, canals and rocks it forms a setting of scenic beauty. The area will become a recreational centre and will give new development impulses for the entire region.

The masterplan introduces a landscape framework formed by different conditions found on the site such as the two lakes with their waterfronts, the canal and road system, the green spaces and the bridges. Enriched with carefully designed elements like public squares, parks, roads and paths a continuous landscape fabric is established which ties the entire development together. Two centres and different residential quarters, offering maximum views to the lakes and landscape features, are embedded in this fabric.

The question is which urban models and what policies can be developed in order to steer rapid green field development in Asia into a sustainable urban future? Are the above mentioned criteria for "urban breeding grounds" valid, applicable and potentially operational? [Fig. 30]

Fig. 30   Nine commands for good urbanism, KCAP.

A Conversation on Architecture South of the Border

Alfredo BRILLEMBOURG and Hubert KLUMPNER
Directors, Urban-Think Tank (U-TT), Caracas
Co-Chairs of Architecture and Urban Design, ETH Zurich

> *It may be true that one has to choose between ethics and aesthetics, but it is no less true that whichever one chooses, one will always find the other at the end of the road.*
> Jean-Luc Godard

Our central question as designers today is whether the informal settlements of the twenty-first century can both contribute to a new definition of social capital in cities and at the same time, improve architectural education?

1: Talking Across Borders
Urban designers and architects are facing a crisis. As Godard points out, it is the critical mediation between an ethical position and an aesthetic formulation that gives rise to a creative product. Architecture is coming to terms with the realization that we have largely ignored how the majority of human beings live. For decades, the focus has rested comfortably on the global north and the norms of Western culture; collectively, designers' books, magazines, and projects have only gazed above the socioeconomic equator. Not only has this limited our field's creative palate, but it has depleted our field's legitimacy. If designers and architects are to improve cities and impart meaningful strategies to subsequent generations, we must begin to look southwards with creative intent.

The slums of Latin America, Asia and Africa, and the recently impoverished suburbs of North American and European cities, cast doubt on the traditional notion of city growth as self-contained and rational, born of the logic of the functional organization of space. Fast growing cities in the developing world and shrinking cities in the developed world present us with two faces of the same coin: the phenomena of informal development.

We have come to an understanding that the conditions and wealth of cities in the Western world are the exception. The rule is what we have documented over the last decade in the cities of the South: urban development without institutional assistance; overstretched infrastructure; lack of resources; and policies of exclusion. Cities, whether deliberately or not, are moving toward a less formal, more flexible order. It is therefore critical that designers recognize that informality provides a large-scale, conceptual framework of cooperation between stakeholders and urban managers if made operational. Such a formulation would establish a global agenda of open-design framework that accepts cultural, social, and ideological differences. Thus, we must shift the emphasis of contemporary architectural practice and education away from form-oriented mentalities to those that are process-driven.

We at Urban-Think Tank (U-TT) praise the productive power and the skills of the inhabitants in slums but we are aware of the fact that there is an urgent need for support. Municipal and national government must provide the financial and the technical expertise to make changes on a larger scale (infrastructure, legal framework, etc.) possible. We are in danger of watching another generation merely survive in cities, rather than flourish in them. The authorities often deliberately ignore potential urban dangers because no easy answers are in sight; the results of these negligent policies are too frequently catastrophic. As slum zones are often constructed in the least favourable areas for formal development—such as land with extreme slopes and weak soil resistance or areas subject to seasonal flooding or earthquake—they are permanently at risk. Entire stretches of neighbourhoods can be lost during a rainstorm, as happened in São Paulo in 2011. Slum zones need to be recognized as urbanized living quarters, and within these zones, we must respond to the need for housing and infrastructure solutions.

Understanding these behavioural processes is critically important to those architects working in the developing world. On the other hand, the so-called 'first world' has the responsibility of creating long-term strategies to assist local stakeholders and professionals to make these cities more resilient. We ask: are young architects being trained to take on these challenges?

Traditionally, architecture has been defined by a lateral exchange in the northern hemisphere. Since the nineteenth century, Europe and the United States (and later Japan) formed a ring of mutual exchange and intellectual stimulation. More recently, new nodes—China, Brazil, India, Korea, Taiwan, and the Emirates—have been added to that ring and have started to distort the geography of architectural education and provided new spaces for production and dissemination.

However, for ambitious students and practitioners of architecture, the elite American schools, and the established European universities continue to be the beacons for advanced design education. For many of the architectural migrants from the South who move to these destinations, the only change is a mental shift to the hegemonic architectural theory and tendencies of neoliberal urbanization. Rather than incubating or exchanging ideas, the schools have become places of passing on pre-packaged formats of intellectual and cultural supremacy. Cultural divides and differences largely remain in place and impede a productive flow of information, skills, and development. In Latin America, U-TT is a witness to the effects of a 60 year legacy of importing Northern-hemisphere ideas to the countries of the South. This system results in a reinforced inferiority complex among many students from developing countries. Additionally, it is often unattractive or impossible for architects of developing countries to consider a career in their cities of origin, only further increasing the perceived distance between the North and the South.

The architectural profession must incorporate the developing world into their understanding and definition of global, urban studies. It is necessary that this exchange of ideas is a two-way bridge between the developed and the developing worlds. Successful change comes from collaboration between international experts and local knowledge. It is essential to have input from a culturally diverse body of consultants and concurrently remain connected to the most advanced solutions in sustainable technologies.

In many ways, this reorientation can most easily happen within the academic model of architectural education. U-TT has increasingly embarked on projects and university studios that are focused on global mega-cities such as São Paulo, Chengdu and Mumbai. What we)re aiming to achieve with research platforms, such as ETH's Future Cities Lab in Singapore, and the Aedes Network Campus in Berlin is the creation of a pragmatic set of intelligent measures and scales that constitute a toolbox of social buildings that respond to a modern, urban experience. The resulting design tools generated from these workshops mark stages in the acquisition of consciousness and meaning. They create a set of priorities, a guiding map for the process of transformation in the informal city and a hope of transcendence in which society still respects what architects do. These developments raise our expectations for a more equitable global exchange of architectural and urbanity ideas. In the future, we anticipate that even more universities and research institutions will show more presence in the developing world. We envision this trend as analogous to the investments—financial and educationally—that built Silicon Valley into a hub of innovation.

In the cities of the global South, large-scale master planning has not resulted in healthier cities. Instead, it has accentuated the existing asymmetries within society and within the city fabric. Approaches that involve rapid, large-scale change such as much of China's recent urbanization—the bulldozing of slums, mass relocation of populations, and infusion of money for major public works—have questionable outcomes. Either the plans are too large to be executed with meaningful attention and adaptations over time, or they are too piecemeal and atomistic. We need plans that work in the middle ground, thinking with a city in mind but evolving coherently on local levels with the complexity of urban life in mind. Many attempted "fixes" fail to address socio-economic inequalities and the deliberate unwillingness of political and economic actors to alter the exclusionary policies of our growing urban planet.

Our experiences have taught us that architects have to work with and become social advocates. They must understand the vulnerability of low-wealth populations yet also engage the community-based organizations that often systematically define social operations in such populations. Architects need to think about architecture in the same way that Nobel Laureate Mohammad Yunus rethought traditional business models in banking and entrepreneurialism. And as Yunus recently proclaimed at the Royal Institute of British Architects, "When things work you do not want to touch it because it is working. When things do not work, then you think about it. If it still does not work, then you kick it! This is the time to kick."[1] As designers, we must transpose this radical questioning of orthodoxy into our work. U-TT strives to do this by becoming advocates for our clients as agents of change. We aim to bring citizens and their cities closer together by creating a greater sense of individual responsibility for a stronger community and an active civil society. All of the investigations we make and solutions we propose are tested by two over-arching questions: are we better understanding the nature of informality, and are we designing affordable solutions that can work within a social business principle?

2: Assembling an Urban Toolbox
Rather than imposing change, our new lab at ETH engages the real world and attempts to provide prototype solutions for urban dwellers in order to give them better control over changes within their environment. Together, with U-TT's office and NGO in Caracas, we are executing local projects that place a strong emphasis on understanding the dynamics and contexts of Latin American cities. This is where we started our research and deepened our experience for over more than a decade. Yet, we have also found that many of the lessons we have taken from our work in Latin America can be implemented in the slums of Mumbai, Kibera, and Amman. This finding points to certain essential and universal qualities that arise in the world's urban zones and the potential for more unified design strategies.

We are not against architecture. Rather, we are opposed to commercially derived branding, that does not play a meaningful role in the creation of a more democratic city. We see the design of processes as a strategic element to prepare the next generation of designers for the challenges of working in contemporary cities. Processes, not brands, are what will join utopia and pragmatism within tangible projects. Change will happen through executed projects rather than their images. It will occur through the definitions of new typologies and programs, and the intelligent incorporation of social needs.

We propose a working method for a new architecture that empowers people at the margins of the global South's emerging cities and promotes sustainable development in the slum areas. Our agenda to devise an urban toolbox has two objectives: to shift the emphasis of contemporary architecture and architectural education from being form-driven to being purpose-oriented; and to eliminate the disconnect between design and its social impact. Simply phrased, we strive to foster activist architecture that enacts positive urban changes.

As U-TT and likeminded partners begin to assemble a robust toolbox, we turn to conceptual and pragmatic devices that have already proven

Figs. 1–2   Metro Cable in Caracas

their merit to urban designers attempting to bridge the North and South. We will highlight some of the tools we have put in our kit of parts such as activist architecture, slum mapping, less invasive infrastructure, vertical public space, and urban generators. Some of our tools are established practices while others possess a more recent history of implementation; we neither glorify nor fear the traditional and novel—rather we value tools that have proven their worth in contemporary cities or strike us as empirically promising. The best way to explain components of our toolbox is to examine two of our projects examples: the urban transport system called *the Metro* Cable Car in the San Agustín barrio of Caracas, Venezuela (2004–09); and our future urban revitalization project for the Grotão *favela* in São Paulo (2008–12).

2.1: Activist Architecture
In 2004, our attention turned to San Agustín, a highly dense and almost century-old squatter territory, located right next to Caracas's formalized centre. With over 45,000 residents in the barrio, the area houses a significant portion of the city's formal and informal workforce. Yet, San Agustín is situated on a large hill that for decades has limited the social and economic vitality of the neighbourhood. Its lack of a 'bridge' to the city centre fostered a real and perceived isolation amongst residents. The *Metro Cable* was the result of a simple question: How to create access to the top of a slum on a steep hillside if there are no roads for public transport and the inhabitants are opposing government plans for road construction which would displace 30 percent of the population. In this context, our strategy was to read the neighbourhood carefully, engage in participative design with residents, develop thoughtful and novel mapping techniques and ultimately, to propose an infrastructural intervention.

We approached the first part of this process by refashioning the traditional tool of urban literacy in conjunction with the anthropological tool of participative engagement. Whether it were the social researchers Charles Booth in London's East End and Jacob Riis in New York at the end of the nineteenth century, or other early Modernist designers, many of history's groundbreaking architects have been careful observers, documenters, and interpreters of data. We maintain that the next generation of researcher-practitioners must interact directly with the individuals that compose the communities they study; research and practice must be community-driven, not just community-pertinent. The architect must develop interdisciplinary expertise in order to build a thesis that goes beyond cursory assumptions.

The first step in exploring and deploying that potential is to ask many questions in person and on the ground. Our idea of participative design is not to ask people what they want but to moderate and animate individuals and community groups. We need greater insight into and have an overview of existing complex infrastructure services. As we developed the design of our Metro Cable project in Caracas, we increasingly relied on the local residents of the San Agustín barrio. The impetus for the project came from direct conversations and meetings there, but as the design process intensified, we sought more creative modes of tapping the community's vision. This took the form of drawing sessions with neighbourhood children to hosting debates at community meeting about both aesthetics and pragmatics. Indeed, as the entire project was a framed in the context of a political retort to the city government's proposal to construct more roads through the barrio, our design process took on the form of an election campaign.

In this case, we functioned as a mediator and interlocutor, establishing the link between top-down infrastructure and bottom-up community development. *The Metro* Cable project originated as a viable alternative to traditional and destructive methods of infrastructure development. Indeed, the state-sponsored, road strategy was only averted after U-TT organized a public presentation and symposium in 2003 at the Central University of Venezuela in Caracas, which attracted architects, planners, university activists, and barrio leaders in order to protest the government's plan. This process demanded careful negotiation between competing requests on behalf of the city, residents, and our own office, but it resulted in what can only be defined as a socially invested design. As more stakeholders contribute to a project's planning and sign off on the process, the outcome's resilience strengthens. Participative design, in this light, is not only morally sounder, but it is more likely to create a lasting product.

2.2: Slum Mapping
Architects generally face unsatisfactory data sets regarding the ecological and social conditions of communities like San Agustín. However, U-TT has also recognized the inadequate mapping techniques that designers have at their disposal when working in such contexts. Scrutinizing the informal city through traditional methods of urban analysis is often fruitless and misleading. Satellite images, for example, are too distant to grasp the complex essences of slum fabric. Other forms of data, such as GIS, ground surveys and census information, have not been linked together in order to show the interrelationships of different layers and modes of understanding. Also, because slums are in a continuous process of transformation; as

Figs. 3–4 "Slum Shader" maps

TOPOGRAPHY

CONSTRUCTION DENSITY

DENSE CONSTRUCTION / TOPOGRAPHY

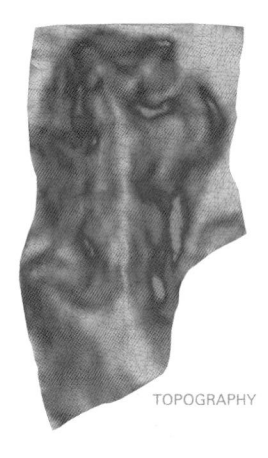

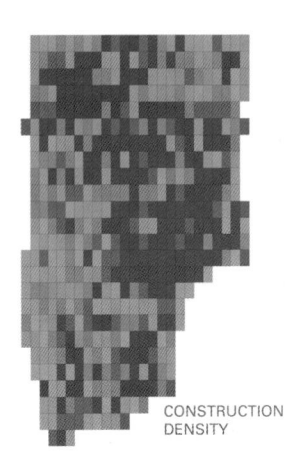

soon as a data set is compiled, it begs updating. Likewise, barrios such as San Agustín resist maps that colour-code functional zones in a modernist fashion, because such graphics only provide two-dimensional images of three-dimensional phenomena.

One mapping tool we created in anticipation of understanding San Agustín was a hybridized mode of representing topography and density called a "Slum Shader". By combining different data sets with the aesthetics of heat maps in mind, we were able to render a complex matrix of statistics in an easily accessible form. This proved useful for both conceptual strategizing and technical decision-making once the cable car project progressed.

We propose an alternative mapping methodology that begins with first-hand experience and exploration. The designers of tomorrow must inquire about vernacular changes in lifestyles, perceptions of local government efficacy, and collectively desired improvements to public and private spaces that often dominate community meetings and initiate social demands. Accurate answers to such inquiries rarely lie within official statistic books or in the speeches of politicians, but rather it must be "read" in the oral history that is inscribed on people's memories and daily lives.

Because these traditional planning and mapping methods fail to grasp the informal, we became increasingly fascinated in combining diagrams that present and juxtapose functional zones, gang territories, risk zones, multi-layered infrastructures, and blurred ownership information. Using GIS, we assembled our own three-dimensional data bank for the San Agustín hill. What we so often find is that the shape of the slum fabric (such as what we found in San Agustín) emerges from a bottom-up process; as density increases, slum dwellers build upward and outward. This pattern results in distinctive variations that merge together to form an architectural unity. With such an evaluation, we were able to finally comprehend San Agustín through a useful metaphor: the community was not a mountain of houses, but rather a house the size of a mountain. Through careful diagnosis, we could draw the necessary conclusion that the people living in this 'house' needed an elevator, as many residents were relatively incapable of trekking down or up the 89-storey hill due to health concerns and lack of resources. The solution—our elevator—was an urban cable car system.

2.3: Less Invasive Infrastructure
As we progressed along the development phase of *the Met*ro Cable project, we began to think about light infrastructure as a broad, urban tool. The need for standardized and consolidated infrastructure presents a cen-

Fig. 5   Metro Cable in Caracas

tral challenge to cities in the developing world. The project we designed with San Agustín was a venture in rethinking customary modes of public transportation development. While the city made an automobile-centred proposal to integrate San Agustín with the rest of Caracas, U-TT saw the opportunity to implement a sensitive form of infrastructure that would act as urban acupuncture. By inserting an above-ground cable car system, integrated with new housing, community recreational centres, and spaces for commercial developments, the barrio would not have to sacrifice its existing fabric or a third of its inhabitable space for mobility.

In essence, *the Metro Cable* project taught us how the macro must serve the micro. Standardizing the design of the stations, we realized, produces greater flexibility within the system as a whole. The self-evident benefits to regularized and predictable infrastructure include easier expansions, changes, and repairs in the future. Less obviously, designers must regularize infrastructure so that it can be consolidated to effectively permeate the informal with a multitude of accessible services. In *the Metro Cable's* case, garbage collections, water, and electricity are bundled with social functions and a cable-car infrastructure. Improved connections between infrastructures of varying scales create a viable support network. Social programming clusters, in proximity to infrastructural upgrades, bolster the network and create a densely public hub that reinforces the built environment through anticipated use. Indeed, *the Metro Cable's* structural backbone permitted us to speculate about the neighbourhood's future path, but it has also allowed community residents to independently adapt their environment and create new spaces of growth. We witnessed this on our last visit to La Ceiba station in San Agustín, where residents have opened small businesses, upgraded their houses, and instigated more efficient systems of water-management. We acknowledged the touristic possibilities inherent within the cable car platform, while at the same interweaving the needs of the community, both prosaic and productive. This is infrastructure performing many roles at once, like a Spanish plaza or town square, reflecting and reinforcing the multifaceted community for which it was built.

2.4: Vertical Public Space
In our second example, U-TT has been developing a proposal for the Grotão *favela* in São Paulo alongside SEHAB, the City of São Paulo Housing Authority, and now in coordination with our research lab at ETH Zurich. Despite its central and urban location, the area of Grotão is connected with only one road to the larger circulation systems of São Paulo, effectively separating it from the formal city, much like the San Agustín barrio of Caracas. Within this separated zone, increased erosion and dangerous mudslides have characterized the Grotão site as one of many low-access and high-risk zones. As a result, the unfortunate but necessary removal of several dam-

Figs. 6–7 Grotão project in São Paulo Paraisopolis favela: landscape and sectional perspective

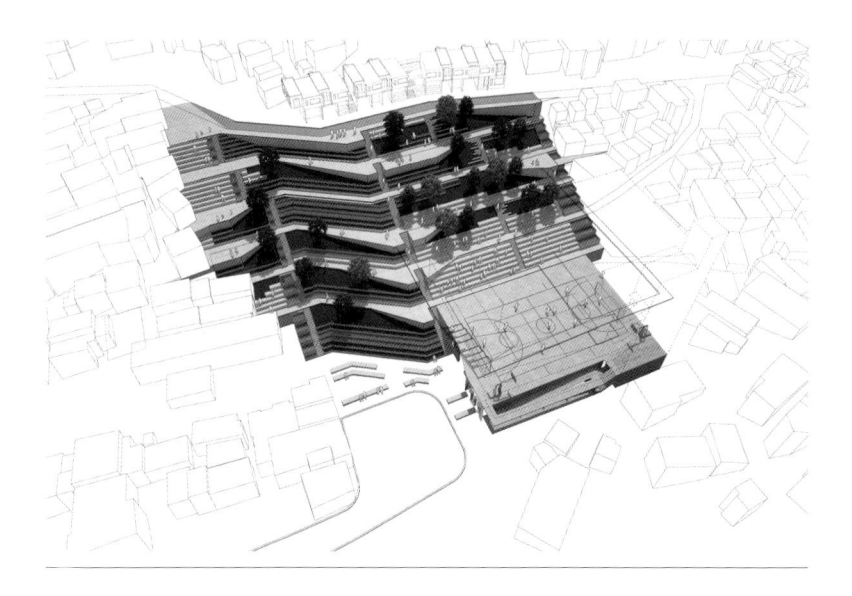

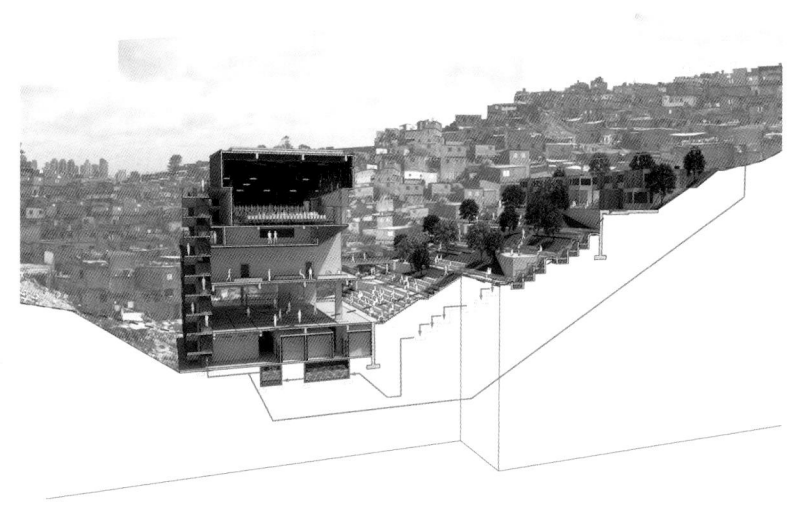

aged housing units has created a void in the otherwise dense fabric.

The new landscape generates the opportunity to transform the vacated space into a productive zone and public space through social design, a process of analysing the conditions of rapid growth and improving marginalized settlements through social infrastructure. In addition to stabilizing the precarious ground and eliminating erosion, the terraced landscape of our proposed park transforms Grotão into a 'natural arena' that encourages diverse community participation in recreational and civic gatherings. The park will serve as a foundation for piecemeal development of sports facilities and a music school that will be built vertically on the site and create different types of parks within the same plot of land.

Grotão will be realized out of a specific context and for a specific community, but it serves as a useful example of what may be done in other similarly situated vertical spaces. Public space, as the New Urbanists reminded us, is not a luxury but a necessity. They reminded us of tenets that early urban planners, like the fifteenth century Spanish, knew so well—creating plazas and courtyards reinforce social bonds with a myriad of functions and utilities. When designed with complexity and density in mind, the parks and recreational spaces of a slum may accomplish much more than what early modernist planners would have estimated possible.

Fig. 8   Grotão project in São Paulo Paraisopolis favela: aerial view

2.5: Urban Generators

The Grotão project initially began as a proposal for the creation of public space, but recently, we have transformed the plan into a full-scale revitalization project, or as we term this class of tools—an Urban Generator. The site will become a focal point for productive changes in the community as a whole—changes that will ripple out and rhizomatically reinforce the area's physical and social instabilities. What was initially an uninhabitable slope will become a public access point for civic engagement and environmental education. It will exhibit—in one installation—a wide bandwidth of ecological technologies and social enhancement programming that will demonstrate the usefulness of small-scale infrastructure and devices along with their connecting ability.

With both recreational space and a centralized building, or hub, the project will consist of a library, repair station, Internet port, retail shop, kindergarten, public restroom. The hub will also be an ecological prototype for the community, as it will model state-of-the-art technologies that demonstrate how to responsibly deal with energy and resources both within and beyond the *favela*. Using a combination of solar cells, water recycling, and gardening habitats, the hub is meant to empower residents and improve the quality of life in the *favelas* by combining education with experimentation. As an urban generator, it will catalyze commercial and social cooperatives within the community. Indeed, we conceive of the hub as Grotãu's own plug-in station, whose assemblage relates to the practices of slum construction and whose components are as cheap as possible, function on a small footprint, and are easily reusable.

3: Opening the Dialogue

We envision a plan for quick-fix urban architecture that functions as a life-support agent for the perpetually changing city. We promote architecture as an event, which can only be fully realized with the active participation of inhabitants and users of space. Architects have to wake up and employ new methods to speed up response times and accept that governments do need our creative and unconventional input to keep all citizens—not just the privileged few—safe.

Activism and politics have to stress that working within informal settlements is also deeply embedded in a complex process of democratization; the inhabitants will always be there to judge our success or failure by the practical aspects of the solutions proposed and their capacity to improve living conditions for everyone. Given that slums operate based on appropriating available space, and thereby starting a process of incremental development upon the existing resources in order to expand, reproduce and generate new structures, they are examples of perpetual growth and transformation. The unrestrained realism of the slum can light a 'spark' in residents and architects alike.

Future generations will judge our success by the applicability of our proposals and their capacity to improve living conditions for everyone, everywhere. The notion of a slum-free world is not optimistic but rather pessimistic. If we can embrace slums as components to cities rather than tumours, perhaps we can find more effective ways to lessen their failures and learn from their successes.

This is the time for architects and designers to recognize that we do not serve one social group, but rather all of humanity, regardless of borders. The global South and global North are antiquated, rhetorical devices, but they help identify certain truths. We include them in our toolbox out of necessity as it is difficult to call attention to wide divisions in our world without speaking in divisive terms. However, we find it crucial to observe the unity of problems and creative solutions that are now emanating from the developing world. We see hybridizations arise from scarcity, where the distinction between production, consumption and living blurs. In this sense, we see that the essence of North-South relations must not always be defined by transactions, but rather redefinitions—reformulating values, boundaries and identities. The hemispheric division, like that between aesthetics and ethics, is only as limiting as our collective imaginations allow it to be.

Notes
1   Yunus, Muhammad. "Talking Without Borders." 75th Annual British Council Celebration. Royal Institute of British Architects. London, England. 29 05 2009. Lecture.

Fig. 9   Metro Cable in Caracas: aerial view

The Edge of Vertical

Rosalyne Shieh
Assistant Professor Taubman College of Architecture and Urban Planning, University of Michigan

In the opening pages of *Architecture of the City*, Aldo Rossi includes a photograph of the rural road leading out of the city of Santiago de Compostela. [**Fig. 1**] Taken from a vantage point above a dense cluster of roofs, it looks out along the road leading out of town. The urban fabric forms an edge beyond which lies a distinctly different landscape of low-lying, rural buildings, dotting plats of open fields. The slightly lofted perspective visually stitches horizontal bands of city, country and sky, juxtaposing and convincingly contrasting them to produce a distinct identity for each part. The view is sweeping and essentially lateral, reproducing the traditional devices of landscape painting by constructing a clear foreground, middle ground and background.

Rossi uses this image to cohere an identity of the city as a thing by presenting the edge at which it becomes a distinctly other condition. For Rossi, the city was not only a built, physical artefact, but also a repository of history. The city is at once a thinkable totality, a concept, as well as a physical, inhabitable, artefact. The city in all its meanings is an embodiment and site of a collective subject that belongs to that city. The building of a city is also the construction of the collective identity of its subjects. Rossi's image frames the city against the non-city, suggesting that the presentation of its limits is important in cohering it as a seat of the collective subject.

If the traditional city of Rossi was well represented by the compositional devices of landscape painting, it may be argued that our cities of the twentieth and twenty-first centuries, made possible by steel and modern construction, suggest a view from a different vantage point. In the vertical city, the top of the highest skyscraper is a hinge upon which the view tilts and is projected back down. Not unlike the manner in which pictures are viewed on the wall, the city is flattened into a textured plane. In contrast to Rossi's traditional European city, the dense, vertical cities of today define a different kind of urban experience. As Michel de Certeau wrote:

> To be lifted to the summit of the World Trade Center is to be lifted out of the city's grasp. One's body is no longer clasped by the streets that turn and return it according to an anonymous law; nor is it possessed, whether as player or played, by the rumble of so many differences and by the nervousness of New York traffic...His elevation transfigures him into a voyeur. It puts him at a distance. It transforms the bewitching world by which one was 'possessed' into a text that lies before one's eyes.[1]

Fig. 1   Rural road leading out of the city of
         Santiago de Compostela.
Fig. 2   Earthrise. December 1968.

De Certeau's view of New York City isn't the sweeping, horizontal one of Rossi's traditional city, but one lofted so high in the air as to flatten the territory into a projection of itself. By an adjustment of distance and perception, the subject completely disengages from its body—the city — looking down to recognize itself across the distance made possible by modern engineering. It is this confrontation of a collective subject with its own image that Rem Koolhaas argues fuelled "the self-awareness in New Yorkers that amplified and fed Manhattan's ambitious and idiosyncratic planning and development."[2]

Scalar shifts bring about representational shifts that produce measurable ripples through our shared consciousness. Take for instance *Earthrise* [**Fig. 2**], the photo taken from the moon in December 1968 by astronauts on the Apollo 8 mission, the first human spaceflight to leave the gravitational field of planet Earth and be captured by the gravitational field of another celestial body. The concept of a spherical Earth dates back to antiquity, but up until this moment, Earth had only been experienced as being horizontally extensive and boundless. The tension between the endless horizon and a bound planet was a contradiction illustrated by the very concept of the horizon as both a limit and a frame and a line at infinity, from which all else begins.

Here, for the first time, one can trace the edges of the Earth, complete the circle around it and grasp it as literally bound: an irrefutably closed and therefore limited, system with limited resources. This was the first visual, photographic evidence of the earth as a discrete object. It is a representation made possible by a real displacement in space, taken from an unprecedented vantage point, giving us a view from a never-before inhabited place. In a way, it was the holding of a great distance between the viewing point and the object that closed the distance between them. So it doesn't come as a surprise that the concept and image of the "Whole Earth" was widely associated with the rise of the environmentalism in the late 1960s and early 1970s. By a stretch of the imagination, one might consider the displacement from the earth to the moon as moving outwards along an axis that passes through the centre of the earth; if so, the position of the view becomes an extreme case of verticality. While slightly absurd, such a thought experiment presents an extreme case that highlights the possibilities of theorizing verticality in architecture.

The relationship between space, knowledge and verticality in architecture

Fig. 3   Kaohsiung Pop Music and Maritime
         Centre, Kaohsiung, Taiwan4

goes back to nineteenth century Scottish urbanist and natural scientist, Patrick Geddes. Geddes' Outlook Tower in Edinburgh was at once observatory, museum and civic laboratory. Geddes believed vision and spatial experience to be bound in the production of knowledge. From top to bottom, the sequence through the Outlook Tower proceeded from the rooftop panoramic overview, followed by the view through the medium of the Camera Obscura and, lastly, details of the city as enhanced by various instruments of measurement and observation. For Geddes, "knowledge of reality may be obtained through projections of a multitude of distinct, specific scientific observations, but this multiplicity must always be reappraised in the light of a synoptic vision encompassing them all."[3]

This idea of a 'synoptic' vision is a model where multiple, sometimes contradictory, understandings of a place or thing can be held together; different images of a place cohere into an assemblage that produces an identity. For example, *Earthrise* added the image of the whole earth as bounded to the lived experience of the horizon as boundless. One does not supplant the other, but rather the bounded and the boundless are held together in a 'synoptic' vision; one that might help us to realize that, as in the horizon view, within any frame or site are flows that pass in and out as continuities rather than objects, but at the same time, as in the object view, the same system forms a whole whose parts are in flux, but are in an overall balance that must be maintained. The simple shift from horizontal to vertical, from the city as lived milieu to bound object, from environment to thing, and all that lies between furnish a rich set of possibilities to construct multiple projections of a reality that make up the contemporary urban experience.

The dominant component of vertical cities is the tower and the transformative possibilities of the iconic tower, its proliferation driven by the engine of finance and profit, have been exhausted. Popular representations of the city favour the skyline, reducing the city to a collection of icons or morphological traces. The iconic tower, as basic component of the vertical city, defines a *type* that implies a particular relationship between representation and use: as icons, they can be reduced to their profile; stamp-like, they are perhaps best represented as two-dimensional, monochromatic figure against an empty ground; their exteriors are iconic while their interiors are generic. A means to produce something other than the iconic, vertical city, might be achieved by representation would be to operate within a logic that is different from the icon. To multiply the layers of experience that make up the synoptic vision of vertical cities, attention should turn to ways to operate beyond the logic of the object.

Adopting a pragmatic strategy to exceed the logic of the iconic tower would be to do so without attempting to supplant or negate it. The tower can be accepted as a given, as the natural geological unit that characterizes the terrain of vertical cities. This establishes two parameters for working on the vertical city: interest and investment in the edge and in-between sites of the vertical city; and, the use of representational modes that drive the design with criteria other than morphology. The rethinking of the vertical city is precisely not situated in the rethinking of the tower as object, but at the moments where vertical meets horizontal. The edges of the vertical city, where it transforms from vertical, to horizontal, extensive and other, become charged sites for leveraging the possibilities of vertical cities.

Project: Kaohsiung Pop Music and Maritime Centre, Kaohsiung, Taiwan4

Our project for a Pop Music Centre in Kaohsiung, Taiwan was located precisely at such an edge. Measuring 145 kilometres at its widest and 378 kilometres at its longest, Taiwan is a dramatic landscape dominated by mountains (the highest peak, Jade Mountain, measures 3952 metres). Most of the urban development is densely concentrated on the leeward plains along the western edge, with a pattern of clustering around a string of central city cores, marked by tall buildings. Taipei is the largest city and lies on the northernmost tip; the financial centre and seat of government, it is a vertical city surrounded by mountains and boasts one of the tallest buildings in the world: Taipei 101. The Tropic of Cancer passes through

Fig. 4   The site
Fig. 5   A vast horizontal monument
Fig. 6   "Scaffold"

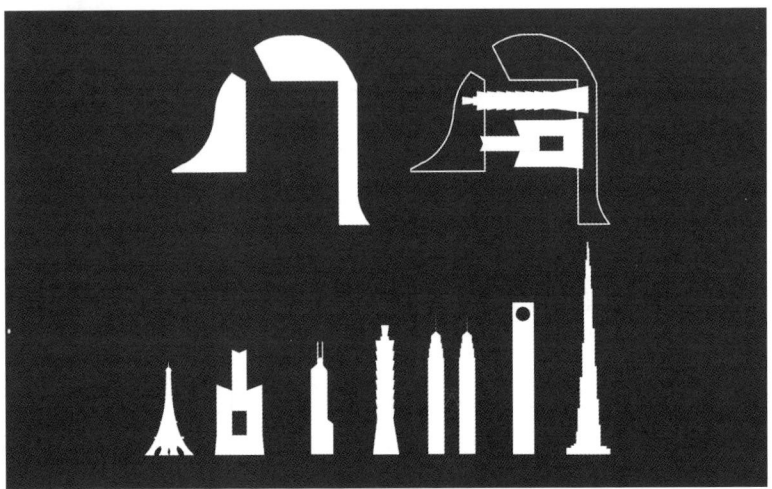

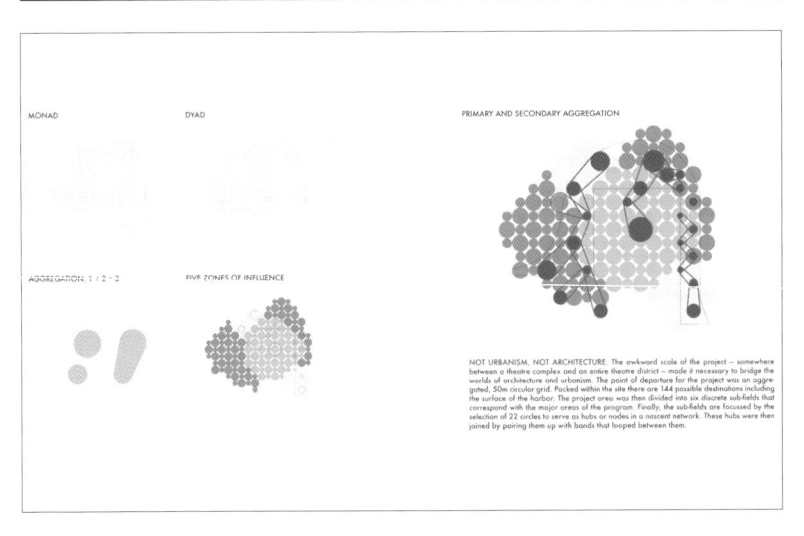

the centre of Taiwan, dividing the island into two distinct climate zones and reinforcing an apparent north-south identity division. As the second city of Taiwan, Kaohsiung is the maritime heart of the south; it is the site of Taiwan's largest seaport, located at the southern end of Taiwan's most expansive plain. Connecting the low-lying, productive lands of Taiwan to the ocean, Kaohsiung is a city that links two horizons.

Fig. 7   Five infrastructural stages

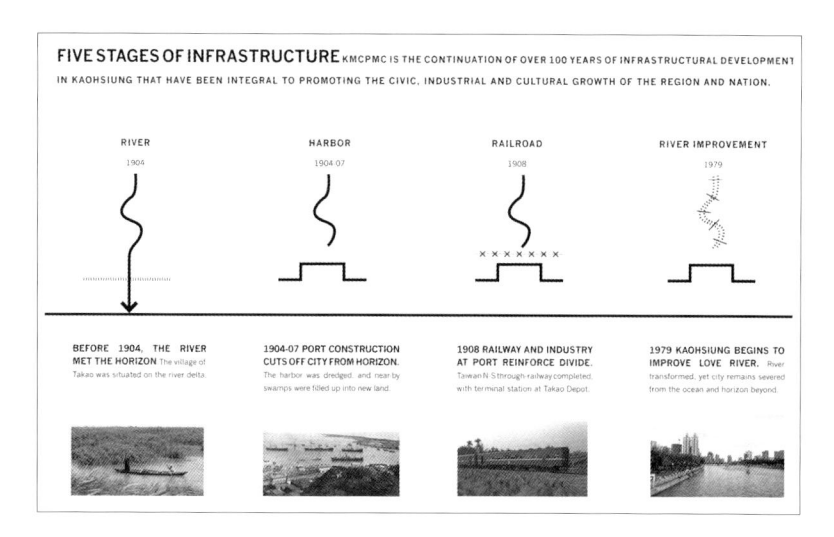

FIVE STAGES OF INFRASTRUCTURE KMCPMC IS THE CONTINUATION OF OVER 100 YEARS OF INFRASTRUCTURAL DEVELOPMENT IN KAOHSIUNG THAT HAVE BEEN INTEGRAL TO PROMOTING THE CIVIC, INDUSTRIAL AND CULTURAL GROWTH OF THE REGION AND NATION.

RIVER	HARBOR	RAILROAD	RIVER IMPROVEMENT
1904	1904-07	1908	1979
BEFORE 1904, THE RIVER MET THE HORIZON The village of Takao was situated on the river delta.	1904-07 PORT CONSTRUCTION CUTS OFF CITY FROM HORIZON. The harbor was dredged, and nearby swamps were filled up into new land.	1908 RAILWAY AND INDUSTRY AT PORT REINFORCE DIVIDE. Taiwan N-S through-railway completed, with terminal station at Takao Depot.	1979 KAOHSIUNG BEGINS TO IMPROVE LOVE RIVER. River transformed, yet city remains severed from the ocean and horizon beyond.

The site of the project is an old industrial wharf, located at the outlet of the cities' major river [**Fig. 4**]. It is defined by a hard edge that frames a square of water at its centre. The Love River enters the site diagonally from the north and a slip opens off to one side; all of this opens onto the larger Kaohsiung Harbour, which links out to the ocean. At Kaohsiung, we wanted to give a legible identity to the city that was linked to the horizon by the land and sea, one that was different from the iconic skyscraper. It was a conscious decision to try to imagine the project as a kind of vast, horizontal monument [**Fig. 5**].

In an explicit move to design the project outside of a logic that reinforces it as a collection of iconic objects, we introduced a "scaffold" capable of organizing variegated design criteria—from forms to processes—across the project [**Fig. 6**]. A scaffold is a synthetic diagram that is introduced into a project to negotiate between sets of design criteria. A scaffold is a temporary lattice that structures and provides points of attachment, and defines the organization of material and movement. Scaffolds are soft in that they fix critical relationships within a larger, more flexible matrix of relations. Their softness is embedded in it as a projective mode of representation: as an underlying diagram of sorts, a scaffold does not manifest into a physicalized, materialized geometry, but facilitates both organization and form; ultimately falling away in the final instance—in fact, a scaffold that has been used successfully should disappear after it has been implemented. For us, the scaffold is the use of representation in architecture to instrumentalize ideas from within the design process; rather than illustrating, it is a something through which a design is projected and constructed.

Our scaffold here was a 50-metre circular grid, with two scalar states—monad and dyad; it provided a range of figures and an underlying metric that to structure a site that was awkwardly scaled somewhere between a building complex and an entire neighbourhood. Located at the mouth of the river, our system also had to integrate natural and infrastructural systems across a horizontal expanse. We framed the transformation of the site over its 100-year development, in five infrastructural stages relative to the horizon [**Fig. 7**]. In the first, pre-industrial stages, the river met the horizon, which was then cut off by the construction of the hard edge of the port, and further divided by the laying of railroad tracks, all of which coincided with a destruction of the river's natural ecologies in its use as a conduit and dumping site for industrial and human waste. About 30 years

Fig. 8   Six subfields
Fig. 9   Interconnectivity
Fig. 10 Local loops

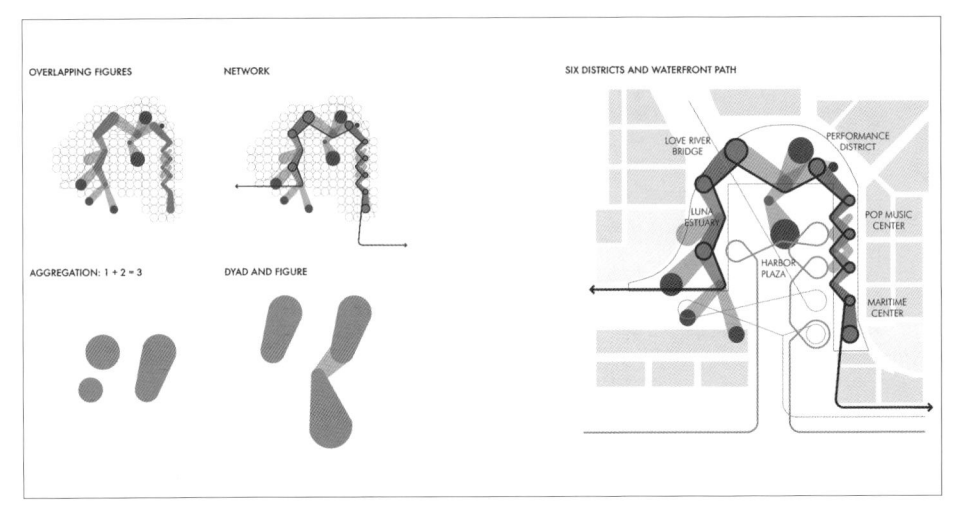

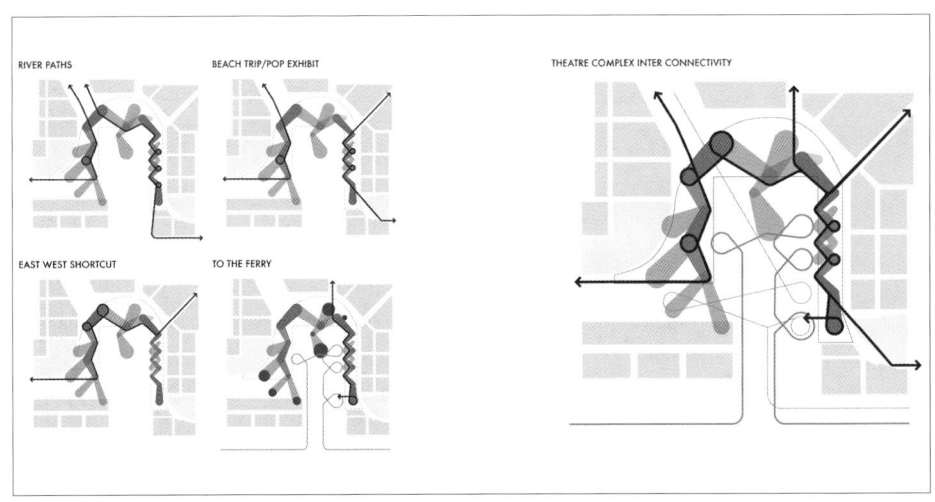

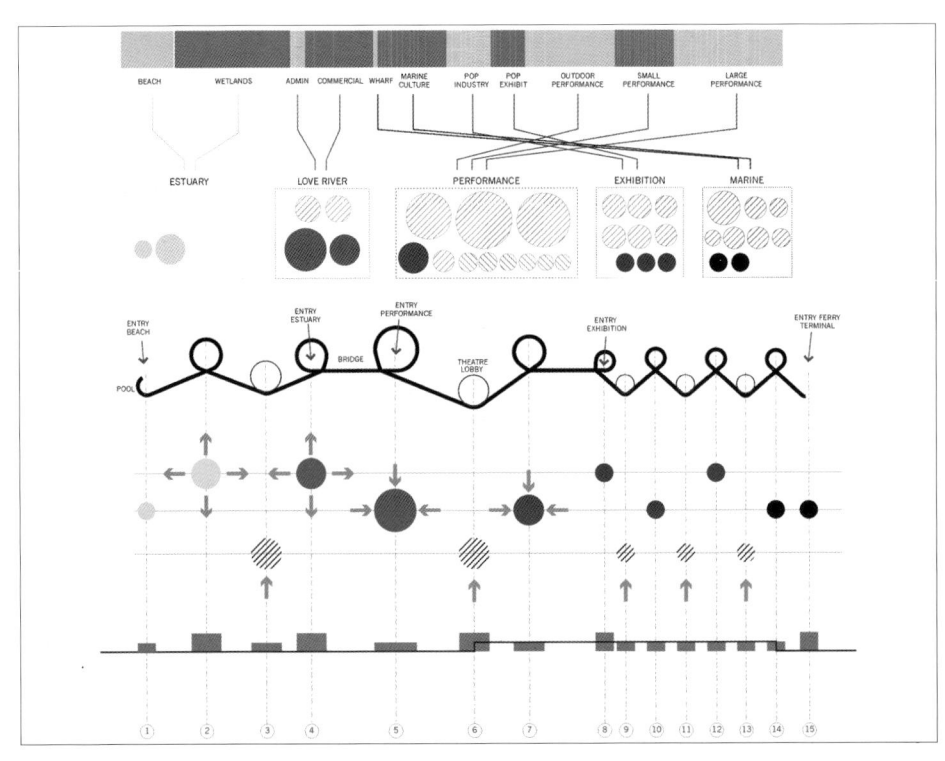

ago, the city of Kaohsiung began to clean up the river, a process which accelerated in the 1990s following political shifts and Taiwan's more general turn into a post-industrial, high-tech economy. Within this narrative, we saw the project as a means of re-connecting the river to the horizon by a low-slung, horizontal monument around the site. The main focus of this was to re-conceive the wharf as a water plaza—a new liquid core for the city, defined by a square of water, facing out to the horizon beyond. The water plaza also gives a destination to the Love River—as a kind of spectacular conclusion to its long rehabilitation.

Using our scaffold diagram, the project was divided into six subfields at a range of scales to produce different neighbourhoods corresponding to major areas of the program. [**Fig. 8**] 22 circles were selected as hubs or nodes within the network. Pairs of nodes were linked in order to create local loops and define building sites; these were also joined together with a path that carried through the entire site which is the primary circulation route that connects each of the local elements into an overall figure [**Figs. 6, 8 & 9**]. The large and rather complex program was grouped into neighbourhoods and organized around nodes strung along the main circuit. The largest and most prominent node is the anchor for the performance centre complex. The design of the project built up from the designation of master and sub-circuits, which were tied into key moments within the city. The introduction of the scaffold at the beginning of the design was fundamental to orchestrating and organizing relationships between all the parts of the project. The distributed point grid—defined by the centre points of the spheres—organize a funnelling or aggregation of the city that is somewhat flexible or soft; that is, the scaffold provides multiple pathways for the entry of pedestrians, cars or bicycles, which are gathered and brought through and around the figures of the project and then moved out and back into the surrounding city.

As a diagram that could work both at the scale of the bottom-up aggregation of urbanism and the top-down, figure of architecture, the scaffold can be considered a global strategy to organize across the three main scales dictated by architecture, urbanism and infrastructure. The overall project is a constructed, thickened landscape punctuated by figural episodes in the form of buildings, bridges, pavilions, and raised paths. The abstraction of the scaffold allows us to integrate across a varied and heterogeneous mix of landscape, buildings and ecologies; it provides the temporary substrate upon which these systems are layered and attach to. The same scaffold is used to layer the estuary, beach, water plaza, various buildings and landforms, all of which are presented against the city beyond.

The figural quality of the project operates from great heights and from the view of the peripatetic subject. It is the verticality of the city that gives meaning to the horizontal and provides the vantage point from which the project becomes legible. The horizon always extends beyond the gaze of the viewer, while the various figures of the project are linked to the different programs and framed within the broader field of the complex as you

Fig. 11 Site plan
Fig. 12 Exploded axonometric
Fig. 13 "Liquid plaza": night view

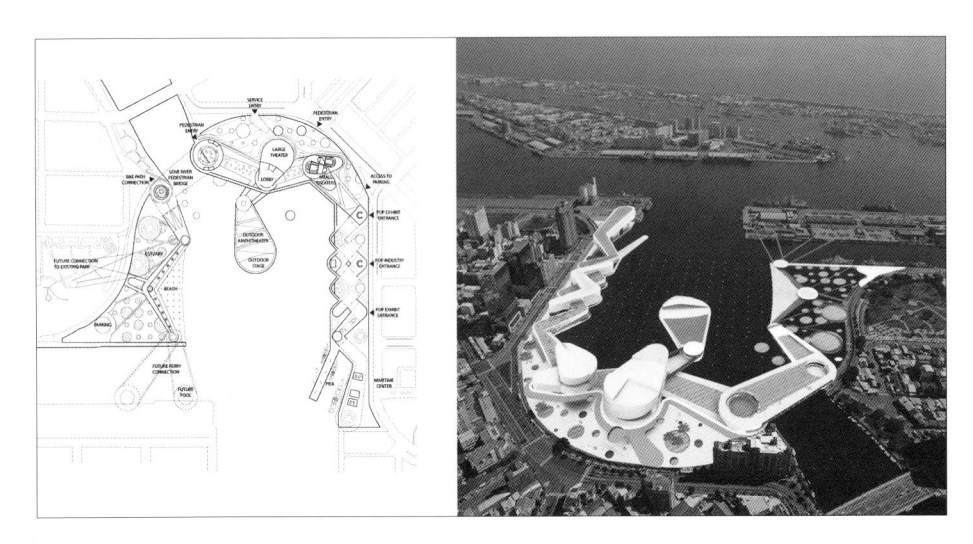

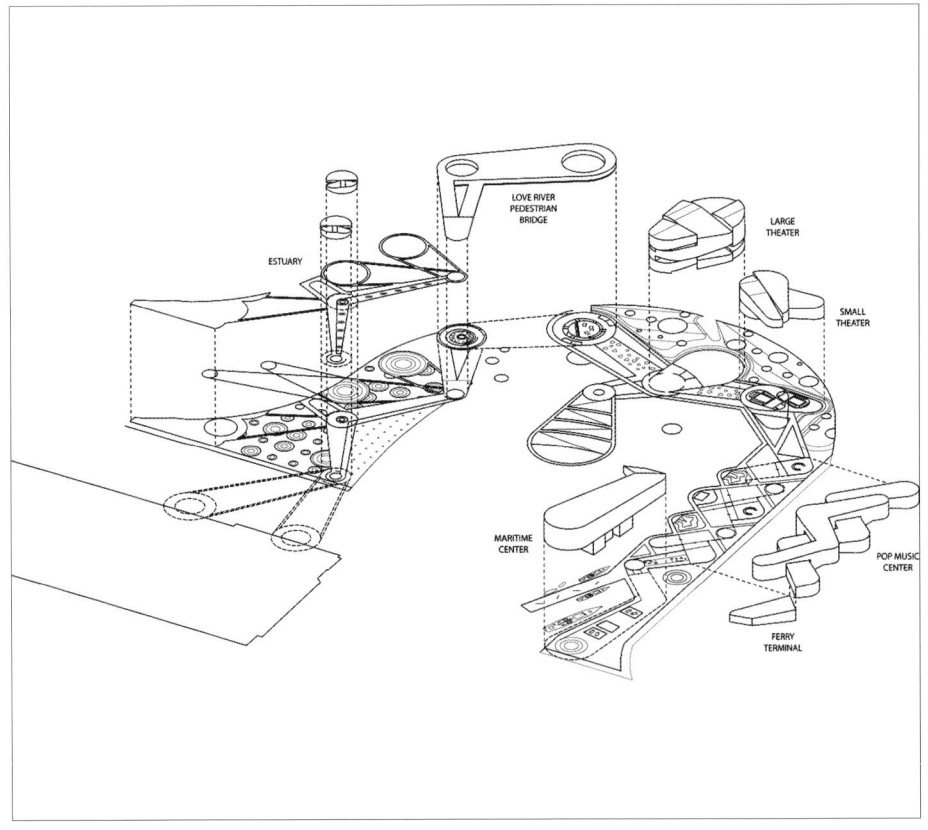

Fig. 14 "Liquid plaza": day view

move around the project. The water is framed as a liquid plaza and focus of the project; as a charged and reflective surface, it makes a second sky to the project [**Figs. 13 & 14**]. Kaohsiung is not a city built around a core of tall buildings; as a water-based city, our intention is for a 'water plaza' at the Kaohsiung Pop Music Centre to define a new core based on water, aptly situated at the edge or seam between land and sea. At Kaohsiung, the spherical grid is then a soft scaffold upon which top-down form can adhere, but is also a means by which architecture is in collaboration with movement. Architecture, the city and natural systems together form a kind of highly charged backdrop against and within which the constantly shifting life and ecologies of the project unfold.

Notes

1   Michel De Certeau, The Practice of Everyday Life, trans. Steven F. Rendall Berkeley: University of California Press, (1988) 92.

2   Rem Koolhaas, Delirious New York New York: Monacelli Press, (1994) 25.

3   Pierre Chabard "The Outlook Tower as an Anamorphosis of the World: Patrick Geddes and the Theme of Vision ," Journal of Generalism & Civics, no. 4, Spring 2004, published online: www.patrickgeddes.co.uk.

4   This project was a joint collaboration between SCHAUM/SHIEH and Albert Pope.

Muddy Skies in Construction: Paper and Projects by Mark Anderson and Peter Anderson

Mark Anderson
Associate Professor of Architecture
College of Environmental Design, University of California, Berkeley

Introduction
There are three primary ingredients essential to working up recipes for rich and healthy vertical cities. Contrary to many assumptions—'ideas are cheap'—the most important requirement is for some messy design imagination to emerge from and then step out beyond the foundational precipice developed through critical inquiry into life's boundless urban complexities. Cities are infinitely important to research and ponder upon, but without some slicing, dicing and cooking up into proposals for architecture, urban planning will always end at reading and writing the menu, and never moving some more fully satisfying meal toward the table. Proposals for urban architecture inevitably risk professional embarrassment and simplistic armchair ridicule, since the issues addressed are infinitely complex, the obstacles to comprehensive solutions are endless, and seductive oversimplification beckons from every theoretical and sub-disciplinary quadrant. Nevertheless, the naïvely optimistic architect's essential step away from the precipice of foundational research into this dangerous void of articulated form and spatial potential is essential to meaningful progress toward radically improved urban construction.

The second requirement is for practical construction ingenuity to wrestle these recognizably messy ideas into affordable and beneficial implementation. The third requirement—as vexing for creative architects as it is to any talented chef interested foremost in cooking as a joy in itself (and woefully burdened by the need to manage the restaurant)—is the application of economic imagination. If someone can invent a strategically-focused profit strategy enabling cities of substantial creative architecture —or better yet, an alternative economic model assigning greater value to health and happy living—then fantastic vertical cities will soon be built with as much dynamic cultural energy as the world has recently witnessed in the creative renaissance of traditional and modern cuisine. Imagine the new vertical possibilities for our urban lives if developing human culture will soon again care so much for its cities and urban architecture as it has so beneficially begun to remember, as expectation and aspiration, for its quality of food (and of course, these issues are actually quite fully intertwined).

This paper outlines design work focused primarily in the first two categories—a little bit of messy imagination struggling equally with practical construction ingenuity. The more imaginative economic strategy cannot be far behind, but in these projects, the economic imperative lies primarily in the logic of construction systemization and the intrinsic logic of working toward more sustainable environmental infrastructure. As a practical matter, the authors of these projects, Mark Anderson and Peter Anderson, have taken a single building block assumption—the ISO standard shipping module—and developed from this flexible base element a series of practical urban construction proposals for high-density low-, medium- and high-rise sustainable construction. Mud of the earth (water and soil), drawn up into more contemporary yet necessarily still muddy human life in the sky, is a central and continuous thread animating this series of basic building block projects, with their sometimes unexpectedly blossoming vertical skins.

Muddy Skies in Construction: Frames and Bladders
The central project in building vertical cities is to bring the vitality of traditional life on earth into an equally vital life in the sky. The project is not so much to invent entirely new ways of life, but instead to take all of the rich tradition of earth bound life with us as we build into the sky. Traditionally, the richest city life has been built most closely integrated with the local earth and weather, embracing a great complexity of interwoven and often contradictory ways of living in a particular place. Muddiness is a particular interest in the following projects, both in terms of the physical structuring of essential soil and water flows into a vertical city face, while also considering this muddiness metaphorically, in terms of enabling complex layers of contradictory and evolving ways of living. With these muddy goals, these series of projects work with two basic and relatively pure systems as underlying infrastructural armature: prefabricated, modular steel frame elements conforming to standardized international shipping geometry, and mechanically active fabric structures interacting with the local weather systems. Utilizing these two basic approaches to system infrastructure, these series of projects explore a range of urban construction proposals uniquely adapted to unique places and cultural conditions.

Wind and water system-structures have been an important component of our work since the late 1980s, beginning in the *Prairie Ladder* series, built in Texas. During the 1990s we built a number of experimental wind and water projects, including *MudMapSnowBlindBladderBladder* in Anchorage, Alaska; *Stick Bladder* in Seattle, Washington; and numerous construction projects with architecture students, including *Clackety-Yak/ Bamboo Wind in Honolulu*; and *ScumBagDirtClodGasHuffPhytoCurtain*, in New Orleans. Working with students at the University of California, Berkeley, in 2005 we built a solar heated outdoor amphitheatre for watching films on foggy evenings, *Hot White Orange*, and in 2006 a self-contained and life-sustaining disaster relief structure, *LifeBean*. Many of these constructions included development of complex plumbing systems, hot and cold radiator systems, large bladder structures, and inflatable mem-

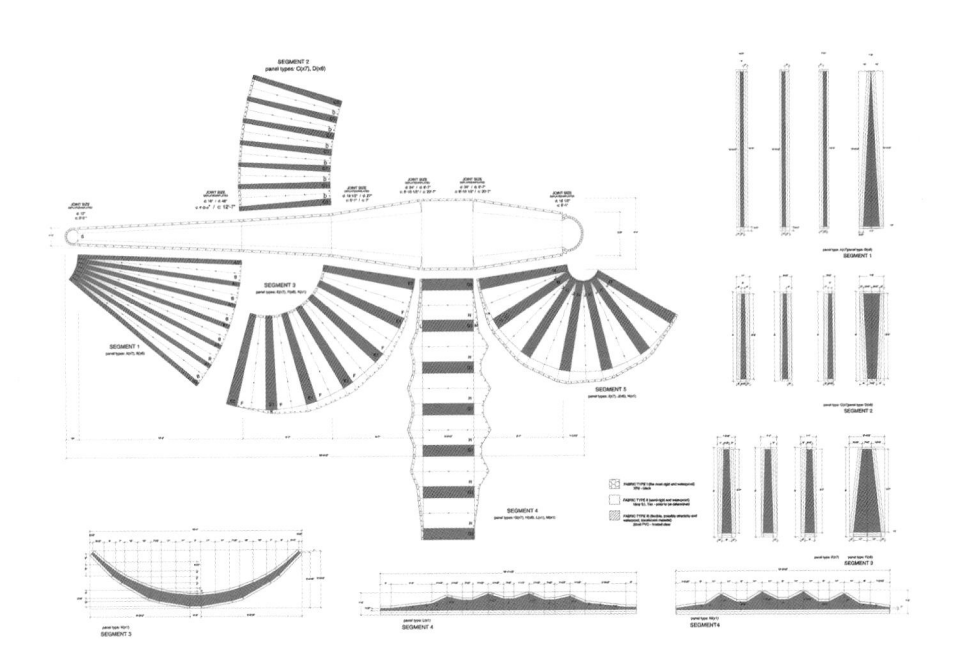

Fig. 1 Sponge Comb: unfolded
Fig. 2 Sponge Comb: deployed

branes. All dealt with site-specific conditions of human experience with local earth, sky, water, climate and weather.

Hurricane Katrina and the resultant flood of New Orleans in the Fall of 2006 brought these active fabric infrastructure construction systems together with our long series of projects on modular steel housing construction methods, still focusing on issues of place and weather. The New Orleans proposal for densely build, rapidly constructed, and weather interactive mixed-use urban housing brought together many of these wind and water threads into a series of related system projects that continue to spin-off into current work. The New Orleans-related high-density modular frame housing projects have incorporated many components, systems and concepts of the earlier experimental weather activated investigations. The first of these post-Katrina projects was a competition proposal, *ShotgunCamelbackSpongeGarden*, for a large mixed-use building on the banks of the Mississippi River in New Orleans, intended to greatly increase population density on the traditional high ground of the city, more protected from future flooding. The integrated building and landscape were designed to act as a vegetal sponge, soaking up and slowing rainfall, and putting the fresh water to practical use. An important system component of this building was its waterfront infrastructure, the *Sponge Combs*, which have since taken on a life of their own independent from their original site.

The *Sponge Combs* are an inflatable levee system that was designed to replace the brittle concrete levee walls that not only proved subject to failure after Hurricane Katrina, but moreover act in very damaging ways to the ecology and daily human life in waterfront cities. The *Sponge Combs* are designed as porous fingers perpendicular to the waterfront, spaced to allow free flow of plants, animals and human views and access during non-flood periods, but utilizing an interior packing of superabsorbent poly-

Figs. 4–6 New Orleans Urban Housing: perspectives

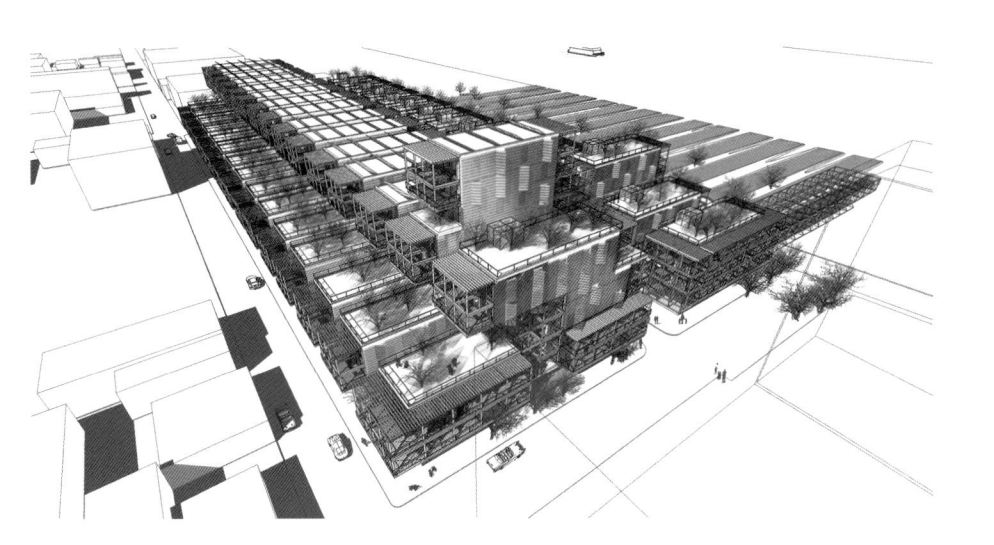

mer to swell and interlock as a watertight dam in moments of high water. The building proposal won first place in the competition, and was later exhibited at the Venice Biennale of Architecture, where large-scale prototypes of the *Sponge Comb* system were exhibited. Since that time, the *Sponge Comb* prototypes have travelled widely in numerous exhibitions, including in Bangkok, Panama City, Los Angeles, San Francisco, New York, Copenhagen, and Hamburg. The wide interest in this proposal has also led to a number of new projects developing various aspects of this system into new ideas and applications, including, *AlamedaLandHandSpongeCombX-BubbleBeach*, and *Poppy Beach, Enormous-PlasticRainFlower (EPRF)*, (San Francisco), *River Dance* (Taiwan), and a current work in progress, *Lips Tower*, which will be discussed in more detail, as a project example, below.

MoMA High Density Prefab Urban Housing Prototype (New York, 2008)

The MoMA prototype project is not the first in this series of high-density steel frame modular housing structures, but is an illustrative example of the fundamental systems and their application in a tight, in-fill application in Manhattan. Unlike the other project examples covered in this paper, this proposal suggests the potential for a relatively basic modular building system to be adaptable to more complex small-site applications in already dense cities, as opposed to presenting a more comprehensive new infrastructure for rapidly developing new cities. The components are exactly the same as in the other project examples, and are deployed as an exhibition of various components offering substantial variation to best integrate with varied urban sites, and varied living programs.

Invited as a proposal for the Home Delivery exhibition at the Museum of Modern Art, this project took the polemical position that in-

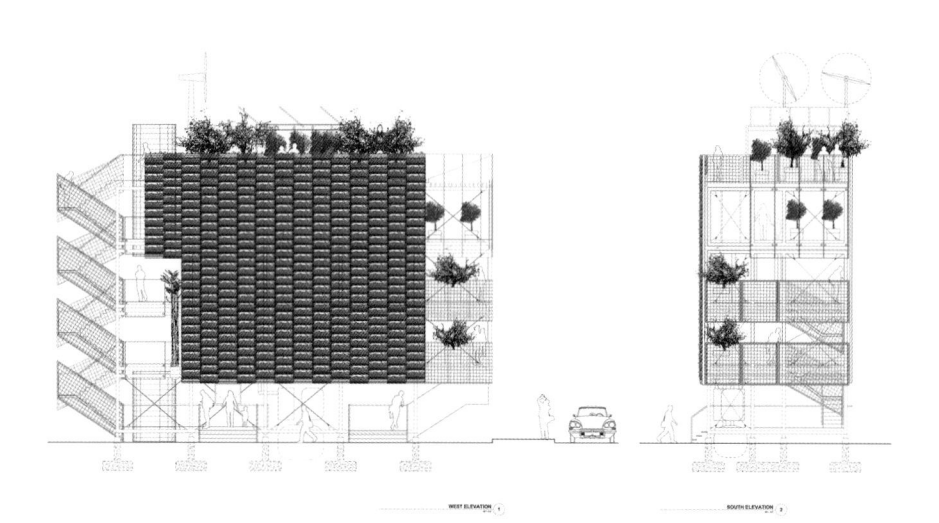

Fig. 4   MoMA Urban Housing Prototype: elevation
Fig. 5   MoMA Urban Housing Prototype: model

dividual housing units were a dead-end for responsible thinking about the future of housing prefabrication, and that future system thinking must place dwelling units into context with a more broadly systemic approach to urban infrastructure as a whole. Rather than proposing an individual dwelling unit prototype as invited, we felt strongly that only a system structure should be exhibited on an urban site, in Manhattan, at the beginning of the twenty-first century, as an example of a significant future for responsible construction systems. The resulting proposal was ambitious as a linked system of nested prefabricated housing, with several individual dwelling units exhibiting the potential for highly variegated individual homes and adjacent public spaces, woven into a cohesive vertical urban system. Although we were eventually able to secure the necessary additional funding required for this larger construction, in the end the polemical position for truly systemic system-housing, as opposed to the mail order individual house, dropped the project from the final exhibition, which became limited to proposals for individual prefabricated dwelling units, in order to maintain a curatorial thematic for the exhibition as whole.

Historically the case that innovative prefabricated housing systems, especially in the United States, have been largely limited to single-family dwellings for suburban landscapes. However, this project clarified in our thinking the important potential for a finer-grained approach to large-scale urban construction. These modular systems presented in these projects embrace both the potential for highly variegated public spaces and individual living units, while placing this potential within a far more comprehensive proposal for dense and broad-scale urban construction. In such terms, these projects lie between the individual particularity of idiosyncratic dwelling and urban construction that we so appreciate in traditional cities, the proto-systemization of the creative, single-family modern house tradition of the early twentieth century, and inflexible, coarse-grained mega-structures of Metabolist and similar urban construction proposals of the late twentieth century. All of the following projects can be viewed with this objective toward a highly flexible and diverse fine-grain construction potential within the practical logic of a more comprehensive industrial, economic, and urban infrastructural recognition.

Wuhan Blue Sky High Density Housing Prototype (Wuhan, 2008)
Wuhan Blue Sky Prototype seeks to provide a highly rationalized steel construction system that is cost effective; appropriate to the current site, program, and project partner production facilities; and readily adaptable to future diverse sites, programs and environmental conditions. As the primary engineering and construction collaborators with whom the next stages of the project will be developed, the *Blue Sky Prototype* has been designed for practical application of the current research interests and production capabilities of China's expanding steel construction industry. The design is adapted and developed in accordance with China's housing and building code requirements, working with local architects and engineers. The construction system, site and building design have developed in coordination with both current codes and with some expansions of current code objectives based on local industry explanations of new national initiatives for housing innovation, land conservation, housing affordability, and interest in expanding the steel construction capacity of China.

Based on these national objectives, the *Blue Sky Prototype* challenges a number of current residential building norms and pushes certain code prescriptions based on the proposal of alternative approaches that will meet or exceed current safety, health and life quality code objectives; further meet new national objectives for affordability, increased density and land conservation; and further create a much higher level of life quality and long term sustainability. The design makes only minor deviations from fundamental building codes with clear offsetting rationale. For example, as a demonstration project innovation, the proposed twelve-storey building configuration achieves greater life-safety and circulation convenience than is provided in code-category maximum eleven-storey buildings; and achieves increased dwelling density, improved sunlight orientation, increased public and private open space and ventilation; and still reduces total land coverage and distance between buildings without shading adjacent dwellings. However, the design will function equally well with the removal of the twelfth-storey if that is required for local conditions. The primary quality of the Blue Sky proposal is not so much in the precise form and space of its configuration for this site, but instead in the broad adaptability that this system provides for efficient design modification for this and future projects without altering the fundamental building components or detail engineering which can be continuously developed and refined in parallel with larger scale planning and program changes.

The first step in producing a healthy, sustainable living environment has involved shaping the space of the building to minimize land use and to optimize orientation to sunlight and natural ventilation. The modular structural system is offset in both plan and section in order to shade the dwelling and community spaces from the hot summer sun, while fully welcoming the low winter sun. This offset geometry further opens the north face to a larger view of the sky and to optimized daylighting and ventilation on all sides of every dwelling unit. The offset further creates a terraced hillside on the north face of the building, planted with trees to provide summer shade and winter wind protection, to create a filtering screen enhancing and modulating natural ventilation, offering a foreground of receding hills and ridges viewed from the balconies, and providing a constructed hillside full of trees as a pleasing presence above the community spaces and public gardens below. This vertical system of gardens and public spaces spills down the hillside of the building to become sunlight and wind modulating screens within the public space below.

The building is organized and detailed to provide maximum daylight and airflow to each unit, and all primary community spaces, stairways and balconies are open air. All rooftops are designed for maximum photovoltaic energy production or for community and private garden spaces, and all roofs collect and filter rainwater for use as non-potable household water. Household grey-water will be filtered and recycled as garden irrigation. Black water and grade-level storm water will both be pre-filtered and partially treated prior to release into the respective city systems, in order to minimize the impact of increased density on existing city services. The intention of the site planning and building systems construction is to minimize adverse impacts on the local urban and natural ecosystems. The construction of the building and its site reaching out into the adjacent park with a water-filtering bio-swale system, edible gardens and orchards is intended as a prototypical approach to the functional and symbolic possibility of sustainable community life in a within a robust natural eco-system.

The form and organization of the building has been developed to encourage community social interaction throughout the building, while also providing desirable levels of privacy for individual dwelling spaces and private outdoor terraces. To best integrate with the larger neighbourhood, the building and site planning is coordinated with the existing planned facilities for a great lawn leading up from the community entrance toward a community gym and shopping centre. These public facilities are integrated with the *Blue Sky Prototype* so that the entire site is planned together as an open-air network of pedestrian streets and public gardens at ground level and winding up into the vertical floor plates.

The organization of the dwelling units places front doors along wide open-air 'streets' in the sky. There are also numerous informal social gathering spaces at all levels within the building. Whereas the typical residential arrangement in China affords excellent solar orientation and through-building ventilation on two sides of each dwelling unit, the resultant circulation system provides a very isolating relationship to neighbours and community, wholly at odds with the communal recent history of China as well as with long-standing traditions of shared community streets, courtyards and gardens integral with daily life and commerce. The *Blue Sky Prototype* attempts to preserve and reinforce the social tradition of streets, community courtyards, dense social interaction, and multi-layered relationships between private and public space. To accomplish these objectives, the dwelling units are organized with a great variety of living options all providing front door access to community 'streets'. The basic module of dwelling units is composed of one or two south-facing flats on

Fig. 6   Wuhan Housing Prototype: perspective
Fig. 7   Wuhan Housing Prototype: model

one side of the street, with two-storey townhouse dwelling with entry doors on the north side of the 'street'. These two-storey units then extend over the top of the flats, so that the primary living spaces of every dwelling in the building all face south, with generous private balconies, excellent sun and daylight, and extensive through-ventilation on a minimum of three sides of each unit, with most units having a full four sides of ventilated window area. All bathrooms, bedrooms and living spaces have direct windows to the outdoors, with the large majority of rooms having cross-ventilation within the room.

This two-storey dwelling organization with 'streets' and elevator stops only every two floors allows substantial savings on initial construction costs and also on long term maintenance and energy costs. Equally important, this arrangement facilitates the density of chance human encounter that is more commonly encountered in a traditional Chinese street, and the resultant layers of overhanging private balconies, open windows in all directions, and a network of alternate travel routes, small and large public spaces, and a variety of populated destination points throughout the building all serve to provide the rich and varied human encounter that is so enjoyable in dense cities when they are full of air and light, full of people, and afford a variety of veiled and semi-veiled private spaces in close proximity to neighbours and the larger community.

To further provide destinations and gathering points throughout the site and building, there are a number of important social spaces distributed at various levels in the public space of the building. The heart of the building itself is a great stairwell and ventilation shaft linking the spaces of the building and providing continually unfolding spatial delight ascending through the dappled light and modulated breezes of this prefabricated steel vertical corridor constructed as a sort of great inhabitable basketwork lantern linking all the parts of the building, encouraging long strolls and minimal elevator use. There are designated locations for a number of shops, restaurants and public gardens at ground level, at various street front levels above, and at the roof top garden. There are suggested opportunities for occasional office spaces along the 'streets of the building', and there are child care spaces with secure playgrounds for small children, a community green house high in the air, a two-storey roof top community social space, and a northern shade garden and a southern sun garden, as well as innumerable small spaces within the winding 'streets' that will be ideal for sitting with friends, playing games or having tea with neighbours beside one's front door. From private terraces one can view streets above and below, through varied densities of screen wall, and all spaces indoor and outdoor, public and private, are provided with abundant vertical and horizontal corridors of light and breeze and view of the larger world. The routes through the building are intended to be endlessly susceptible to exploration, strolling, mingling and enjoyment of light, air, clouds, trees, distant landscapes, community and architecture.

The public 'streets' and steel rod screen wall system that defines and modulates spaces within the residential building is continued out into the adjoining ground level shopping and community centre area where the same system is used to link the primary outdoor spaces of the project and to create two large domes—one over the community pool and gym area at the head of the great community lawn, and the other smaller dome creates an intimate, shaded open-air courtyard surrounded by shops, restaurants and the community centre entrance. Viewed form the public spaces of the tower above, viewed from the community centre and shopping spaces below, or viewed from any distant point within the community, the visual and spatial continuity of this public thread from ground to sky creates a strong image of sustainable public community woven into the neighbourhood.

The *Wuhan Blue Sky Prototype* has been designed and critically reviewed at each step to address issues of design adaptation efficiency, site footprint efficiency, material efficiency, factory production and shipping efficiency, job site erection efficiency, and simplicity of mechanical systems and finishes. In addition, long-term cost-effectiveness is addressed through high levels of energy conservation and positive on-site energy production; standardization and minimization of distinct parts along with simple and sturdy detailing to keep maintenance and repair costs low; and integration of the residential system with mixed-use commercial, restaurant, office, and public community social space in order to help finance initial construction costs and long term maintenance costs.

The proposed configuration of the residential building and its integration with the adjoining commercial and community spaces is expected to yield a total construction cost in line with current average construction costs in Wuhan. Assuming that only the moment frame steel framing modules and cladding/glazing panels are prefabricated, without full prefabrication of major plumbing, mechanical system and cabinetry within the core module, then total construction costs are estimated to be just 5 percent above average local construction costs, even with the generous public space, ventilation corridors and private outdoor living areas. If the maximum prefabrication of just the core modules is achieved for this or for future projects, then total construction costs are estimated to become substantially lower than current costs for similar affordable housing.

**Punggol Green Hills City Prototype
(with Jyanzi Kong, Singapore, 2010)**
To illustrate the flexibility of the *Blue Sky* system, the *Punggol Green Hills* proposal in Singapore presents a much larger "New Town" application, in a tropical location with very different climatic and landscape conditions.

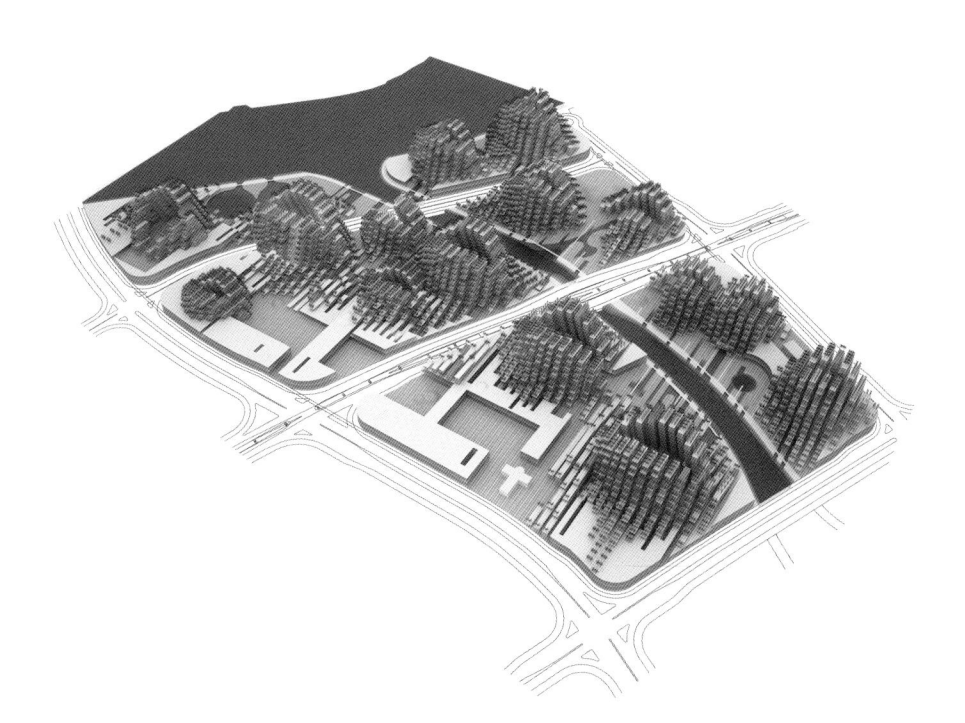

Fig. 8   Punggol Green Hills City Prototype: axonometric
Fig. 9   Punggol Green Hills City Prototype: perspective

In this project, the self-shading, south facing 'cliff-form' of the Wuhan site is transformed into a concentric series of 'volcano-shaped' towers and shaded public court spaces, protected from the equatorial path of the overhead sun.

When Alfred Russell Wallace, the naturalist scientist who landed on the island of Singapore in the mid-1800s, he saw "a multitude of small hills, three or four hundred feet high, the summit of many of which are still covered with virgin forest. The vegetation was most luxuriant, comprising enormous forest trees, as well as a variety of ferns, caladiums, and other undergrowth, and abundance of climbing rattan palm. This exceeding productiveness was due in part no doubt to some favourable conditions in the soil, climate and vegetation, and to the season being very bright and sunny, with sufficient showers to keep everything fresh".[1]

Wallace was perhaps one of the greatest Western literary figures to have rendered an alternative picture of the tropics: a reality that is devoid of conceptual appropriation. For him, the tropics offered a context of incorporation and collaboration with nature at its highest levels, involving visualization, socialization and sublimity of rite and ritual among its inhabitants.

Reorienting the temporal standards of society to be more compatible with the temporality of the planet does not mean going back to a pre-modern mode of existence, as some would suggest. It does mean developing a far more sophisticated and elegant temporal orientation: one that combines traditional wisdom and our newly found ecological awareness with a new generation of institutional arrangements and technologies that can sustain the planet and restore our sacred relationship to it.

Much has been said on Global Warming and the pending havoc that the Planet will create. Perhaps the primary single factor affecting Planet Earth is human construction altering the natural environment. In land-scarce Singapore, the greening program of the nation may take on a complete overhaul in developing not just a garden city but a city of gardens: orchard, plantation and rain forest. Furthermore, the greening program may be layered from skyward to seaward—greening all buildings and public spaces with planting on every available surface.

The tropical land mass is fragile and tends to break down in the weather if ecosystems are disrupted. Stripped of its vegetation, the tropical landform simply 'melts' under heavy downpour and can transform into a tropical desert with intense sunlight. Singapore, with scare natural resources, more so than any other surrounding nation, will have to look for specific new solutions to her national development in the next millennium. To exist successfully as a nation does not mean emulating the same form of construction in every region of the earth. Rather than looking for universal models or prototypes elsewhere, Singapore must look to its own primordial roots, and invent forward from there into entirely new forms of living upon a rich new earth of natural urban density.

Singapore *Punggol Green Hills* seeks to provide a highly rationalized construction system that is cost effective, appropriate to the current site and program, adding system components that are additionally adaptable to future diverse sites, programs and environmental conditions. *Punggol Green Hills* proposes alternative approaches that will meet or exceed current safety, health and life quality code objectives; further meet new national objectives for affordability, increased density and land conservation; and further create a much higher level of life quality and long term sustainability. An important quality of the *Punggol Green Hills* proposal is not so much in the precise form and space of its configuration for this site, but instead in the broad adaptability that this system provides for efficient design modification for this and future projects without altering the fundamental building components or detail engineering which can be continuously developed and refined in parallel with larger scale planning and program changes.

San Francisco High-Life Farming Block (San Francisco, 2010)
A final example of this modular urban system approach is located as one component of a planned new urban community in San Francisco. A primary objective of the design process for this project was to apply the modular system as a test project in a master-planned new town designed by Skidmore Owings and Merrill (SOM). SOM hired us as one of six architecture firms collaborating with them to design individual buildings within the community master plan, in order to create initial architecture diversity with this area of the city, and to fully study and engage the SOM master plan guidelines in order to test the flexibility of their master plan as a viable long-term planning vision that will allow future flexibility.

Our experience in the design of a building for our site—based on an-

Fig. 10 San Francisco High-Life Farming Block: section
Fig. 11 San Francisco High-Life Farming Block: perspective

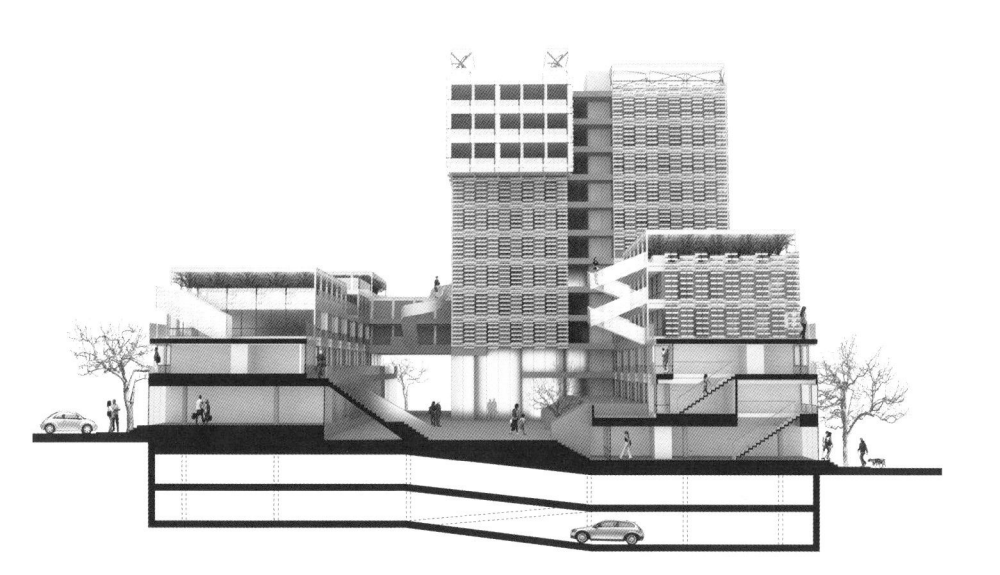

alytical climate studies and based on the overall design process – has confirmed in our minds the clarity and effectiveness of the SOM master plan in specifying building massing that is climate- and topography-logical as well as clearly reinforcing the intended urban logic of defined, secure streets, pedestrian corridors and public spaces, with a coherent neighbourhood focus on local nature, sustainability, and local food and energy production. In parallel, placing our approach to a modular urban system as a single building project within a more variously conceived urban plan, has confirmed the flexibility of a modular approach to act as an idiosyncratic urban in-fill approach just as effectively as a more comprehensive urban community structure such as *Punggol Green Hills*. Our experience in this design process confirms the potential for a great deal of design flexibility and individual creative potential at the building scale, while maintaining the strength and logic of an overall existing or planned community of a character different from the modular armature that we have proposed. Based on the SOM master plan guidelines, we have concentrated this design proposal on the following issues:

- Maximizing sunlight access and wind protection for the master plan public park space designated for our block, on the adjoining site designed by Stanley Saitowitz/Natoma Architects. To accomplish this, the design process began with extensive analytical modelling in solar and computational fluid dynamic wind studies of the site and potential building mass organization.

- Defining urban street quality with continuous building frontage, emphasizing building/street relationship to provide urban neighbourhood vitality and 'eyes on the street' neighbourhood security.

- Placement of the master plan commercial space designated for our site, directly facing onto the public park space, onto the adjacent street, and also facing onto the two designated mid-block pedestrian throughways—the public east-west paseo and the semi-public north-south 'open-sky' corridor—in order to mutually reinforce the activity and identity of these public and commercial spaces at the heart of the block. The placement of the commercial space and adjoining public space is such that it is through-visible from all three streets and both pedestrian corridors on our site, as well as from the building lobby, from all major building corridors, common spaces and terraces, and from most apartment units.

- Organization of the semi-public courtyard space of our building to be animated and secured with direct frontage and view lines from the building lobby, adjacent streets and pedestrian corridors, the majority of building common space and apartment units on all levels, and by the commercial space and commercial space terraces (commercial space is configured in this design to work well as a neighbourhood, two-storey restaurant bar with outdoor dining areas fronting onto the public park, public pedestrian corridors, and semi-public building courtyard).

- Organization of the building mass to maximize sunlight and prevailing wind orientation for the commercial space and terraces, individual apartment units (there are no solely north-facing units), semi-private common courtyard, roof terrace, commercial agriculture and energy generation systems.

- Organization of the building program to maximize "eyes on the street" frontage to secure and animate adjacent streets, pedestrian corridors, the adjoining public park space, and all semi-private corridors, courtyards and rooftop terraces: The building lobby is a three-sided glass space at street level fronting onto the street, and the semi-public pedestrian corridor and building courtyard; The commercial space is a three-sided glass space opening onto the street, the public park, both pedestrian corridors, and the building courtyard; The elevator lobby and adjacent service core are glazed on every level and look onto the building courtyard and roof top terraces, and toward the public park, commercial space terraces and pedestrian corridors; common space stairs and corridors are primarily outdoors and open onto the building courtyard and adjacent pedestrian corridors and look toward the commercial terraces and public park space; The three facing streets, pedestrian corridors, building courtyard and public park space all have prominent and direct street front entries and continuous overlooking windows and balconies from individual apartments, the building lobby, and the commercial spaces, so that there are no blank, closed or un-animated building faces at street and ground level.

- The parking garage ramp is placed adjacent and within the building lobby. This animates, secures, brightens and clearly identifies the garage ramp along the street wall and within the public face of the building.

- All roof top areas are utilized based on their orientation and adjacencies: The tower roof (above view level) is fixed with wind turbines and a continuous field of photo-voltaic and solar thermal panels; Lower roof top areas are utilized in small areas as common social spaces (adjacent to areas that are designed to serve as either apartment unit spaces or as alternative income generating spaces such as gyms, child-care or other uses), but are primarily developed for practical commercial agriculture activities (see below).

- Wall surfaces are optimized to provide the best light, air and views to individual dwelling units, with variation based on orientation, structural system and program adjacency: Glass walls at street, courtyard and roof terrace levels to maximize public space security and liveliness; View, sunlight and ventilation windows for primary living spaces; Shaded wall areas for secondary living areas, provided by vertical agricultural planting walls.

- Street level apartment units are designed as continuous glass walls to super-animate the building relationship to the street. These street front units are typically two-storey townhouse units that can be utilized as commercial space, live/work space, or strictly residential use. While the continuous glass walls at street level may be disconcerting to some potential tenants, they will be unique opportunities for the more socially inclined, and will radically enliven the street if a culture of open windows develops. Unlike some of the cladding system in the upper levels, which subtly distinguish individual units, the street level units are intentionally undifferentiated within the continuous ribbon of glazing, in order to provide a play of anonymity within the public/private porosity.

- To maximize affordability as well as sustainable, long-term component reusability, the building is designed to be constructed using a system of modular, prefabricated frame assemblies. This system is highly adaptable to varying levels of prefabrication, from simple frame assemblies to speeding the framing process only, to more fully pre-assembled units complete with a majority of plumbing,

Fig. 12 Le Corbusier' sketch of Janus face. 1948.

wiring, fixtures and surfaces. No part of building design is limited or constrained by this building method, but the construction schedule, cost, energy, waste, long-term maintenance and management savings are potentially very significant in a building this size, and enormously significant if considered for multiple buildings.

- In addition to systematizing the building structure and dwelling units as prefabricated modules, the same approach is taken to modularizing the cladding, glazing, energy production and commercial agriculture components of the project. This modularity affords maintenance and component replacement logic and savings for all of the building parts, but the practicality for the energy and farming modules is particularly valuable: On-site energy production equipment will rapidly evolve and improve over the life-time of the building, and these modules are designed to be easily lifted off the structure and upgraded as the financial amortization versus efficiency improvement of equipment dictate; Commercial agriculture integrated with urban dwelling structures affords great symbiotic potential, but only if practical working methods and access systems are integrated – this design proposes a modular system of high-value, long growth-period, nursery-style tree and plant farming, with plantings placed and harvested by mobile crane, quickly lifting and replacing whole farm fields in a matter of hours and on an infrequent basis, with minimal disruption to the streets or community. This ever-changing landscape provides income for its maintenance and substantial potential for positive income as well.

- The green rooftop and vertical farming panels terrace back and upward from the public park space, multiplying the green space of the park into a large, planted urban valley incorporating much of the block. These green surfaces are designed to gather and filter water from rain and fog, and to put this water to work before gently landing remaining water into the neighbourhood street swales. The image, surfaces and structure of the building and landscape are all intended to evoke and deliver a unique quality of self-sustaining urban/natural life in vertical gardens on the ocean coast.

An Expanding System of Diverse Vertical Landscape Infrastructure
Architecture and cities require far more than just practical system making. They cannot be designed, or anticipated, by narrowly conceived logic alone. In 1948, Le Corbusier sketched a Janus face—half threatening, snake-haired Medusa, half benign yet world-weary sun. This image has long been a haunting touchstone in our thinking about architecture and culture. Le Corbusier drew this face at a moment just following the devastation of World War II, amidst the

Fig. 13 Lips Tower: elevation diagram

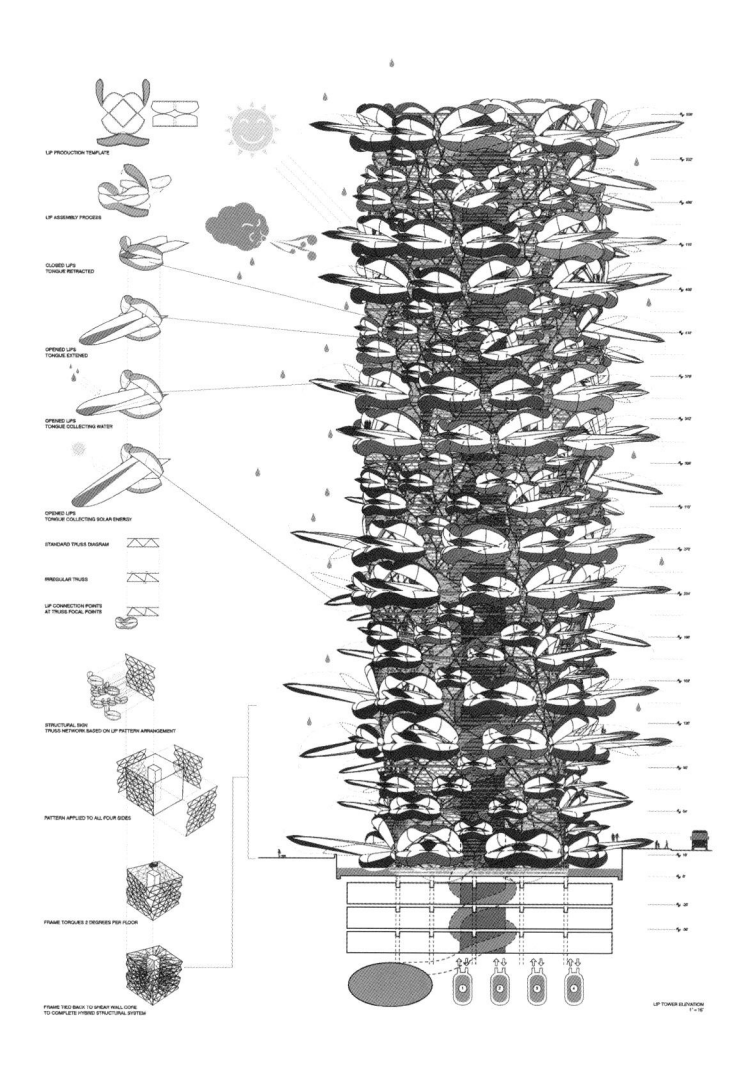

dwindling optimism of peace congealing into Cold War angst, when artists and intellectuals throughout the world confronted imagination and creation in the face of existential terror and shattered foundations. This moment is seminal in Le Corbusier's shift from self-confident modernism into work that emerged far rawer, more primitive, impure and soul-searching than the previous esprit nouveau. This sketch represents for us the face of a post self-certain world, and the clearest existential protest against the sort of pious self-satisfaction represented in so much of the skin-deep conservatism of traditional urban form-making "preservation" pastiche, or for that matter, of the simplistic reductivism of safe, modernistic gloss or decorative modernistic jubilance. It is necessary to work with two faces, and to embrace optimistically constructive logic as well as recognition of critical uncertainty and the muddy multiplicity of desire, fear and imagination of the unknown.

Lips Tower (San Francisco and Torino, 2009–present)

As fresh water resources rapidly diminish worldwide, cities require new strategies for collecting, storing and distributing clean drinking water. This issue is most pressing in dense urban areas with limited available ground space, increasingly distant from secure and efficiently available natural aquifers. In most cities substantial energy resources are expended in routing and pumping distant water sources into urban areas. This long

Fig. 14 Lips Tower: model

distance tapping of precious lake, river and ground water also exacerbates water rights disputes between cities, farmers, fishermen and advocates of environmental conservation. Beside the need to develop new sources of water, creating these sources locally will greatly reduce energy consumption, transport costs, evaporation and leakage losses, and reduce damage to natural eco-systems, landscapes, agricultural production and traditional rural culture and economies. Saving water and creating new alternative sources of water parallels and supports similar efforts in energy resource conservation and the development of local, low-impact energy production. *Lips Tower* addresses these issues as a proposal for a resource-efficient, high-rise office tower intertwined with water and energy harvesting and storage systems.

Lips Tower works as a thirsty urban utility sucking water and solar energy from the sky. Operable Teflon lips open and close to modulate internal building temperatures with gentle airflows ducted past gravity fed circulating water coils into soft fabric windpipes cooling the building's interior floor plates. As the sun circles the tower operable fabric tongues extend past their lips to expose photovoltaic skin while simultaneously shading the building face and preventing direct heat gain. As the sun moves on, tongues on shaded portions of the building retreat back into their lips, maximizing ambient work light for the building interior. On rainy days, on wet windward walls, tongues swell out to full extension, rising to gather raindrops into rivulets piped to water bladders banking gravity-battery potential energy, with surplus streams winding down around the building core, cooling the building and running into storage tanks and city water mains beneath the tower foundations. On foggy nights and cloudy humid days the tongues extend again with cool, tendriled skin to lick condensation from heavy, moisture-laden air.

The mechanism of these fabric machines is relatively simple and requires minimal energy. Micro-sensors on the building skin evaluate microclimate conditions and dictate optimal positioning of each operable utility element. The lips, tongues, internal throats, wind pipes and pleated building skins are all constructed of UV stabilized, Teflon-coated industrial fabrics with a projected useful life-span of forty tears, and are detailed for simple bolted installation and replacement. The lips and tongues are mechanized with interior bladders shaped and activated either by compressed air, or in some applications with hydrophilic, superabsorbent polymer packing, causing the pleated, hinged and folding skin panels to rise, fall, swell, contract, extend, shrink and retract as required to coordinate usefulness with localized atmospheric conditions. The top surface of the tongues is faced with flexible, fabric-adhered, photovoltaic. As the lips open and close, they draw with them the fabric building skin, to maintain a weather-tight seal. Accommodating this movement, the insulated skins are created of pleated fabric panels carrying elliptical windows in aluminium frames. The flexible fabric between the window panels allows the skin to hinge and bend along a horizontal arc. The vertical expansion and arcing is accommodated with horizontal pleats in the fabric, which also act as hoods or eyelids partially closing and shading the windows. As the lips open on warm days to maximize gasping intake of cooling air, the stress in the building skin is reduced, relaxing the pleats and hooding the windows at this moment when reduced daylight and reduced heat gain is most welcomed. When the lips close on cooler days to reduce air intake, the adjacent building skin tightens, arcs further outward to match the geometry of the lips, stretching the pleats and un-hooding the windows. This varied play of maximized utility acting in microclimate efficiency across the face and around the corners of the tower give substantial life and comprehensible narrative to a street view of the building dancing with its sky. Firmness. Commodity. Delight. Why should architecture be any less than this?

Notes
1 Alfred Russell Wallace, The Malay Archipelago. (1868)

DESIGN

COMPETITION

Design Competition

The Vertical Cities Asia International Design Competition encourages design explorations and deliberations into the prospects of new architectural, urban design and planning models for the dense and intense urban environments in Asia. The continent is undergoing a dramatic and rapid urbanization. We are observing an unrelenting, large scale migration from the countryside to the cities. Asian cities are getting denser and growing taller at a scale and intensity without historical precedent. The existing urban architectural and planning models struggle to accommodate the increased population. To continue recycling these models in the face of this challenge will lead to devastating effects on land, infrastructure, and the environment.

Basic Framework

The overall topic is complex and multi-faceted, and Asia itself has very heterogeneous cultures. This calls for a sustained and comprehensive exploration of the major issues. For this reason, every year for the five years, a one square kilometre territory from a different Asian country will be the subject of the design competition.

This area, to house 100,000 people living and working, forms the basic framework for tremendous research and investigation into the different aspects of urban density, verticality, domesticity, work, food, infrastructure, nature, ecology, structure, and program – their holistic integration and the quest for visionary paradigm will be the challenges of this urban and architectural intervention. This new environment is expected to have a full slate of live-work-play provisions, with the residential component making up to half of the total floor space.

Everyone Needs Fresh Air

In addition, the theme selected for inaugural edition of the Vertical Cities Asia programme is "Everyone Needs Fresh Air". In the congested cities of Asia, urban sprawl, traffic congestion and environmental pollution have threatened the prospects of biodiversity, greenery, liveability and general well-being of the inhabitants. Until the Severe Acute Respiratory Syndrome (SARS) crisis occurred in late-2002, there has been little study or consideration of air flows through highly urbanised areas. Since then, Asian governments are paying more attention to how urban design and planning can optimise the local wind environment for urban air ventilation. Indeed, the Hong Kong government has taken the lead in establishing and adopting an "Air Ventilation Assessment (AVA) System" which is now being studied by a number of Asian countries.

Chengdu, China

For the inaugural edition of the Vertical Cities Asia programme, the selected site is located in Shuangliu County, 16 kilometres southwest of the city of Chengdu, the capital and largest city of the China's Sichuan province. Sichuan is one of China's largest provinces by area and by population. It is about the size of Spain, and has a population of over 80 million.

Like many other Chinese cities, Chengdu is experiencing rapid population growth in recent years, primarily due to rural-urban migration. Between 2005 and 2010, the urban population grew from 10.8 to 14 million, nearly a 30 percent increase in just five years. With no major geographical obstacles, Chengdu is a textbook example of the concentric ring-road urban development model familiar in many Chinese cities. The outward sprawl facilitated by this model, coupled with the population increase, has led to the construction of sterile high-rise residential precincts in Chengdu and the surrounding counties. These residential-only precincts are quite at odds with the reputation of Chengdu as a lively city of tea gardens and (within the Chinese context) a 'laid back' lifestyle. Another negative consequence of the existing development model is the amount of traffic congestion, and the attendant pollution. Given that Chengdu has one of the lowest levels of sunshine in China, the overall quality of life has been adversely affected.

Competition and Symposium
The inaugural edition of the design competition was formally launched in January 2011. Participating universities were invited to submit two proposals. In addition to the general brief and the theme of "Fresh Air", the proposals were to be evaluated if they had considered the following issues in a holistic and integrated manner:

> Sustainability: The design should examine a closed loop paradigm, ecological and resilience attributes in their solution.

> Quality of Life: The consideration for inclusiveness and sense of community.

> Technical Innovation: The appropriate and innovative use of technology and technique.

> Relationship to Context: Sensitive consideration of the place, climate and cultural context.

> Feasibility: The rigour of the research and criticality of design in addressing the issues.

The jury members convened were:

> Alan Balfour, Professor and Dean of the College of Architecture, Georgia Institute of Technology.

> Ken Yeang, Chairman of Llewelyn Davies Yeang (UK) and Principal of Hamzah & Yeang (Malaysia).

> Joaquím Sabaté Bel, Professor and Chair of Town Planning, Polytechnic University of Catalonia.

> Wang Shu, Professor and Dean of the School of Architecture, China Academy of Art, Hangzhou

> Wong Mun Summ, Founder, WOHA Architects, Singapore

This page
Prize winners, sponsors and the guest-of-honour for the inaugural Vertical Cities Asia competition.

The Symposium was held in Singapore in July 2011. The teams from the participating universities and the accompanying faculty travelled to Singapore to present their proposals. The faculty and the jury also presented papers at the Symposium. At the end of the Symposium, the Jury awarded the prizes to the following proposals:

First Prize:
"Symbio City" - ETH Zurich (Team B)

Second Prize:
"The Wall" - Delft University of Technology (Team B)

Third Prize:
"Boundless City" - Tongji University (Team B)

Honourable Mention:
"Village City" - National University of Singapore (Team A)

First Prize

SymbioCity

University
Swiss Federal Institute of Technology (ETH) Zurich

Tutors
Kees CHRISTIAANSE (Professor)
Alfredo BRILLEMBOURG (Professor)
Hubert KLUMPNER (Professor)
Nicolas KRETSCHMAN (Teaching Assistant)
Michael CONTENTO (Teaching Assistant)

Team B
Carmen BAUMANN
Alessandro BOSSHARD
Julianne GANTNER
NING Hug
Selina MASE
Louis WANGLER

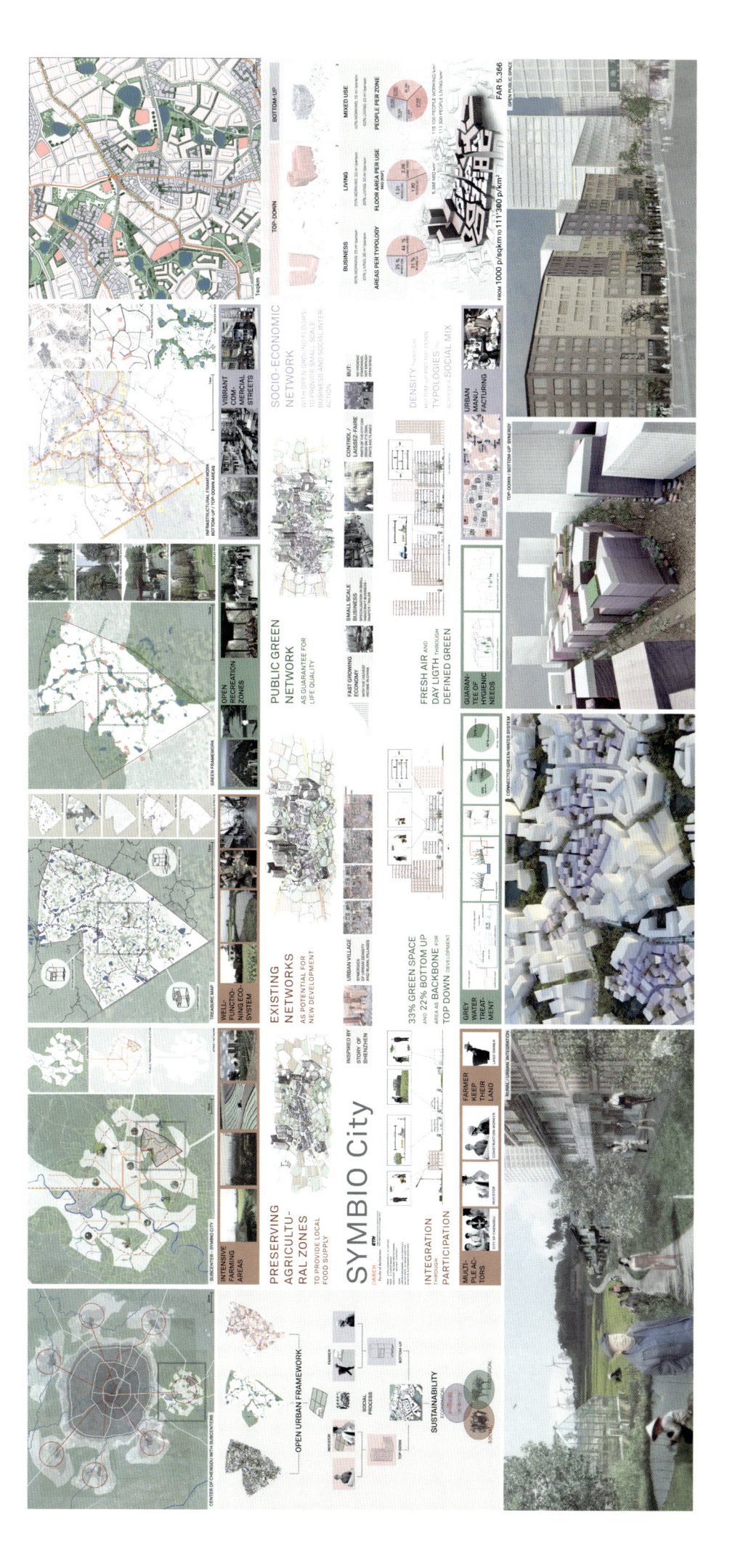

SYMBIO City

ETH Zurich
Team B

Panel
Detail 1

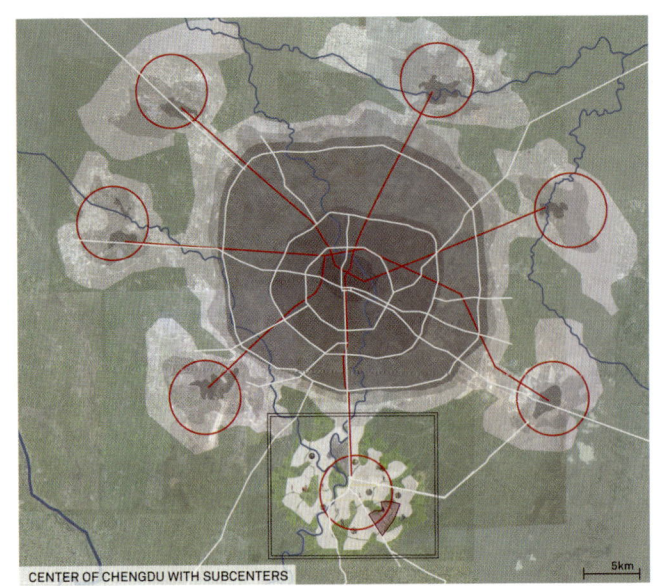

CENTER OF CHENGDU WITH SUBCENTERS
5km

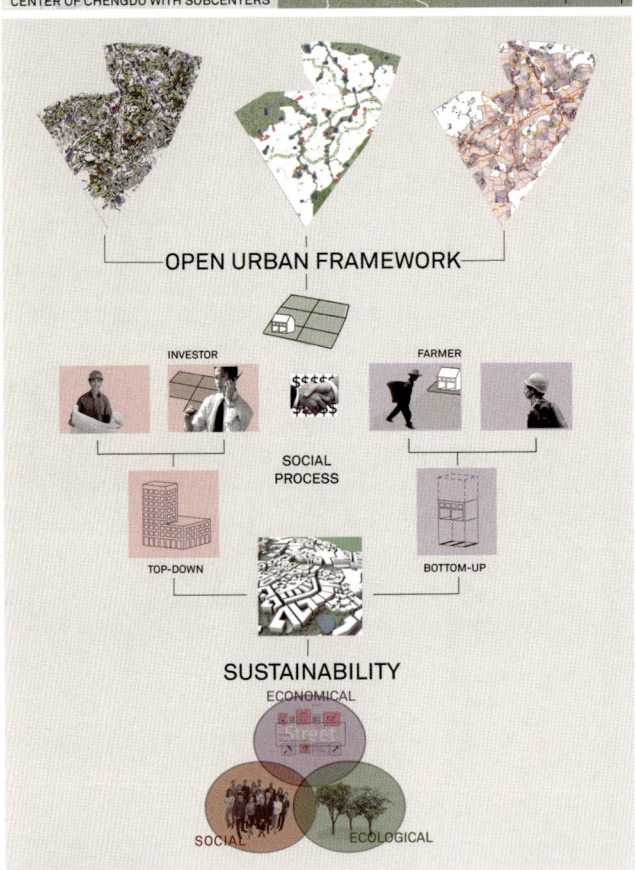

OPEN URBAN FRAMEWORK

INVESTOR   FARMER

SOCIAL PROCESS

TOP-DOWN   BOTTOM-UP

SUSTAINABILITY

ECONOMICAL
SOCIAL   ECOLOGICAL

162

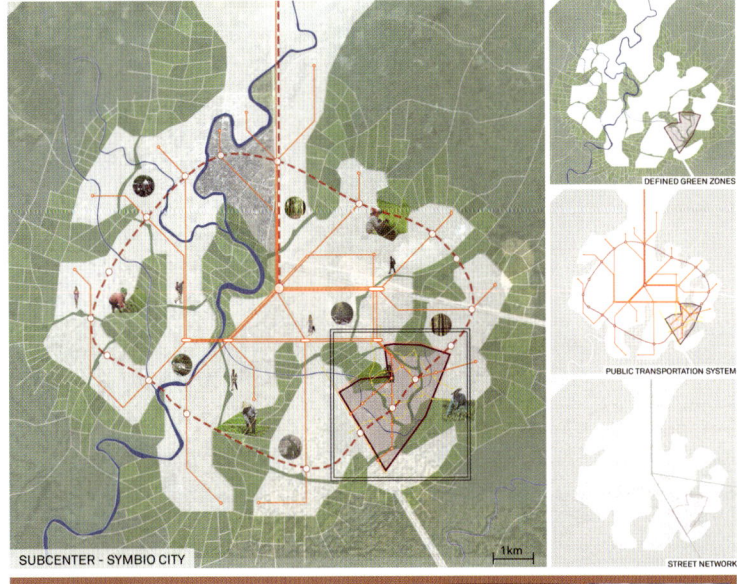

Panel Detail 2

SUBCENTER - SYMBIO CITY 1km

DEFINED GREEN ZONES

PUBLIC TRANSPORTATION SYSTEM

STREET NETWORK

INTENSIVE FARMING AREAS

PRESERVING AGRICULTU-RAL ZONES

TO PROVIDE LOCAL FOOD SUPPLY

SYMBIO City

INSPIRED BY STORY OF SHENZHEN

DARCH **ETH**
Faculty of Architecture
Eidgenössische Technische Hochschule Zürich
Swiss Federal Institute of Technology Zurich

PROF. A BRILLENBOURG H. KLUMPNER
PROF. K. CHRISTIAANSE
ASISTENT. NICOAS KRETSCHMANN
MICHAEL CONTENTO
TEAM:
CARMEN BAUMANN, LOUIS WANGLER
SELINA MASÉ, JULIANNE GANTNER
NINA HUG, ALESSANDRO BOSSHARD

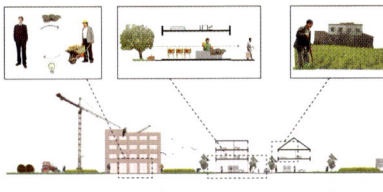

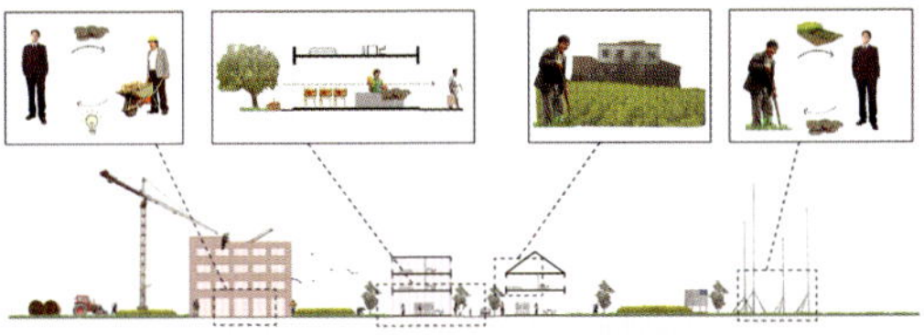

INTEGRATION
THROUGH
PARTICIPATION

| MULTIPLE ACTORS | CITY OF CHENGDU | INVESTOR | CONSTRUCTION WORKER | FARMER KEEP THEIR LAND | LAND OWNER |

RURAL / URBAN INTEGRATION

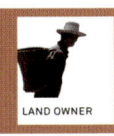

ETH Zurich
Team B

Panel
Detail 3

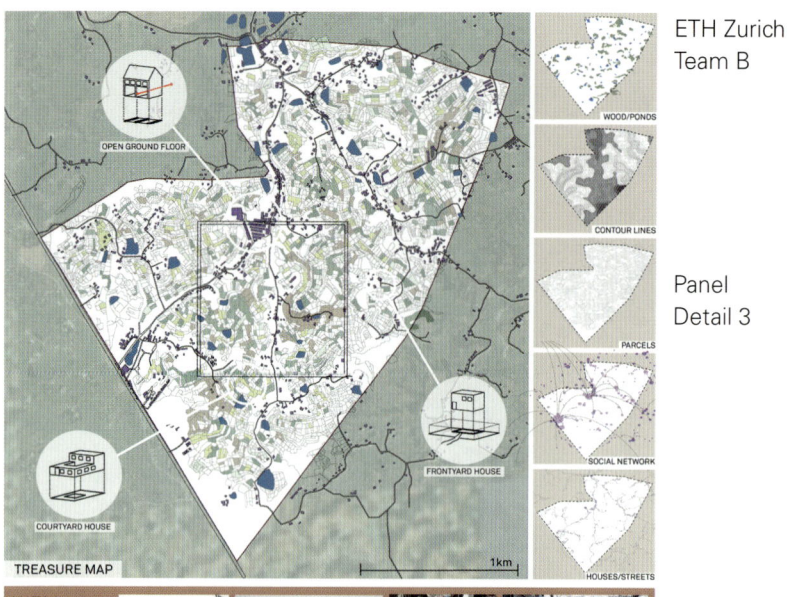

TREASURE MAP

WOOD/PONDS
CONTOUR LINES
PARCELS
SOCIAL NETWORK
HOUSES/STREETS

OPEN GROUND FLOOR
FRONTYARD HOUSE
COURTYARD HOUSE

WELL-FUNCTIONING ECOSYSTEM

EXISTING NETWORKS
AS POTENTIAL FOR NEW DEVELOPMENT

URBAN VILLAGE
SYNERGIES OF URBAN DENSITY AND RURAL VILLAGES

2002 | 2003 | 2004 | 2005

33% GREEN SPACE
AND **22% BOTTOM UP**
AREA AS **BACKBONE** FOR
TOP DOWN DEVELOPMENT

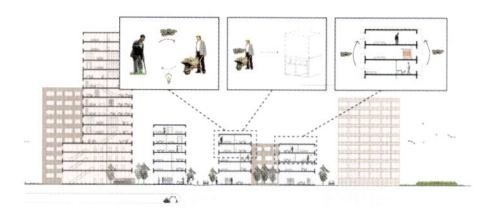

GREY WATER TREATMENT

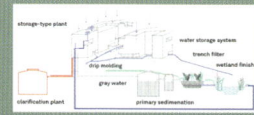

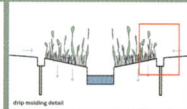

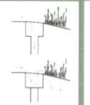

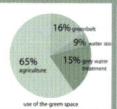

storage-type plant | water storage system
drip molding | trench filter
gray water | wetland finish
clarification plant | primary sedimentation | drip molding detail

16% greenbelt
9% water use
65% agriculture
15% grey water treatment
use of the green space

33% green space
67% building structure
ratio city / freestructure

CONNECTED GREEN/WATER SYSTEM

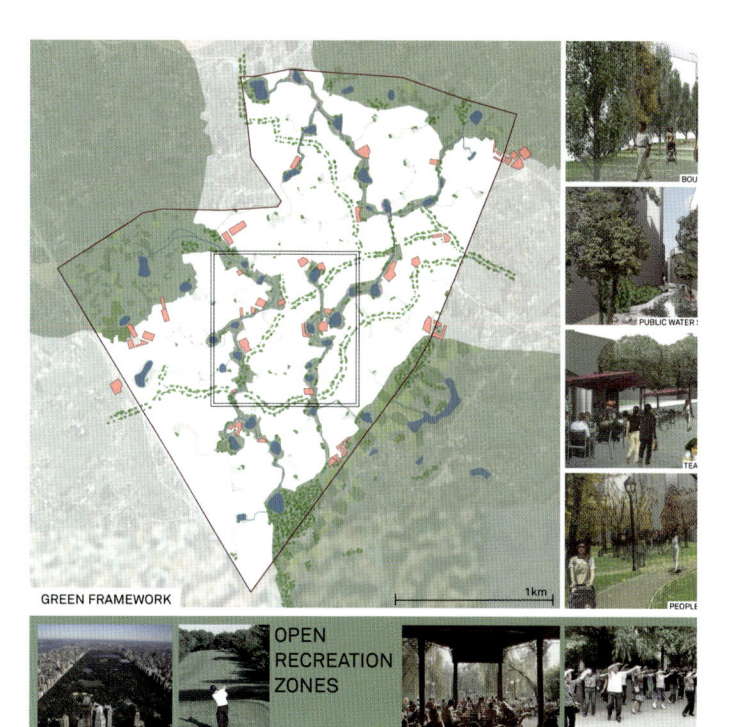

Panel Detail 4

GREEN FRAMEWORK 1km

OPEN RECREATION ZONES

PUBLIC GREEN NETWORK
AS GUARANTEE FOR LIFE QUALITY

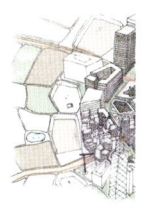

FAST GROWING ECONOMY
WITH THE HIGHEST INCOME IN CHINA

SMALL SCALE BUSINESS
SPECIALISATION IN SMALL HANDCRAFT BUSINESS - PAINTER / TAILOR

FRESH AIR AND DAY LIGTH THROUGH DEFINED GREEN

GUARANTEE OF HYGIENIC NEEDS

drip molding used for evaporation   heat island effect used to create wind

ETH Zurich
Team B

Panel
Detail 5

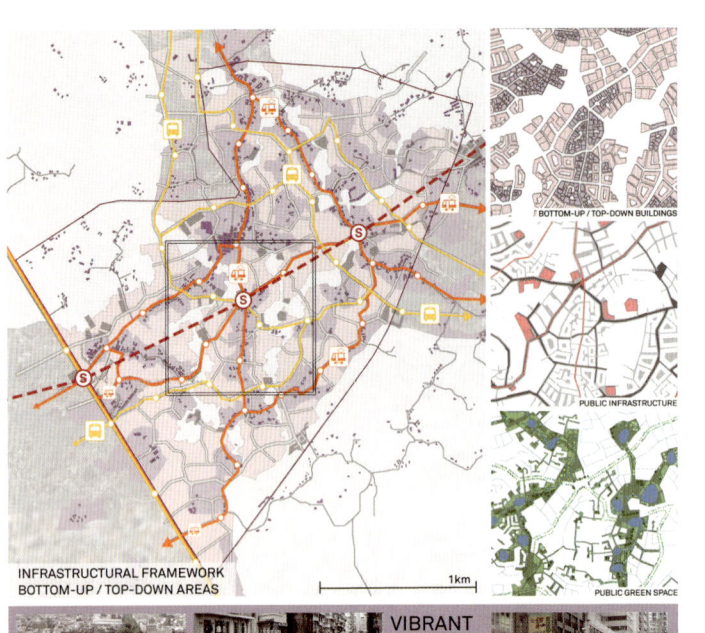

INFRASTRUCTURAL FRAMEWORK
BOTTOM-UP / TOP-DOWN AREAS
1km

BOTTOM-UP / TOP-DOWN BUILDINGS

PUBLIC INFRASTRUCTURE

PUBLIC GREEN SPACE

VIBRANT COMMERCIAL STREETS

SOCIO-ECONOMIC NETWORK

WITH OPEN GROUND FLOORS TO PROVIDE SMALL SCALE BUSINESS AND SOCIAL INTERACTION

CONTROL / LAISSEZ-FAIRE
PARTS OF THE CITY CAN GROW ON IT'S OWN, PARTS ARE PLANED

BUT:
NO HYGIENIC STANDARDS, NOT ENOUGH OPEN SPACE

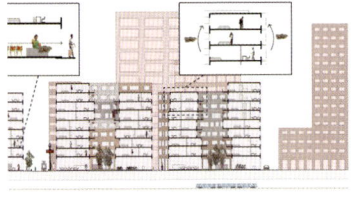

DENSITY THROUGH BOTTOM-UP AND TOP-DOWN **TYPOLOGIES** TO ACHIEVE A **SOCIAL MIX**

URBAN MANUFACTURING

TOP-DOWN / BOTTOM-UP SYNERGY

166

Panel
Detail 6

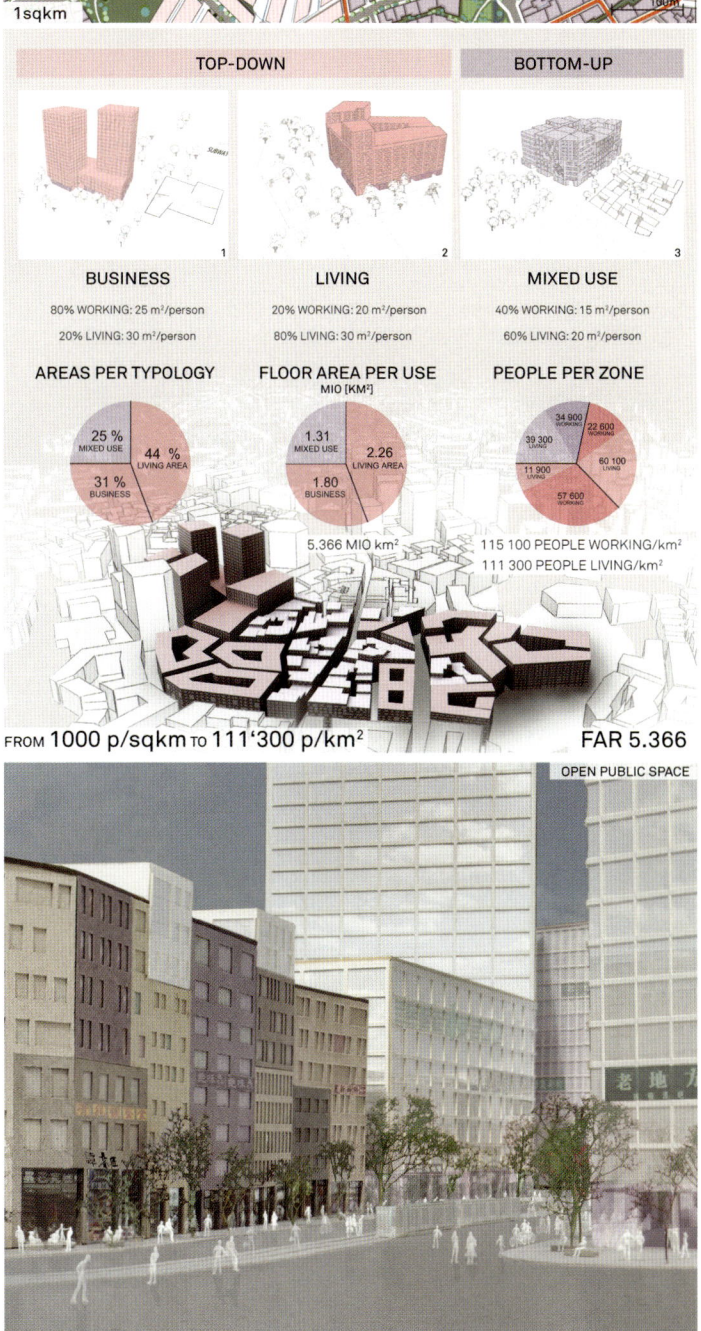

1sqkm

TOP-DOWN		BOTTOM-UP
BUSINESS	LIVING	MIXED USE
80% WORKING: 25 m²/person	20% WORKING: 20 m²/person	40% WORKING: 15 m²/person
20% LIVING: 30 m²/person	80% LIVING: 30 m²/person	60% LIVING: 20 m²/person

AREAS PER TYPOLOGY
- 25 % MIXED USE
- 44 % LIVING AREA
- 31 % BUSINESS

FLOOR AREA PER USE
MIO [KM²]
- 1.31 MIXED USE
- 2.26 LIVING AREA
- 1.80 BUSINESS

5.366 MIO km²

PEOPLE PER ZONE
- 34 900
- 22 600 WORKING
- 39 300 LIVING
- 60 100
- 11 900 LIVING
- 57 600 WORKING

115 100 PEOPLE WORKING/km²
111 300 PEOPLE LIVING/km²

FROM **1000 p/sqkm** TO **111'300 p/km²**   FAR 5.366

OPEN PUBLIC SPACE

Second Prize

The Wall

University
Delft University of Technology

Tutors
Karin LAGLAS (Professor and Dean)
Henco BEKKERING (Professor)

Team B
Bart van LAKWIJK
Herman PEL
Jasper NIJVELDT

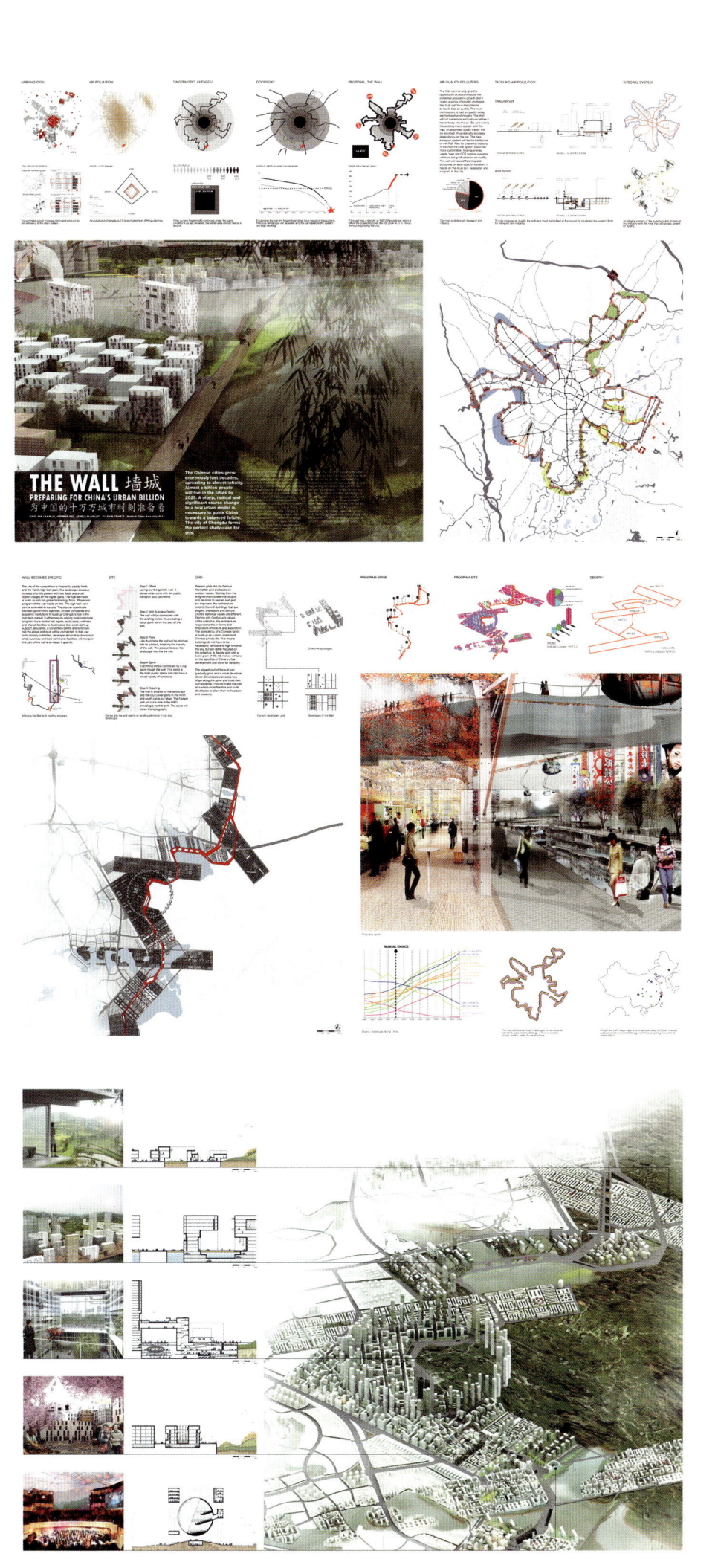

THE WALL 墙城
PREPARING FOR CHINA'S URBAN BILLION
为中国的十万万城市时刻准备者

The Chinese cities grew enormously last decades, spreading to almost infinity. Almost a billion people will live in the cities by 2025. A sharp, radical and significant course change to a new urban model is necessary to guide China towards a balanced future. The city of Chengdu forms the perfect study-case for this.

URBANIZATION

Concentrated growth increases the overall productivity and efficiency of the urban system.

AIR POLLUTION

Air pollution in Chengdu is 2.5 times higher than WHO guidelines.

FINGERMODEL CHENGDU

If the current fingermodel continues under the same conditions as last decades, the urban area almost needs to double.

DOOMSDAY

Expanding the current fingermodel does have negative implications. Precious landscape will be eaten and the car-based traffic system will stop working.

PROPOSAL: THE WALL

156 KM2

If the wall has a density of 100,000 people per sqkm, it offers the possibility to let the city grow to 27.5 million, without expanding the city.

AIR QUALITY POLLUTERS

The Wall can not only give the opportunity to accommodate the projected population growth, but it is also a series of parallel strategies that truly can have the potential to tackle bad air quality. The main contributors to bad air quality today are transport and industry. The Wall will cut emissions and capture before it blows freely into the air. By connecting the existing metro system with the wall, an expanded public-transit will be provided, thus radically decrease dependency on the car. This new transport system will be the backbone of the Wall. Also by clustering industry in the Wall the total system becomes more sustainable. Sharing energy, waste, heat and CO2 capture systems will have a big influence on air quality. The wall will have different spatial outcomes on each specific location. It reacts on the local soil, vegetation and program in the city.

The main polluters are transport and industry.

TACKLING AIR POLLUTION

TRANSPORT

INDUSTRY

To truly increase air quality the polluters must be tackled at the source by clustering the system for transport and industry.

INTEGRAL SYSTEM

An integral system of the existing public transport and industry with the new Wall will greatly benefit air quality.

TU Delft
Team B

Panel
Detail 1 & 2

THE WALL 墙城
PREPARING FOR CHINA'S URBAN BILLION
为中国的十万城市时刻准备着

BART VAN LAKWIJK, HERMAN PEIJ, JASPER NIJVELDT · TU Delft TEAM B - Vertical Cities Asia July 2011

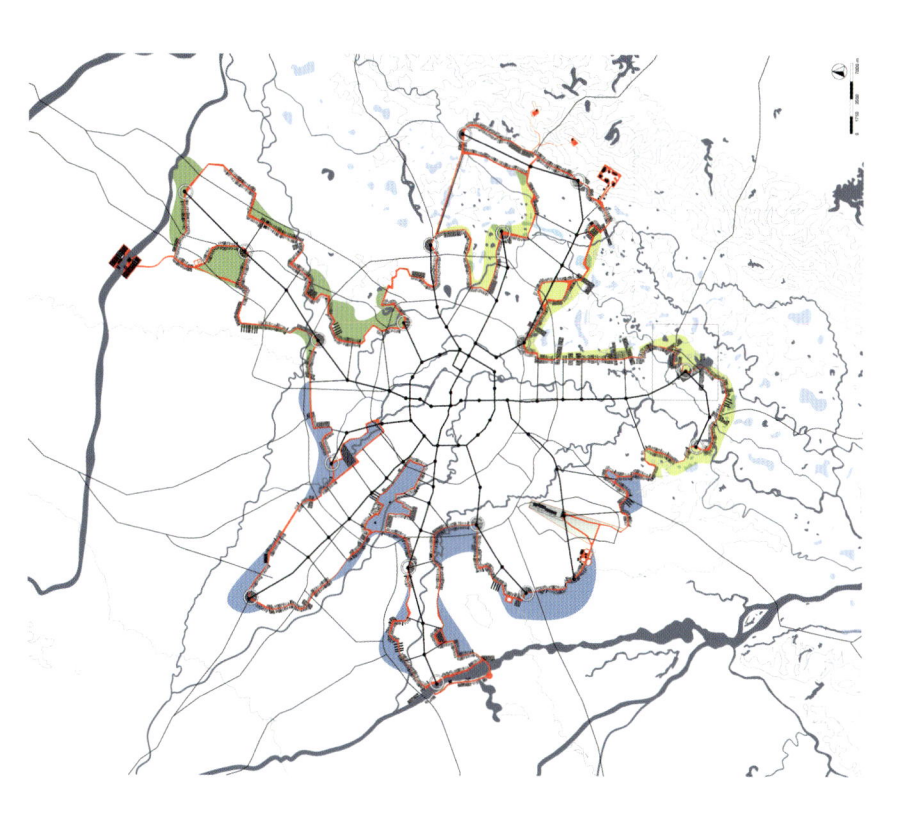

The Chinese cities grew enormously last decades, spreading to almost infinity. Almost a billion people will live in the cities by 2025. A sharp, radical and significant course change to a new urban model is necessary to guide China towards a balanced future. The city of Chengdu forms the perfect study-case for this.

TU Delft
Team B

Panel
Detail 3

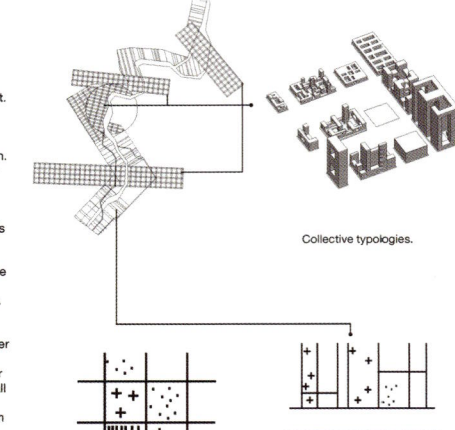

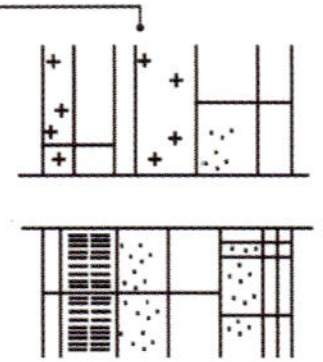

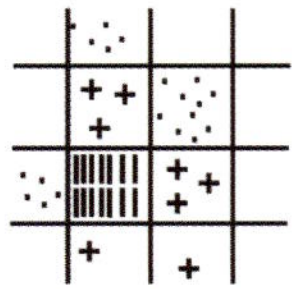

Collective typologies.

Developers in the Wall.

Current developers grid.

GRID

Western grids like the famous Manhattan grid are based on western values. Starting from the enlightenment where individuality and devotion to heaven and god are important, the architecture reflects this with buildings that are elegant, impressive and vertical. China's historical values are different. Starting with Confucius's values of the collective, the architecture responds to this in forms that emphasize enclosure and separation. The domesticity of a Chinese family is build up as a micro cosmos of Chinese private life. This means buildings do not have to be necessarily vertical and high towards the sky, but are rather focused on the collective. A flexible grid with a basic grain of 30x 80 metres will take on the specifics of China's urban development and allow for flexibility.

The biggest part of the wall can gradually grow and is more developer driven. Developers can easily buy strips along the spine and build their own paradise. This will make the wall as a whole more feasible and invite developers to show their enthusiasm and creativity.

SITE

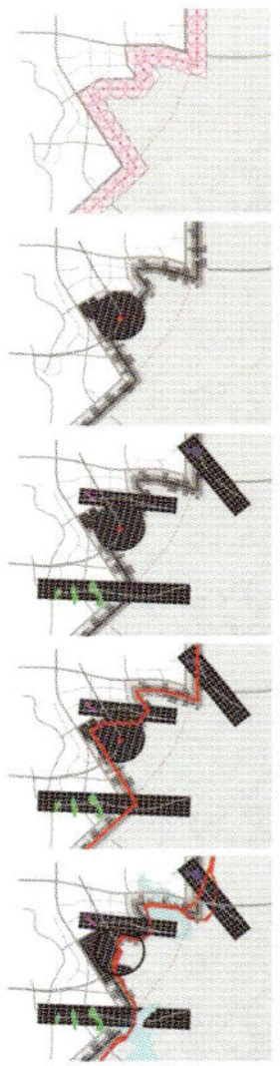

Step 1 Offset
Laying out the generic wall. A dense urban zone with the public transport as a backbone.

Step 2 Wall Business District
The wall will be connected with the existing metro, thus creating a focus point within this part of the wall.

Step 3 Piers
Like duck tape the wall will be stitched into its context, breaking the linearity of the wall. The piers embraces the landscape into the the site.

Step 4 Spine
Everything will be connected by a big spine trough the wall. This spine is the main public space and can have a mixed variety of functions.

Step 5 Reacting
The wall is shaped by the landscape and the city. Lower parts in the north and south carve out lakes. The highest part will cut a hole in the WBD, providing a central park. The spine will follow the topography.

On the site the wall reacts on existing elements in city and landscape.

WALL BECOMES SPECIFIC

The site of the competition is shaped by paddy fields and the Tianfu high tech park. The landscape structure consists of a hilly pattern with rice fields and small ribbon villages on the higher parts. The high tech park is build up with top global technology firms. Shape and program of the wall reacts on this. The high tech zone can be extended to our site. The site can coorcinate between government agencies, private companies and academic institutions to build up Chengdu's role in the high tech market. Furthermore by adding local communal program, like a market hall, opera, restaurants, wellness, and shared facilities for businesses like, small start-up support, education, a convention centre and exhibition hall the global and local will be connected. In that way institutionally controlled, developer-driven (top-down) and small business and local communal facilities, will merge in this part of the wall and makes it specific.

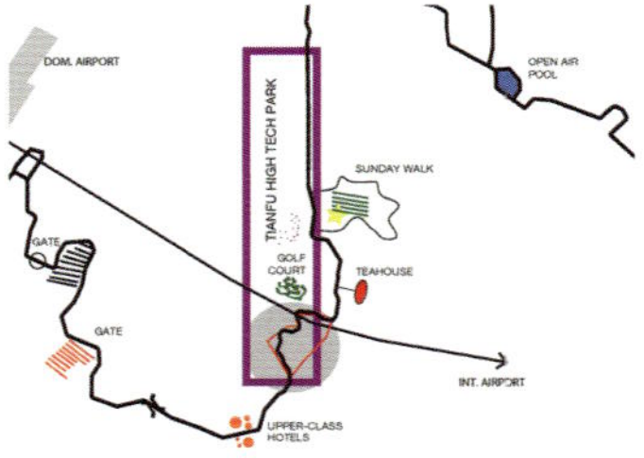

Merging the Wall with existing program.

172

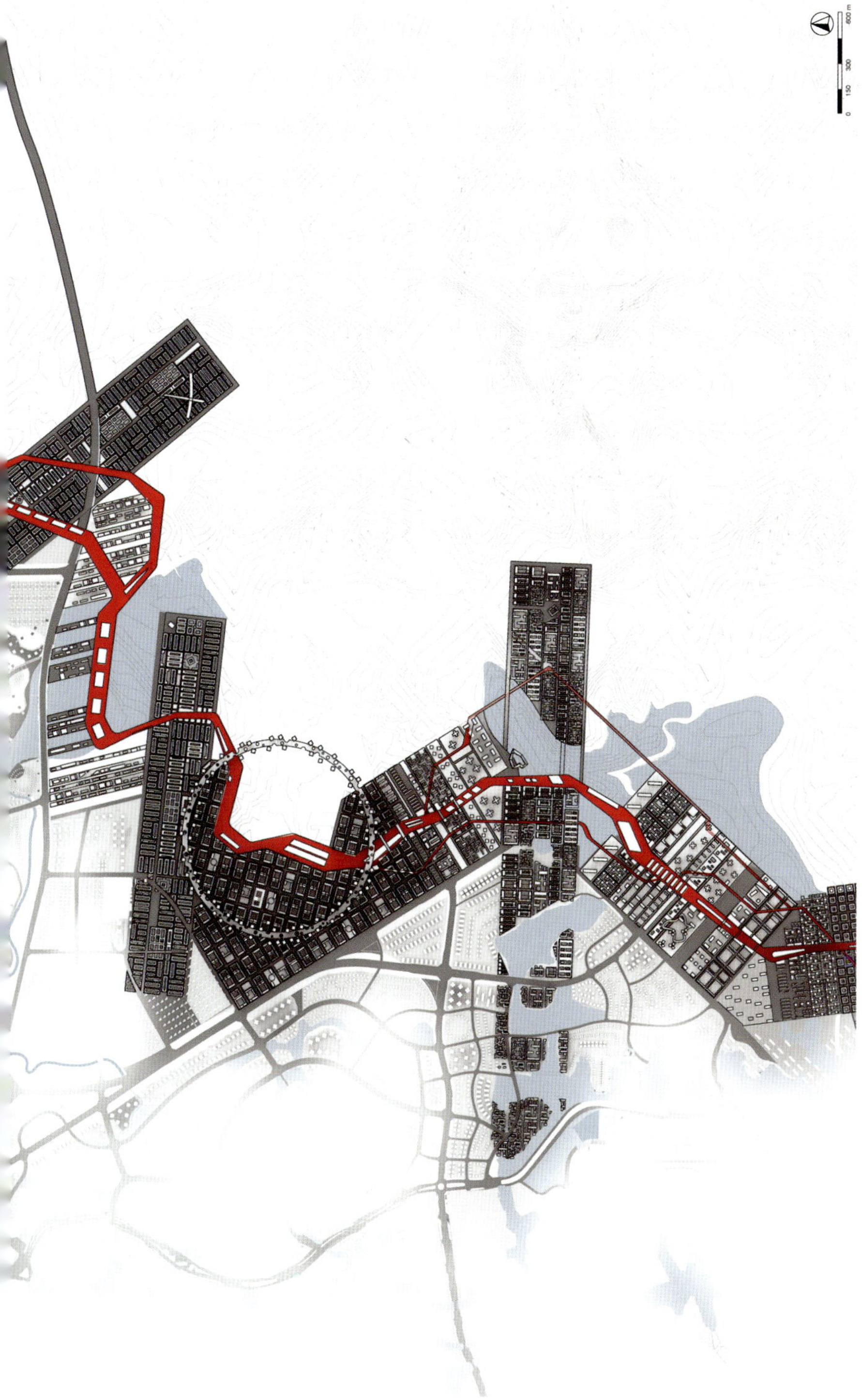
0
150
300
600 m

TU Delft
Team B

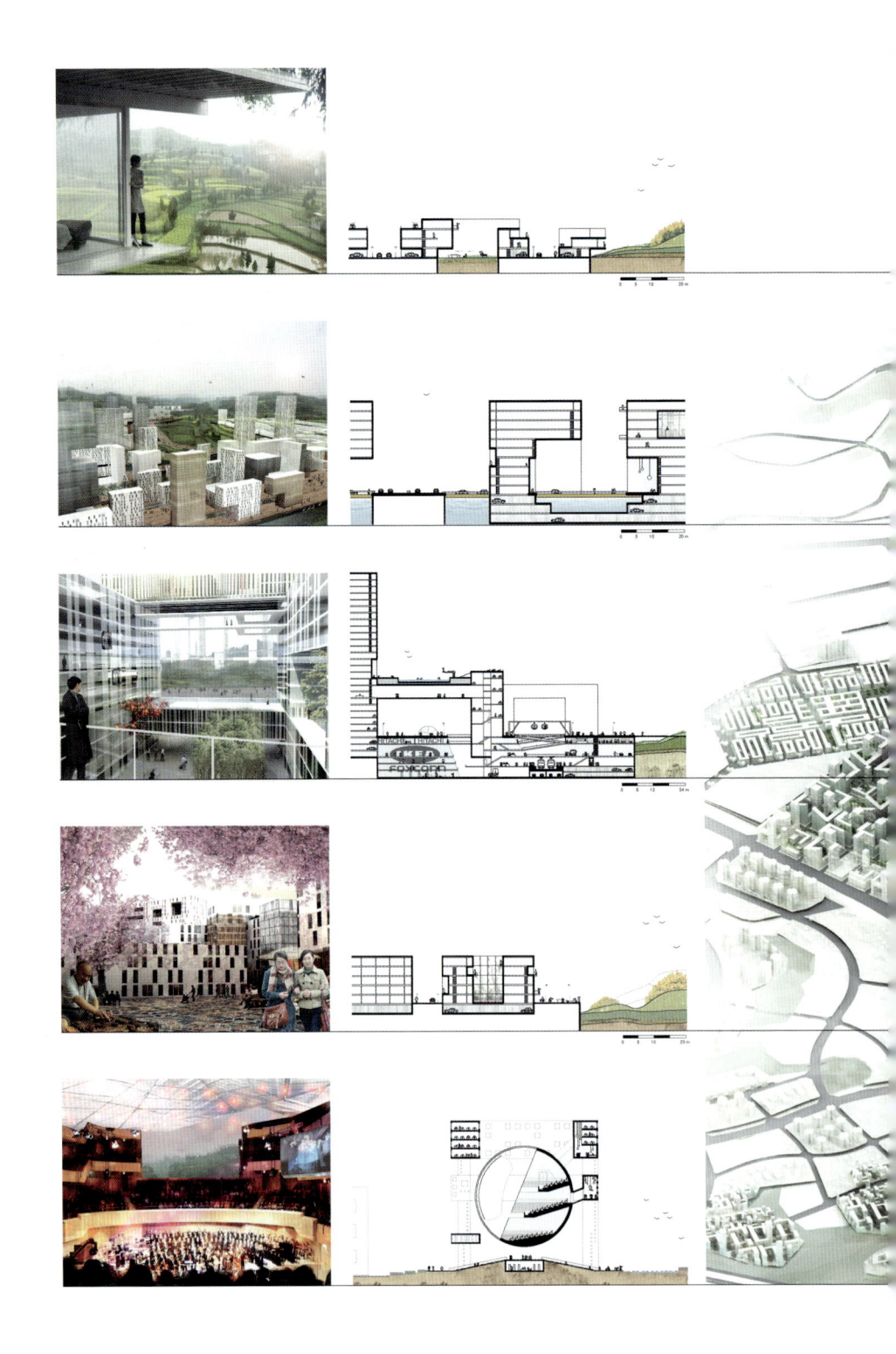

Panel
Detail 4

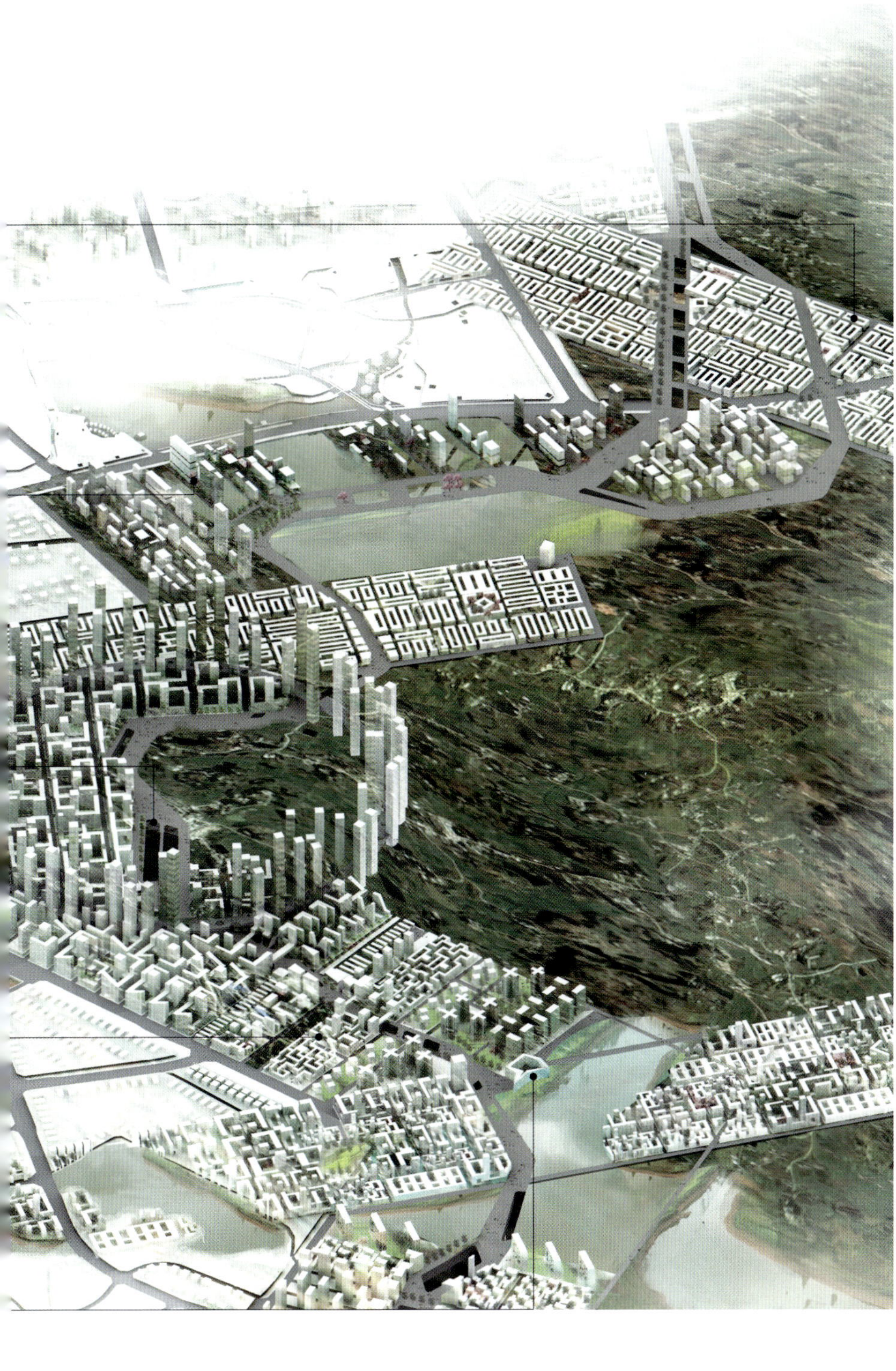

TU Delft
Team B

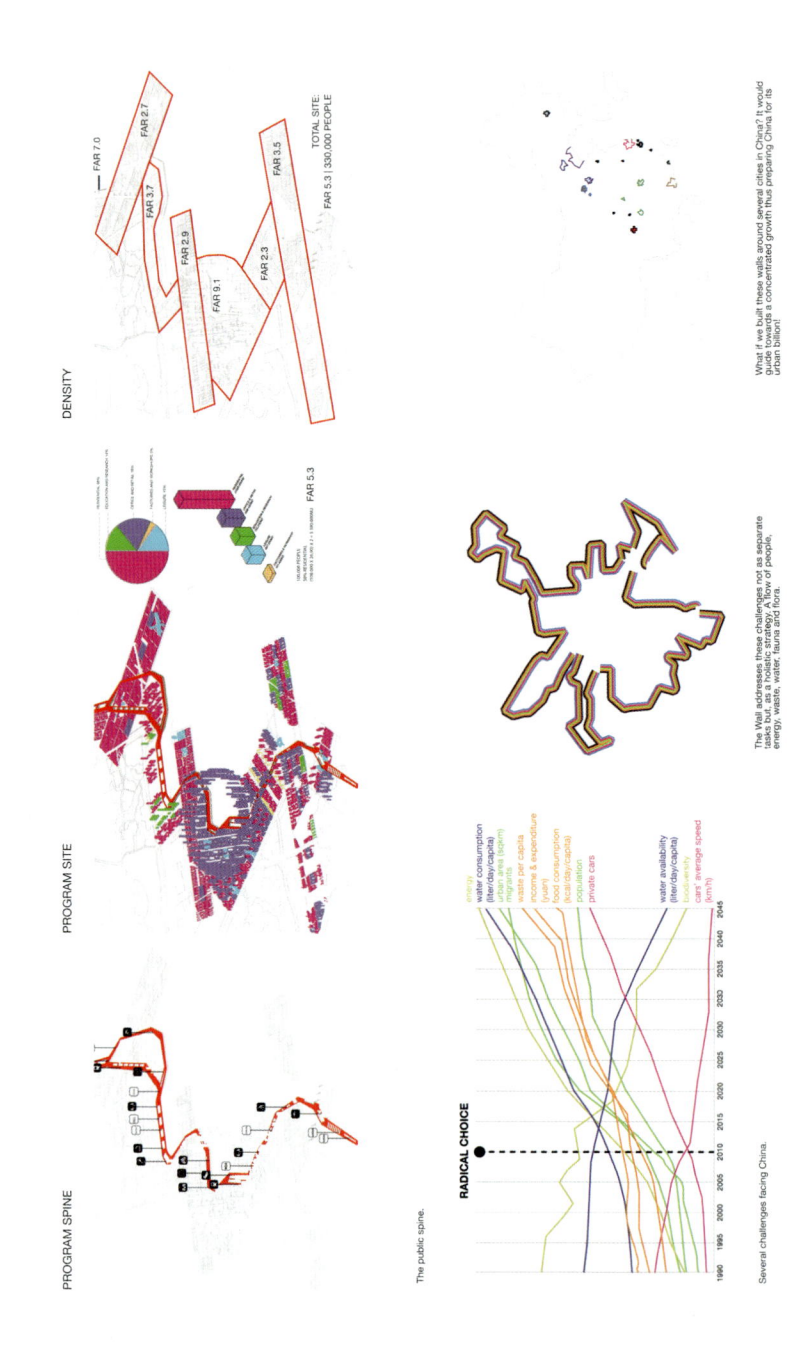

Panel
Detail 5

PROGRAM SPINE

PROGRAM SITE

DENSITY

FAR 7.0
FAR 3.7
FAR 2.7
FAR 2.9
FAR 9.1
FAR 2.3
FAR 3.5

TOTAL SITE:
FAR 5.3 | 330,000 PEOPLE

FAR 5.3

The public spine.

RADICAL CHOICE

energy
water consumption (liter/day/capita)
urban area (sqkm)
migrants
waste per capita
income & expenditure (yuan)
food consumption (kcal/day/capita)
population
private cars
water availability (liter/day/capita)
biodiversity
cars average speed (km/h)

1990 1995 2000 2005 2010 2015 2020 2025 2030 2035 2040 2045

Several challenges facing China.

What if we built these walls around several cities in China? It would guide towards a concentrated growth thus preparing China for its urban billion.

The Wall addresses these challenges not as separate tasks but, as a holistic strategy. A flow of people, energy, waste, water, fauna and flora.

176

Panel
Detail 6

Third Prize

Boundless City

University
Tongji University

Tutors
HUANG Yiru (Professor and Vice-Dean)
LI Linxue (Assoc Professor)
YAO Dong (Lecturer)

Team B
WANG Meng
LIAO Kai
YANG Xu
CHEN XingFeng
CHEN Jiao

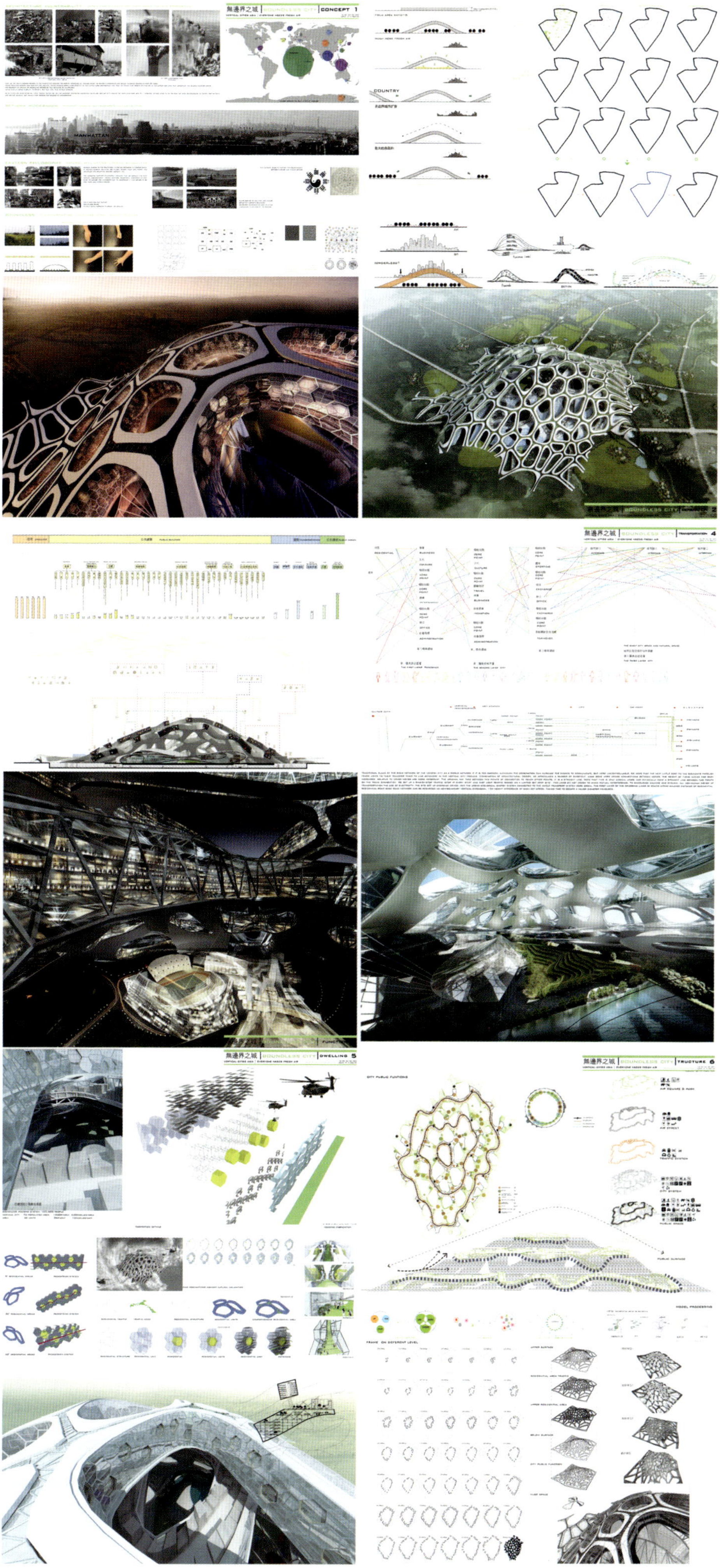

Tongji University
Team B

Panel
Detail 1

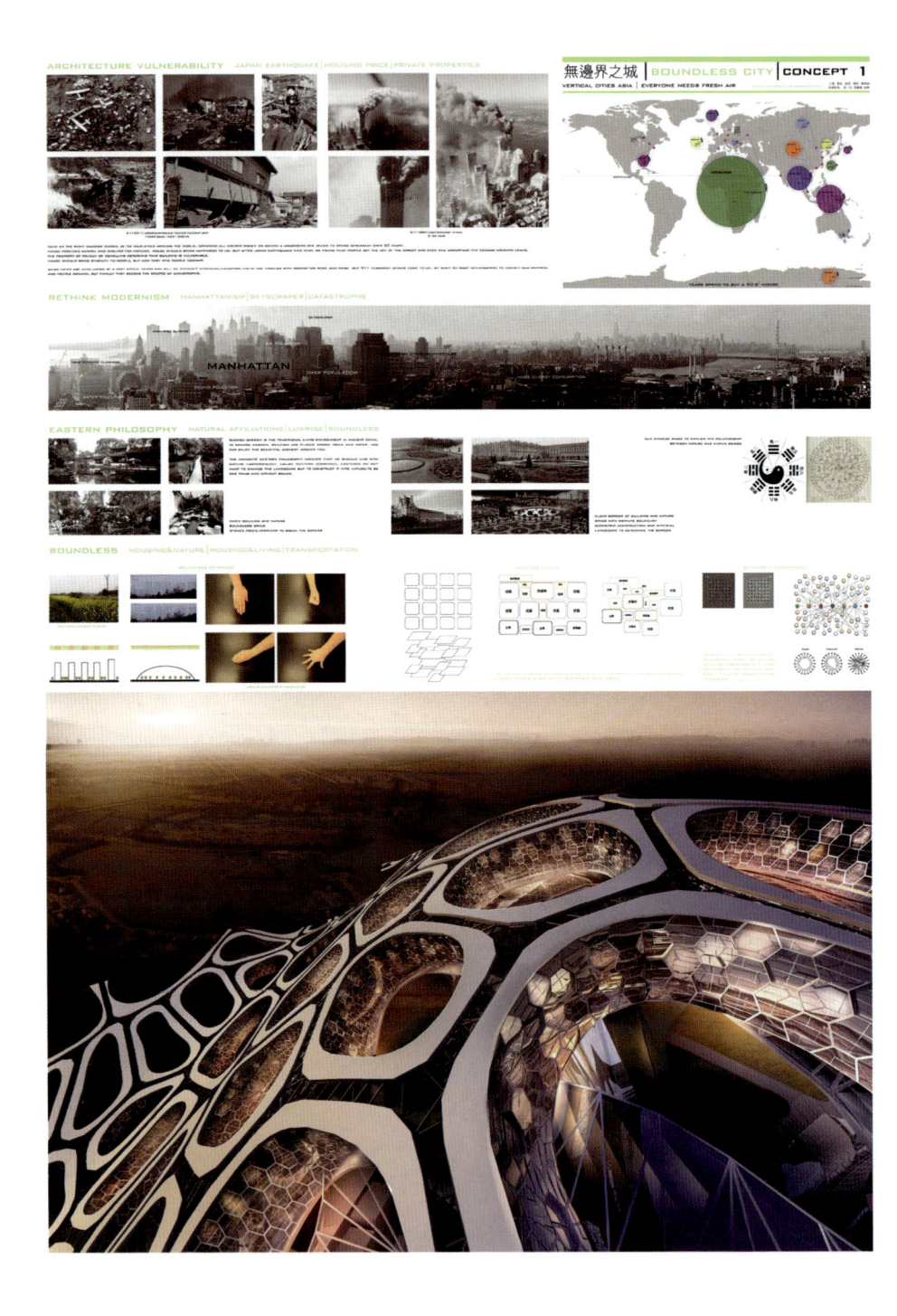

Panel
Detail 2

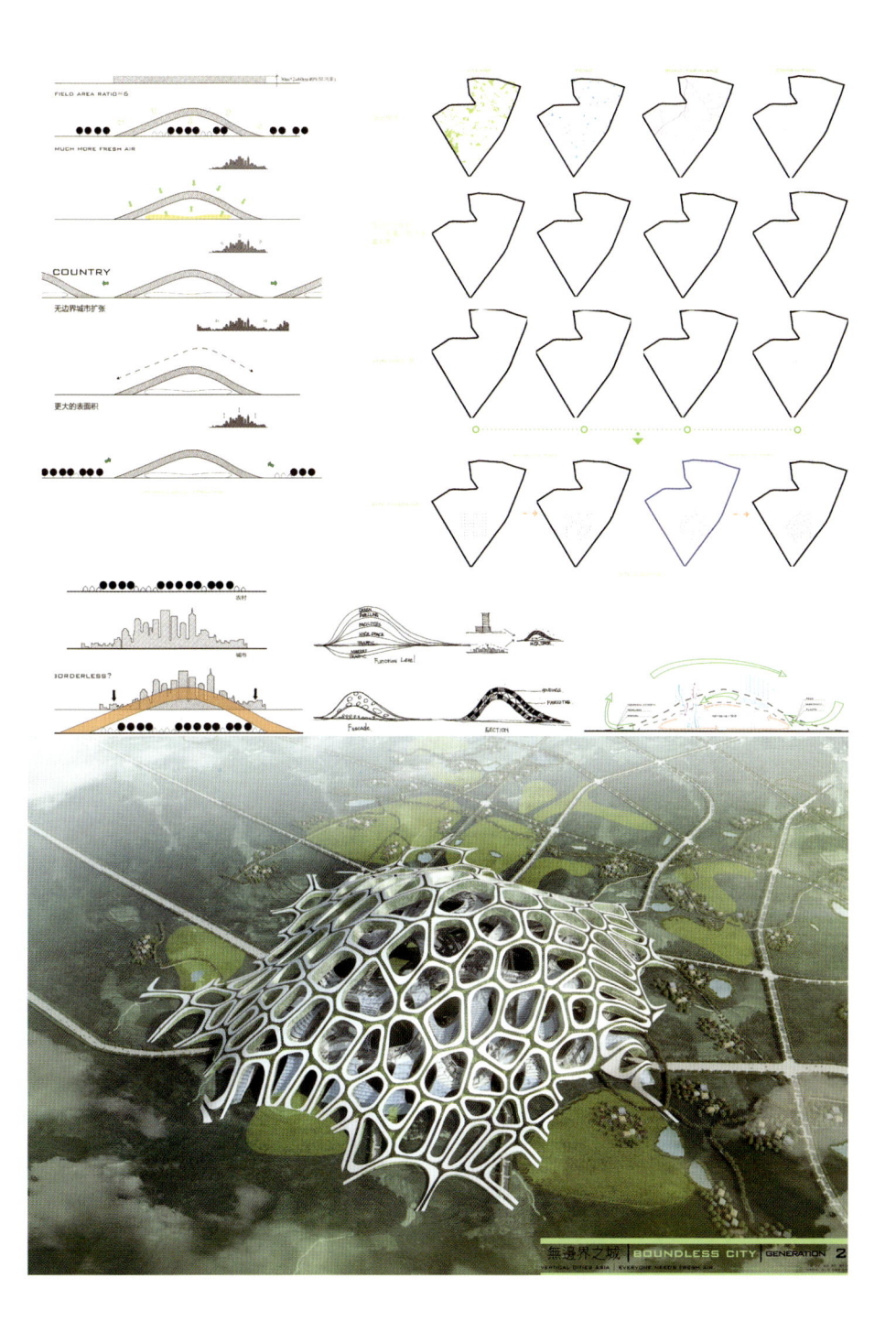

Tongji University
Team B

Panel
Detail 3

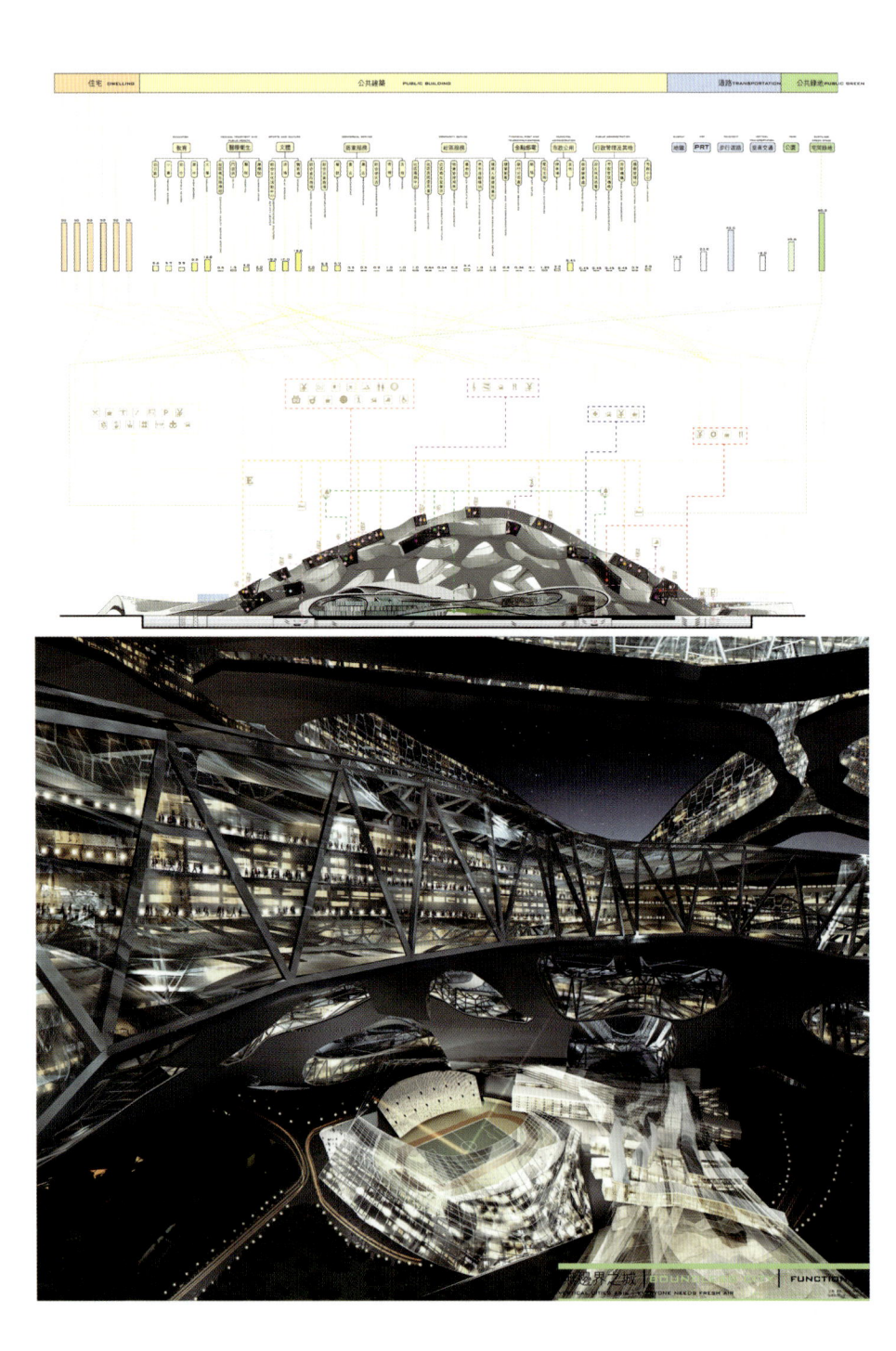

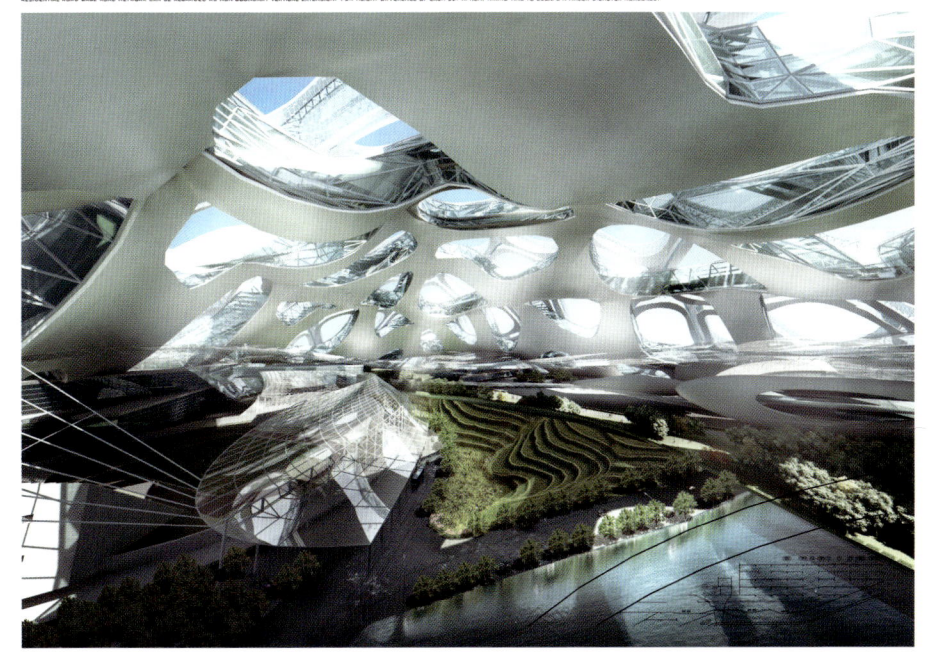

Panel
Detail 4

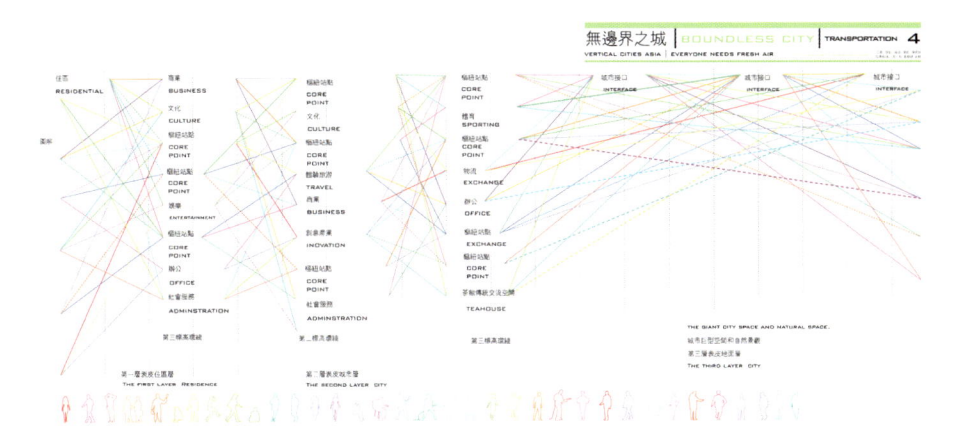

Tongji University
Team B

Panel
Detail 5

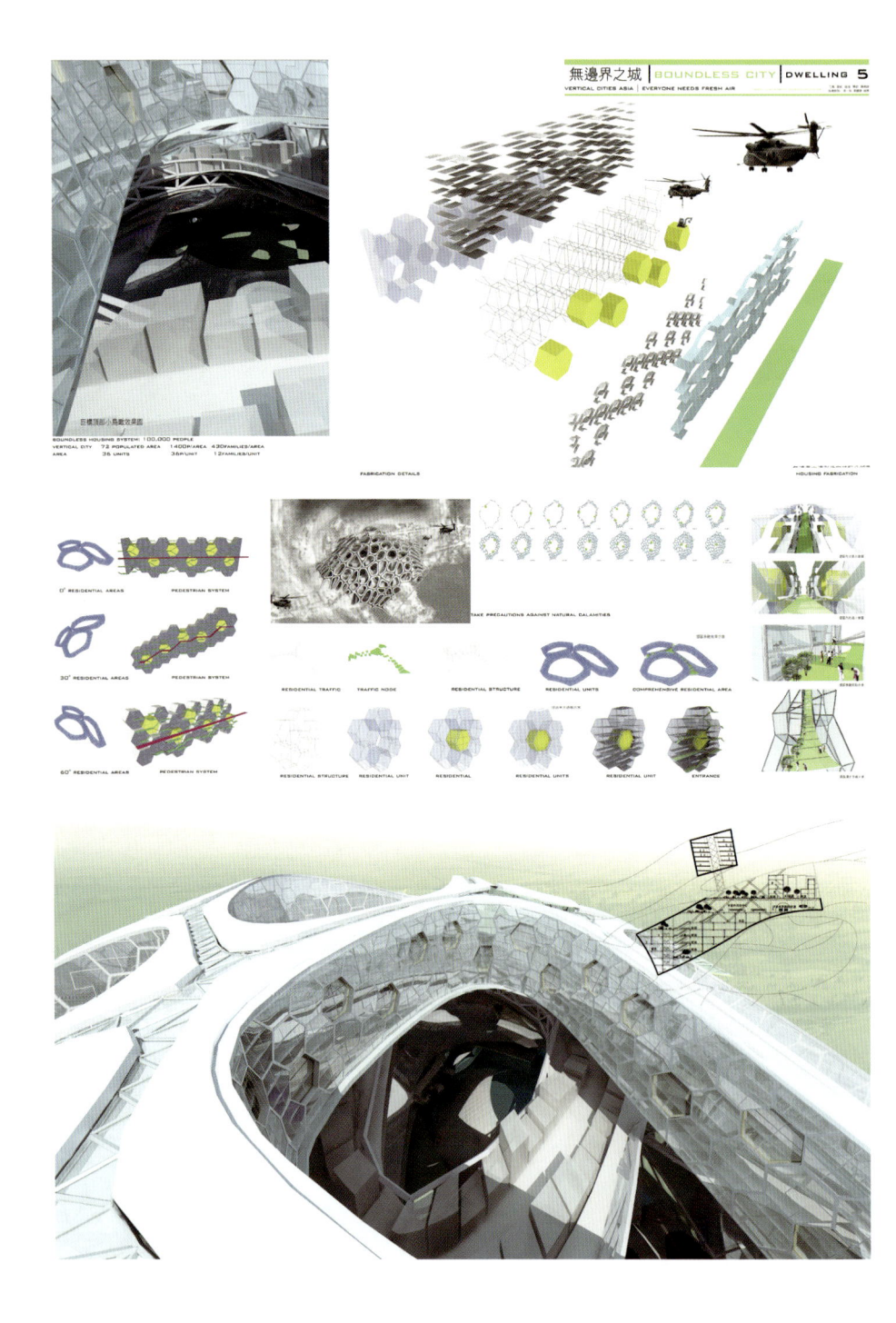

Panel Detail 6

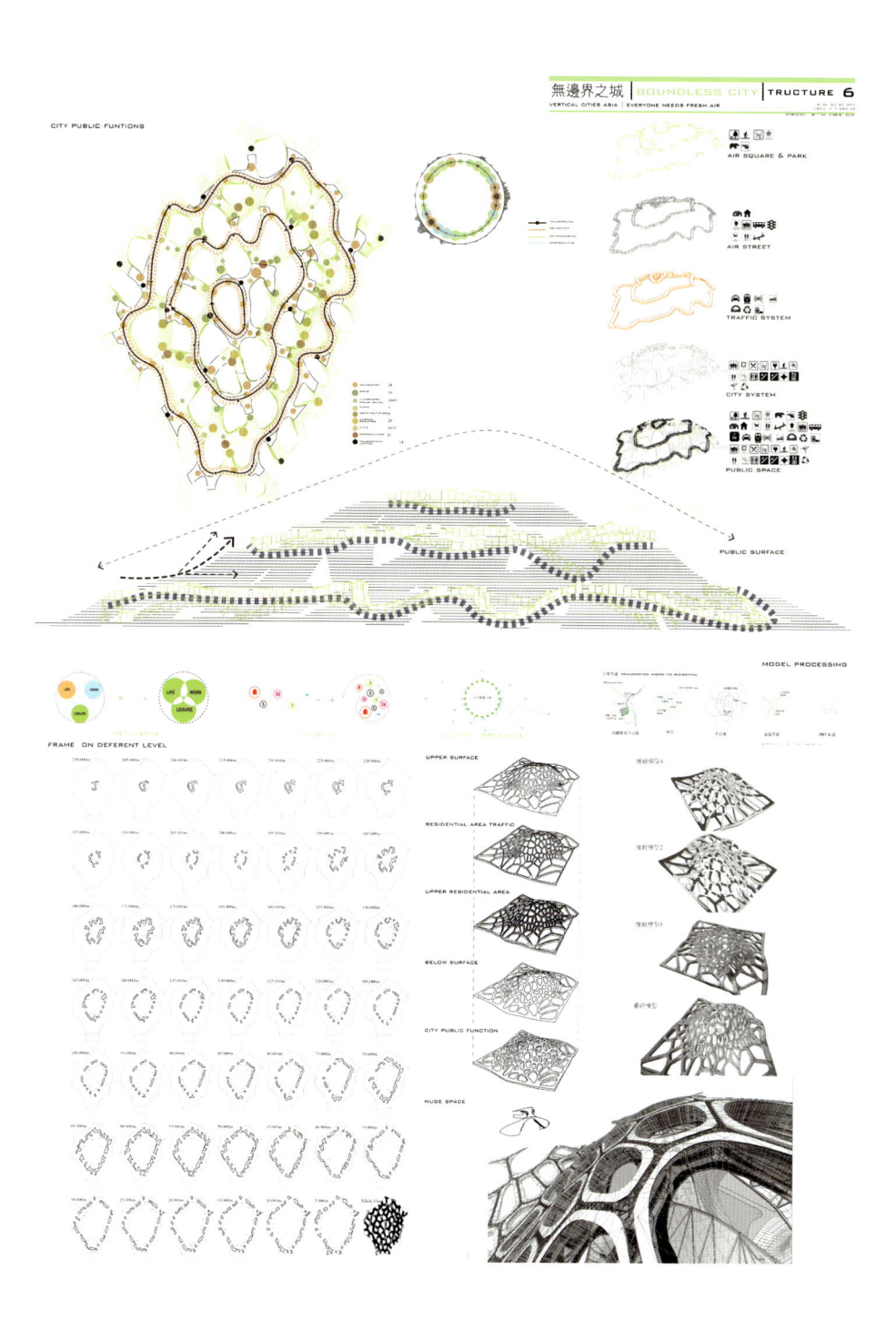

Honourable Mention

Village City

University
National University of Singapore

Tutors
NG Wai Keen (Assoc Professor)
LOW Boon Liang (Senior Lecturer)

Team A
Susanto SOENJOYO
XIA Wan Nao
Harvey LUKMAN

VILLAGE CITY
The coupling of village and city

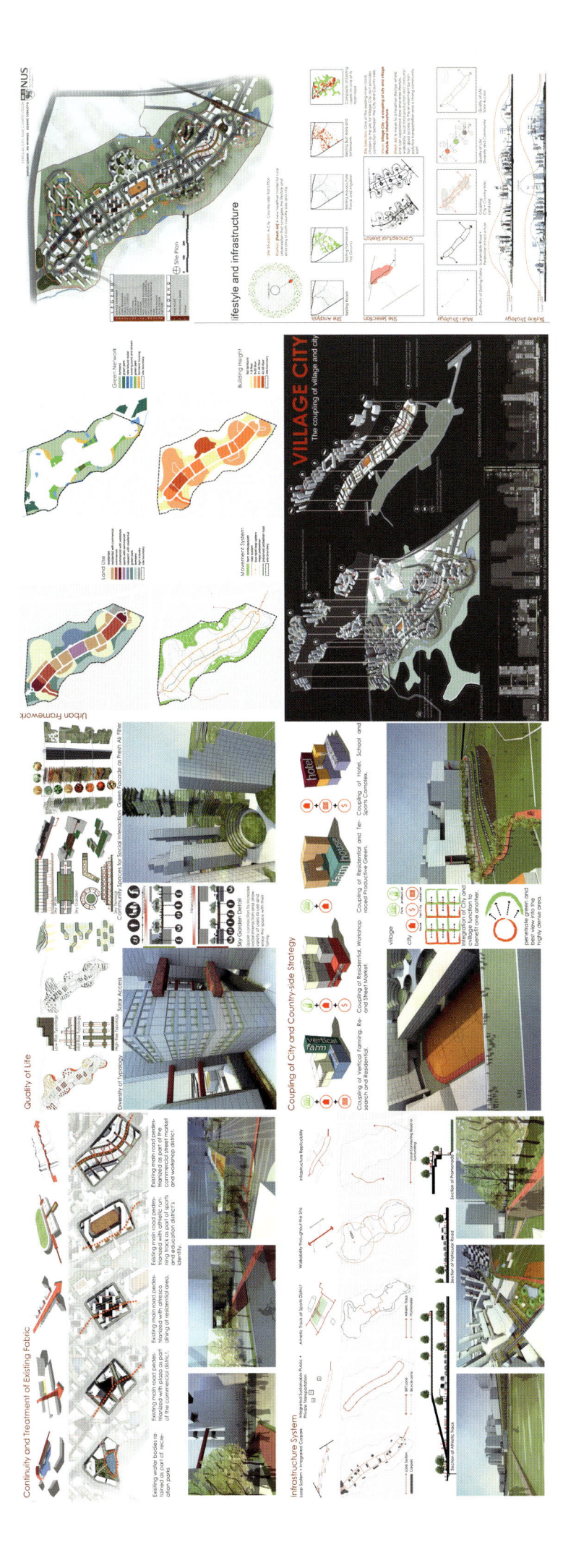

lifestyle and infrastructure

Site Plan

Site Analysis

Site Selection

Conceptual Sketch

Main Strategy

Skyline Strategy

Urban Framework

Green Network

Building Height

Land Use

Movement System

Quality of Life

Diversity of typology

Community Spaces for Social Interaction. Green Facade as Fresh Air Filter.

Sky Garden Detail

Solar Access

Coupling of City and Country-side Strategy

Coupling of Hotel, School and Sports Complex.

Coupling of Residential and Terraced Productive Green.

Coupling of Residential, Workshops and Street Market.

Coupling of Vertical Farming, Research and Residential.

Integration of City and village function to benefit one another.

Continuity and Treatment of Existing Fabric

Existing water bodies retained as part of recreation park.

Existing main road pedestrianized with plaza as part of the commercial district.

Existing main road pedestrianized with athletic running track as part of sports and education district's identity.

Existing main road pedestrianized with athletic running track as part of residential area.

Existing main road pedestrianized as part of the commercial street market and workshop district.

Infrastructure System

Local System + Singapore Corridor

Integrated Sustainable Public + Private Transportation

Walkability throughout the site

Athletic Track at Sports District

Infrastructure Replicability

Section of Promenade

Section of Connecting Road

Section of Vehicular Road

Section of Athletic Track

National University
of Singapore
Team A

Panel
Detail 1

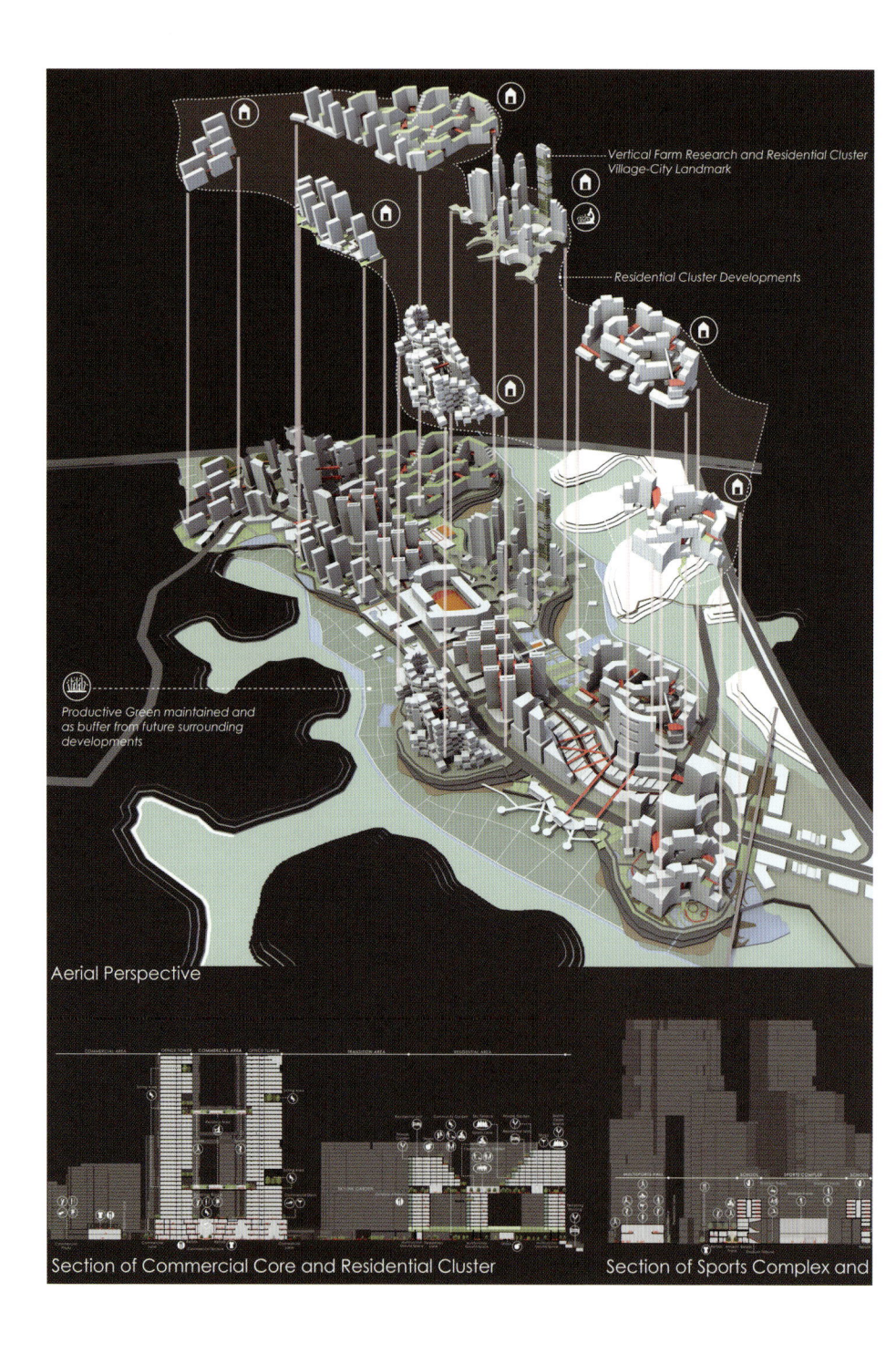

Vertical Farm Research and Residential Cluster
Village-City Landmark

Residential Cluster Developments

Productive Green maintained and
as buffer from future surrounding
developments

Aerial Perspective

Section of Commercial Core and Residential Cluster

Section of Sports Complex and

Panel Detail 2

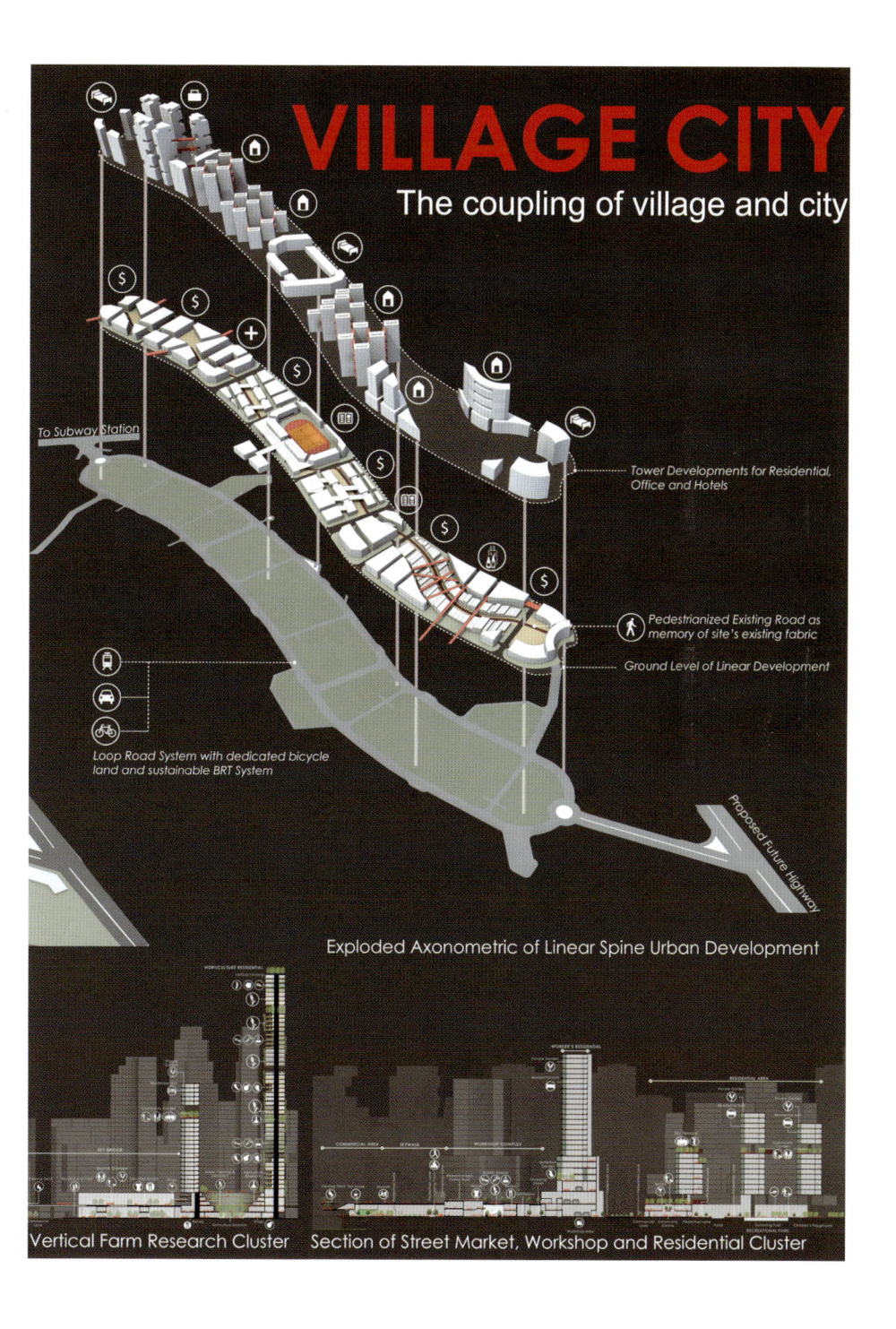

VILLAGE CITY
The coupling of village and city

- Tower Developments for Residential, Office and Hotels
- Pedestrianized Existing Road as memory of site's existing fabric
- Ground Level of Linear Development
- Loop Road System with dedicated bicycle land and sustainable BRT System
- To Subway Station
- Proposed Future Highway

Exploded Axonometric of Linear Spine Urban Development

Vertical Farm Research Cluster

Section of Street Market, Workshop and Residential Cluster

National University
of Singapore
Team A

Panel
Detail 3 & 4

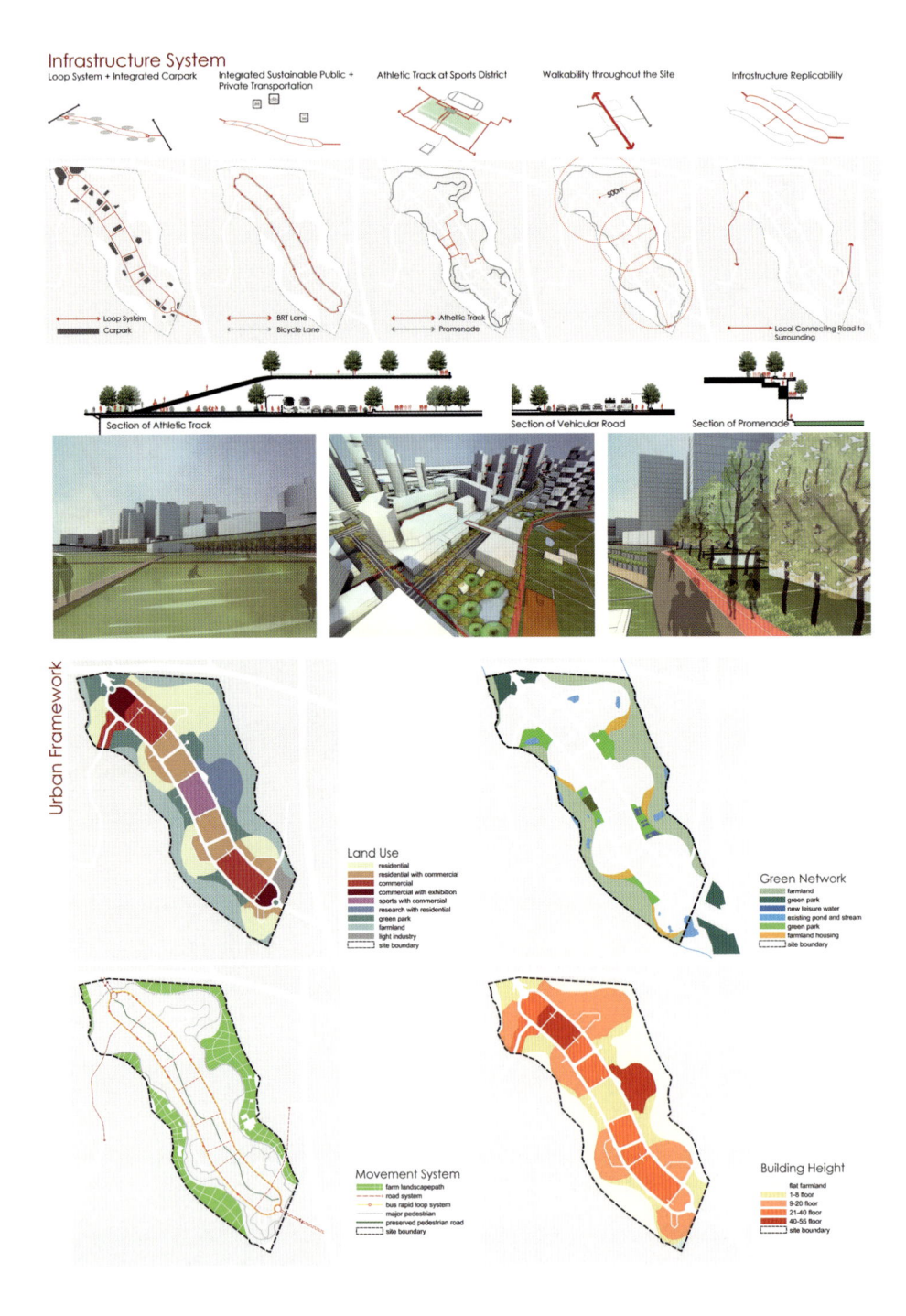

Infrastructure System

Loop System + Integrated Carpark | **Integrated Sustainable Public + Private Transportation** | **Athletic Track at Sports District** | **Walkability throughout the Site** | **Infrastructure Replicability**

- Loop System
- Carpark
- BRT Lane
- Bicycle Lane
- Athletic Track
- Promenade
- Local Connecting Road to Surrounding

Section of Athletic Track | Section of Vehicular Road | Section of Promenade

Urban Framework

Land Use
- residential
- residential with commercial
- commercial
- commercial with exhibition
- sports with commercial
- research with residential
- green park
- farmland
- light industry
- site boundary

Green Network
- farmland
- green park
- new leisure water
- existing pond and stream
- green park
- farmland housing
- site boundary

Movement System
- farm landscapepath
- road system
- bus rapid loop system
- major pedestrian
- preserved pedestrian road
- site boundary

Building Height
- flat farmland
- 1-8 floor
- 9-20 floor
- 21-40 floor
- 40-55 floor
- site boundary

VERTICAL CITY ASIA COMPETITION
HARVEY LUKMAN . XIA WANNUO . SUSANTO SOENJOYO

NUS National University of Singapore

LEGEND
A SERVICE APARTMENT
B OFFICE
C CORE RESIDENTIAL
D PUBLIC FACILITY
E SPORTS COMPLEX
F HOTEL
G EDUCATION
H STREET MARKET
I WORKSHOP
J EXHIBITION
K WEST CLUSTER RESIDENTIAL
L WEST CLUSTER COMMERCIAL
M EAST CLUSTER RESIDENTIAL
N HORTICULTURE RESIDENTIAL
O PARK
P SPORTS FACILITY
Q TRAIN STATION
R CAR PARK

LEGEND
1 FARM HOUSE
2 PRODUCTIVE GREEN
3 STREAM

Site Plan
0 100 200 400m

lifestyle and infrastructure

Site Situation: A City - Country-side Transititon

Position: **[Fresh Air]** A new healthier model for rural urbanization that synergizes the lifestyle and economy of both country-side and city.

Site Analysis

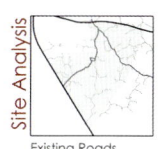

Existing Roads  | Existing Farmland on Flat Ground  | Existing Aquaculture Ponds and Irrigation 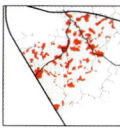 | Existing Built Area and Settlements 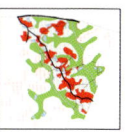 | Composite of Existing Layers on one of its main road

Site Selection

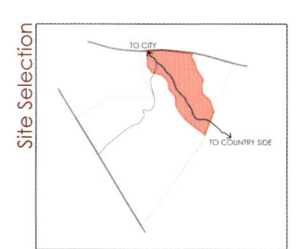

Site Selection: One of the existing main roads chosen as the site for Village City; as it provides connection between the City and Country-side.

Vision: **Village City - a coupling of city and village lifestyle and infrastructure.**

[Fresh Air] A mean to a healthier lifestyle where one can experience slow and relax lifestyle, walkability, local food production and consumption, good access to the environment by non-pollutive transportation and a strong community spirit.

Conceptual Sketch

Main Strategy

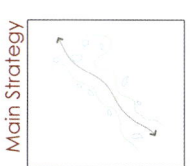

Continuity of Existing Fabric 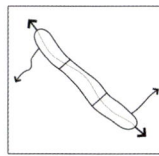 | Sustainable Road + Pedestrian Infrastructure 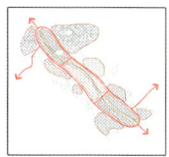 | Coupling: City + Country-side; Land Use 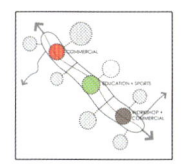 | Quality of Life: Diversity and Community 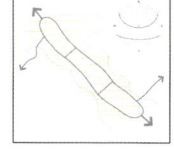 | Quality of Life: Solar Access

Skyline Strategy

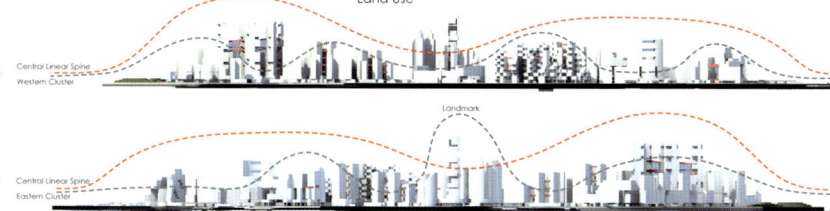

Central Linear Spine
Western Cluster

Landmark

Central Linear Spine
Eastern Cluster

Continuity and Treatment of Existing Fabric

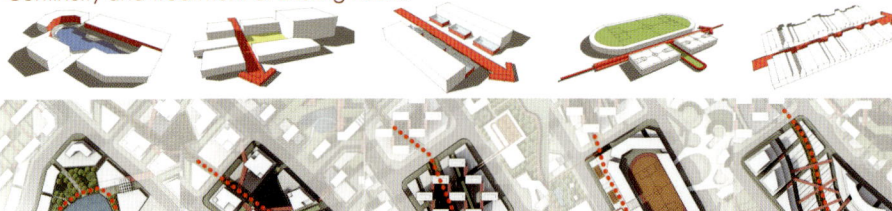

Existing water bodies retained as part of recreation parks

Existing main road pedestrianized with plaza as part of the commercial district.

Existing main road pedestrianized with alfresco dining at residential area.

Existing main road pedestrianized with athletic running track as part of sports and education district's identity.

Existing main road pedestrianized as part of the commercial street market and workshop district.

Coupling of City and Country-side Strategy

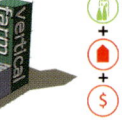

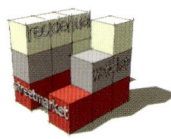

Coupling of Vertical Farming, Research and Residential.

Coupling of Residential, Workshop and Street Market.

Coupling of Residential and Terraced Productive Green.

Coupling of Hotel, School and Sports Complex.

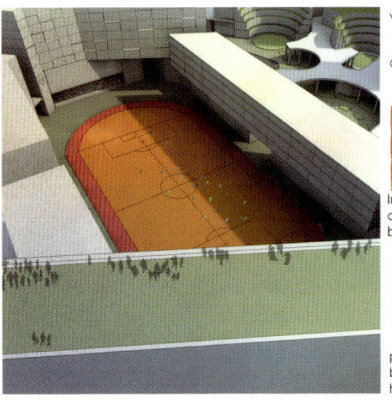

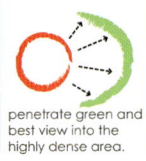

Integration of City and cvillage function to benefit one another.

penetrate green and best view into the highly dense area.

Quality of Life

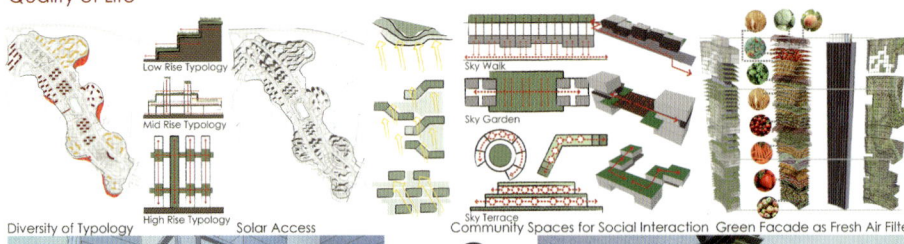

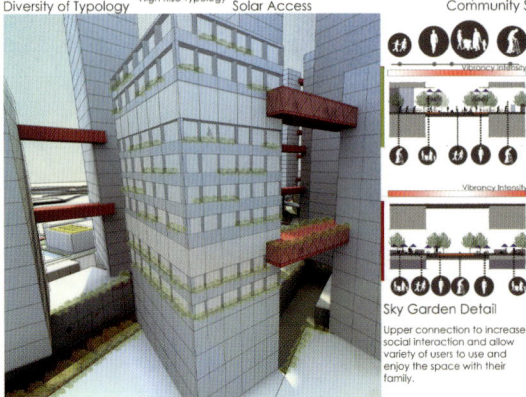

Diversity of Typology — Low Rise Typology, Mid Rise Typology, High Rise Typology

Solar Access

Community Spaces for Social Interaction

Green Facade as Fresh Air Filter

Sky Walk / Sky Garden / Sky Terrace

Sky Garden Detail
Upper connection to increase social interaction and allow variety of users to use and enjoy the space with their family.

National University
of Singapore
Team A

Panel
Detail 5

Compact Paragenetic Ecology

University
The Chinese University of Hong Kong

Tutors
HO Puay Peng (Professor and Dean)
Marisa YIU (Asst Professor)

Team A
LAM Yan-Yu Ian
LEUNG Yin-Ming, Ivan
TAM Yin-Shan Isabella
LI Kai-Min Kenneth
LEE Kung-Yau, Kung
WAN Ka-Wan, April

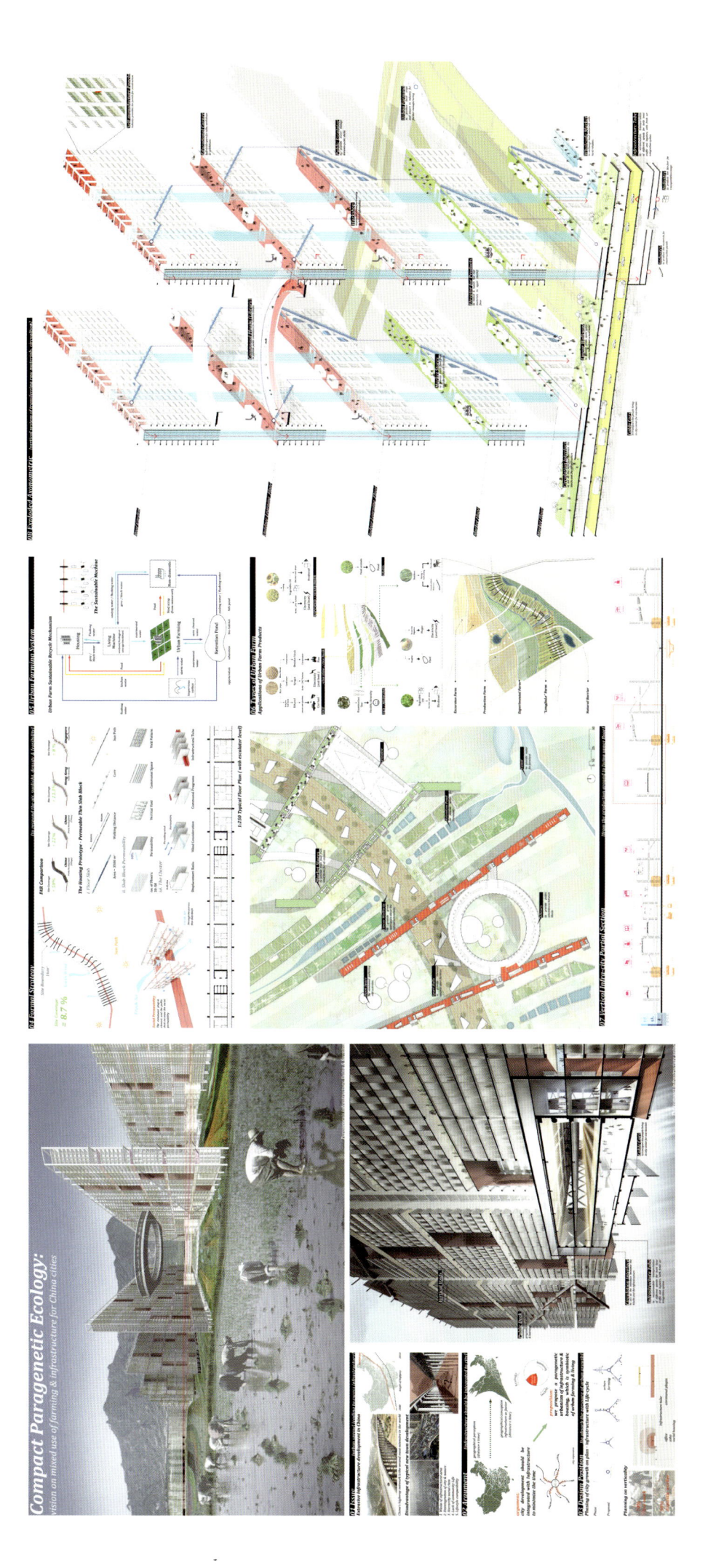

Compact Paragenetic Ecology:
vision on mixed use of farming & infrastructure for China cities

Agropolis

University
Delft University of Technology

Tutors
Karin LAGLAS (Professor and Dean)
Henco BEKKERING (Professor)

Team A
Joeri SLOTS
Xin DOGTEROM
Ronald ROELOFS
Drazen KRICKOVIC

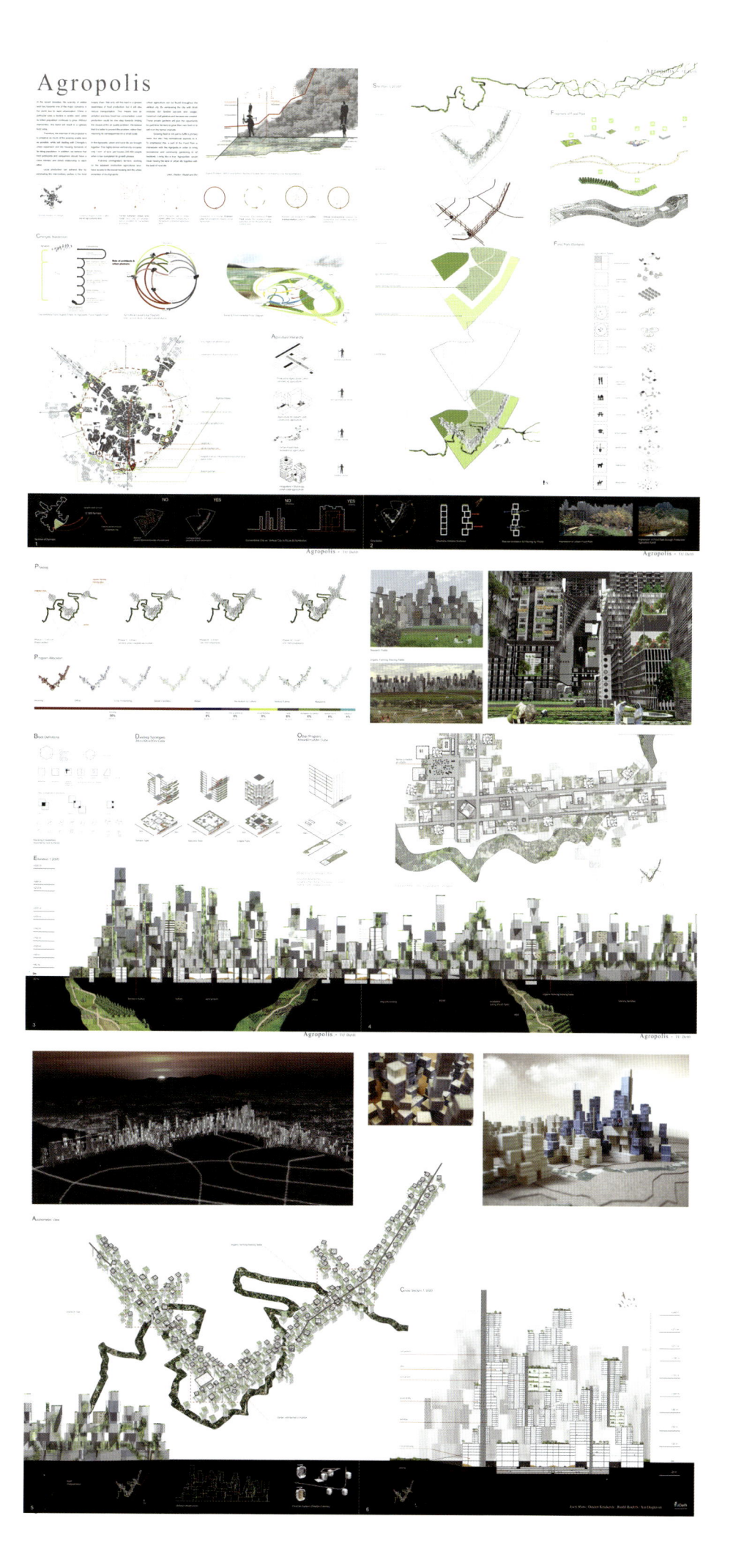

Agropolis

AgroCity

University
National University of Singapore

Tutors
NG Wai Keen (Assoc Professor)
LOW Boon Liang (Senior Lecturer)

Team B
Welly BUDIMAN
PING Lei
Vignesh KAUSHIK

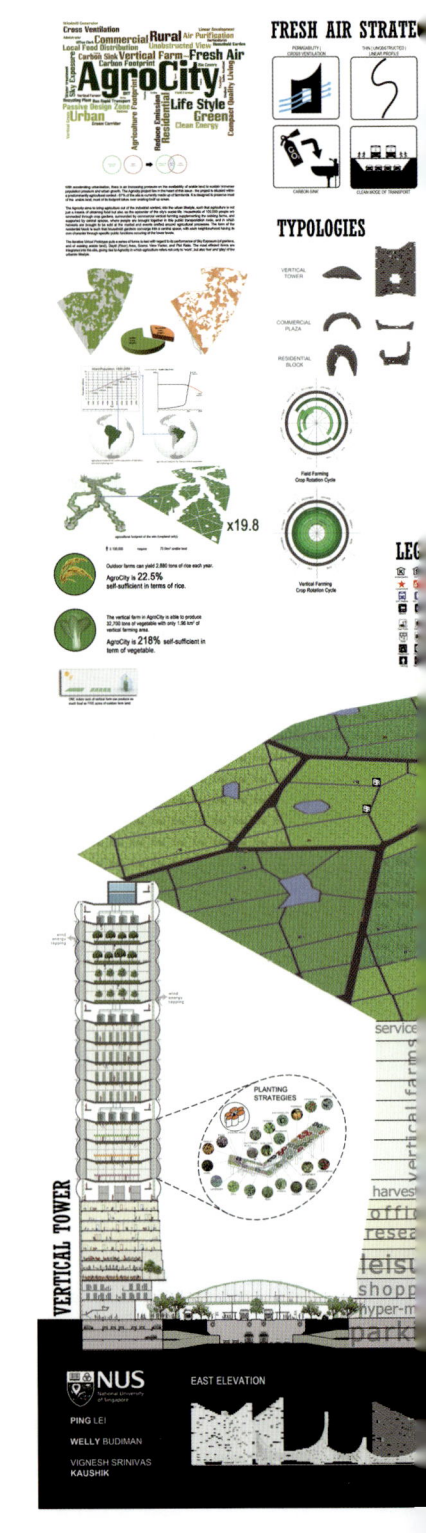

DEVELOPMENT

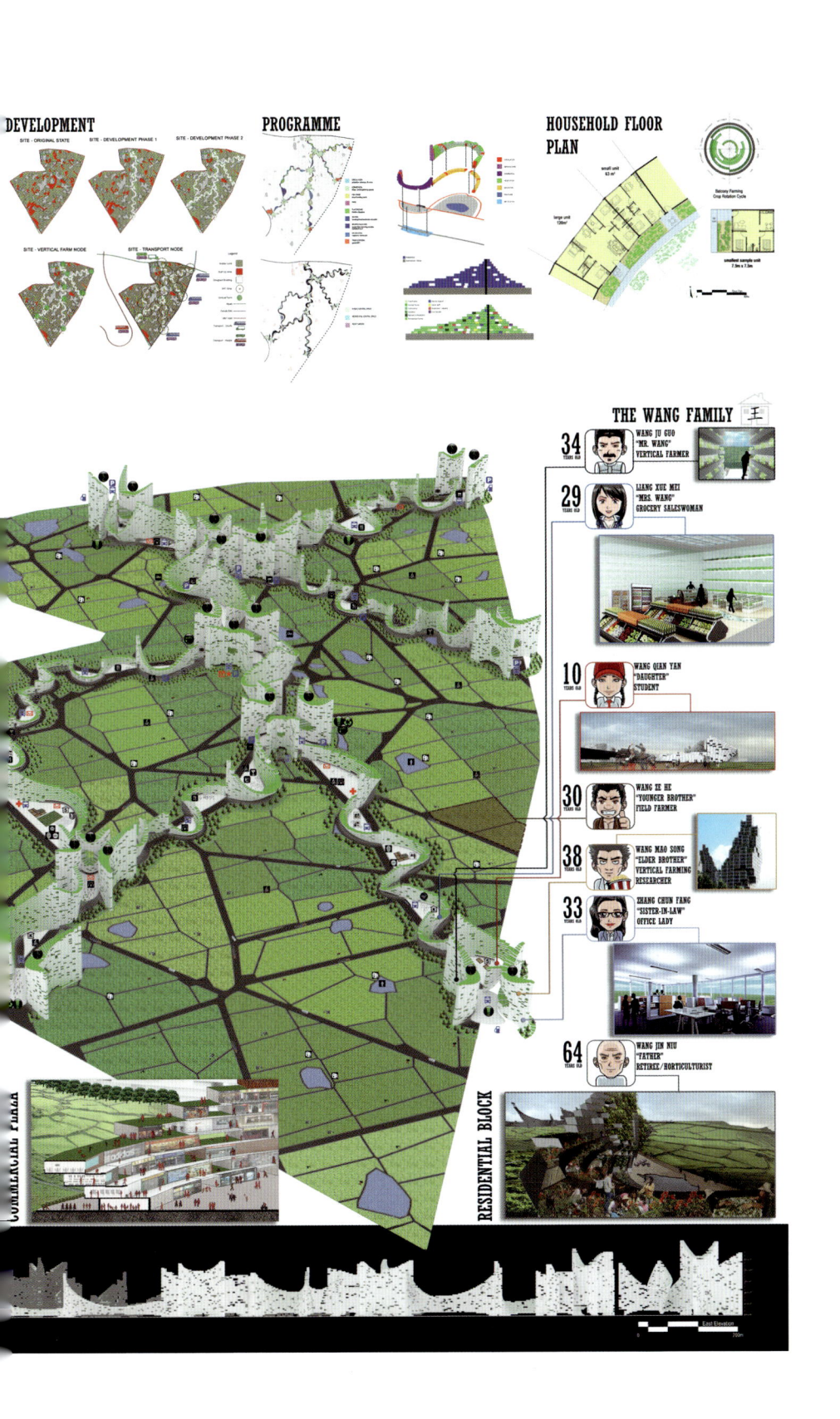

SITE - ORIGINAL STATE
SITE - DEVELOPMENT PHASE 1
SITE - DEVELOPMENT PHASE 2
SITE - VERTICAL FARM NODE
SITE - TRANSPORT NODE

PROGRAMME

HOUSEHOLD FLOOR PLAN

small unit 63 m²
large unit 126 m²
Balcony Farming Crop Rotation Cycle
smallest sample unit 7.3m x 7.3m

THE WANG FAMILY 王

34 YEARS OLD — WANG JU GUO "MR. WANG" VERTICAL FARMER

29 YEARS OLD — LIANG XUE MEI "MRS. WANG" GROCERY SALESWOMAN

10 YEARS OLD — WANG QIAN YAN "DAUGHTER" STUDENT

30 YEARS OLD — WANG ZE HE "YOUNGER BROTHER" FIELD FARMER

38 YEARS OLD — WANG MAO SONG "ELDER BROTHER" VERTICAL FARMING RESEARCHER

33 YEARS OLD — ZHANG CHUN FANG "SISTER-IN-LAW" OFFICE LADY

64 YEARS OLD — WANG JIN NIU "FATHER" RETIREE/HORTICULTURIST

RESIDENTIAL BLOCK

COMMERCIAL FLOOR

East Elevation

Osmosis

University
Swiss Federal Institute of Technology (ETH) Zurich

Tutors
Kees CHRISTIAANSE (Professor)
Alfredo BRILLEMBOURG (Professor)
Hubert KLUMPNER (Professor)
Nicolas KRETSCHMAN (Teaching Assistant)
Micheal CONTENTO (Teaching Assistant)

Team A
Daniel FUCHS
Sascha TOETLY
Adrian POLLINGER
Luis HILTI

OSMOSIS
THE SEED FOR FUTURE URBAN LIFE

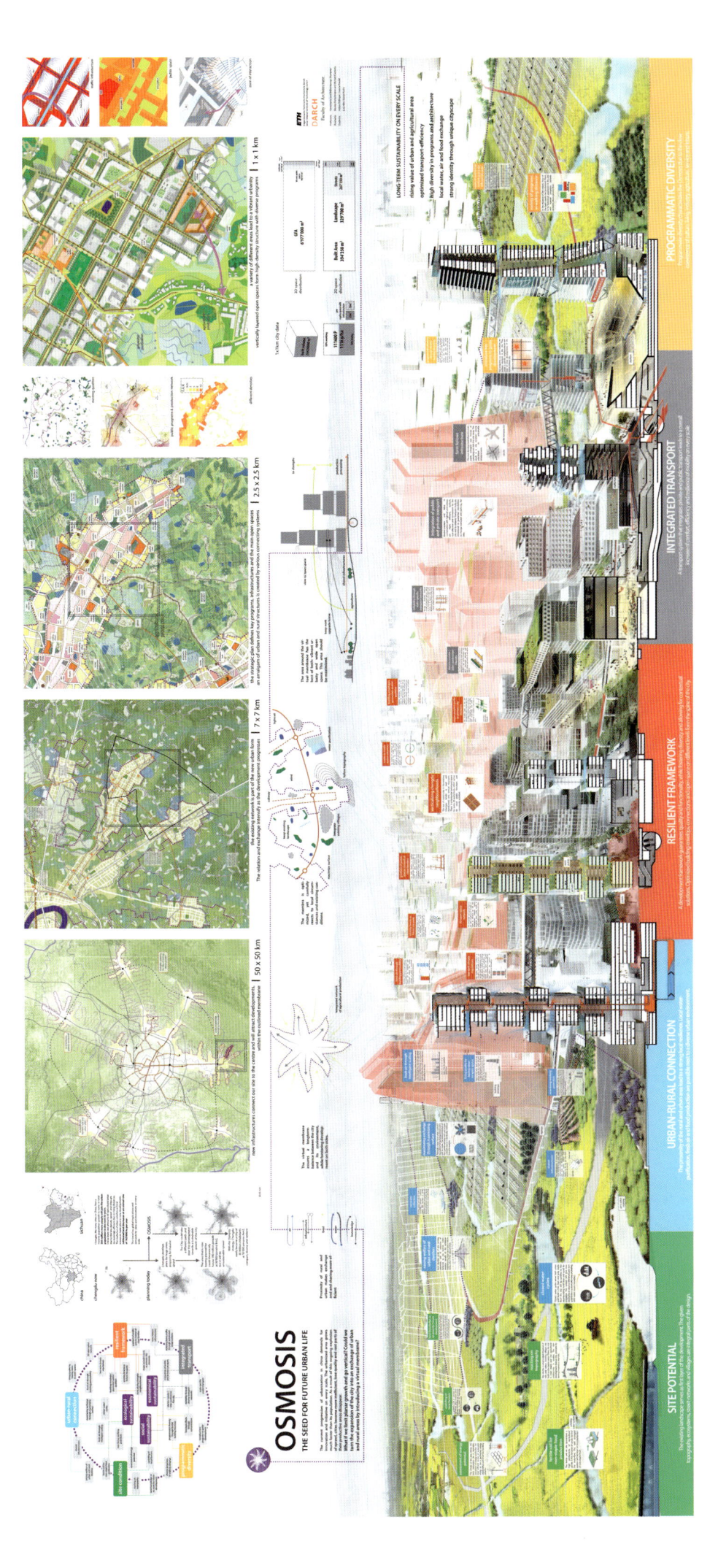

SITE POTENTIAL · URBAN-RURAL CONNECTION · RESILIENT FRAMEWORK · INTEGRATED TRANSPORT · PROGRAMMATIC DIVERSITY

LONG-TERM SUSTAINABILITY ON EVERY SCALE

Democratic City

University
Tongji University

Tutors
HUANG Yiru (Professor and Vice-Dean)
LI Linxue (Assoc Professor)
YAO Dong (Lecturer)

Team A
YAN Wenlong
LI Jie
FAN Yinghui
DING Fan
LIU Ying

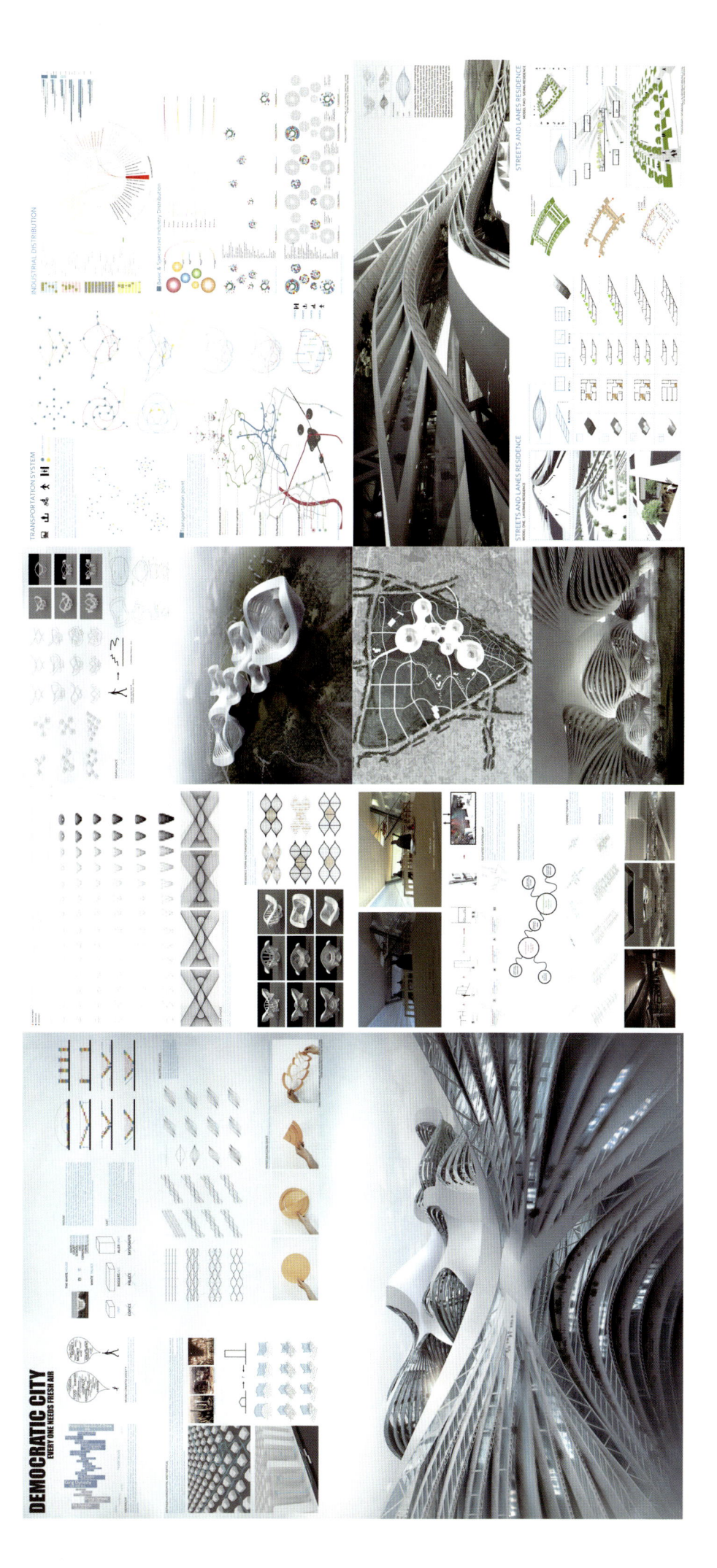

DEMOCRATIC CITY
EVERY ONE NEEDS FRESH AIR

VertiCO Urbanism

University
Tsinghua University

Tutors
WANG Hui (Professor)

Team A
WANG Shenhao
LU Chenchen
LIU Lun

VERTiCO-urbanism
A COOPERATION OF URBAN AND RURAL AREAS

CO-eco
CO-develope
CO-nstruct
CO-live
CO-nflict

URBAN-RURAL CONFLICT

STRATEGY

Bamboo Commune

University
Tsinghua University

Tutors
WANG Hui (Professor)

Team B
WAN Junzhe
LIU Haijing

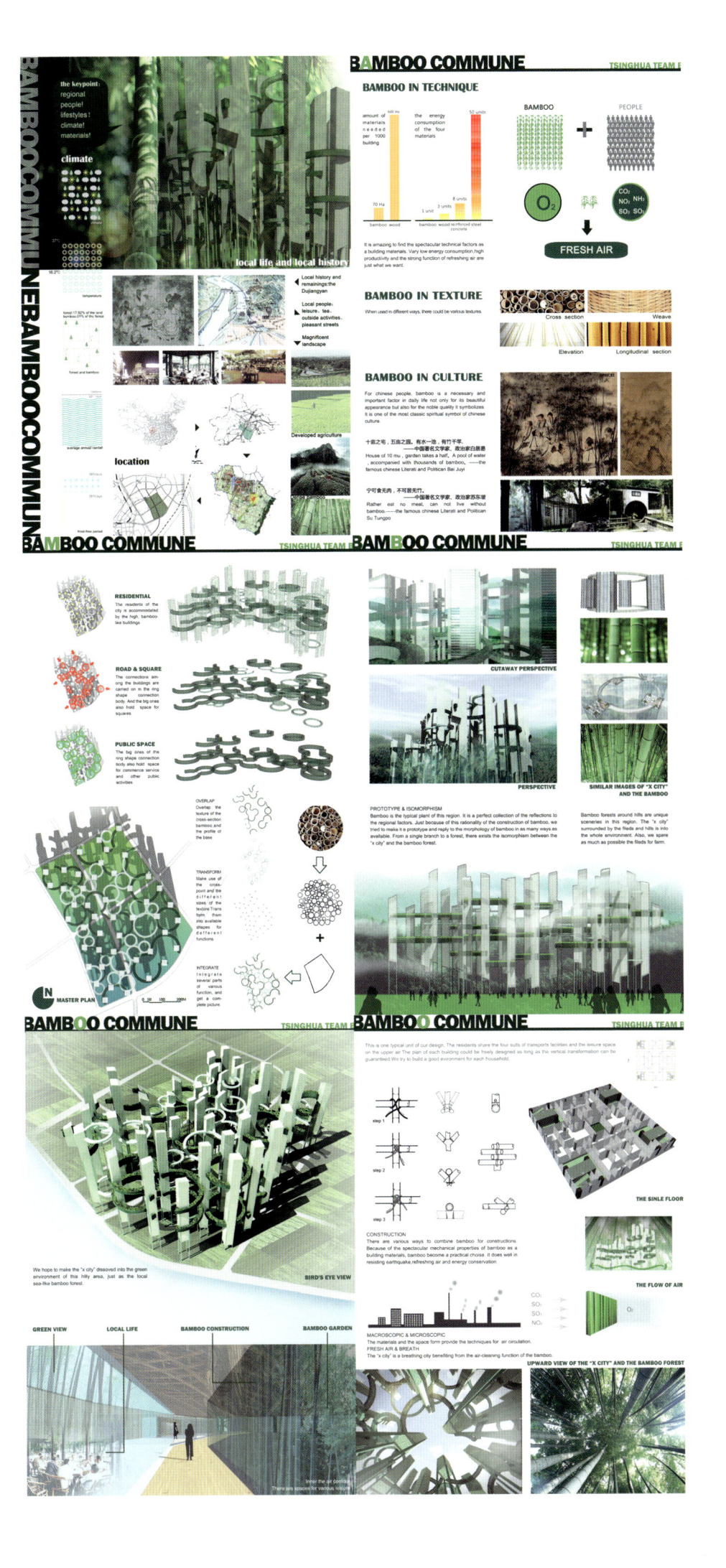

BAMBOO COMMUNE

TSINGHUA TEAM

BAMBOO IN TECHNIQUE

It is amazing to find the spectacular technical factors as a building materials. Vary low energy consumption, high productivity and the strong function of refreshing air are just what we want.

BAMBOO + PEOPLE → FRESH AIR

BAMBOO IN TEXTURE

When used in different ways, there could be various textures.

- Cross section
- Weave
- Elevation
- Longitudinal section

BAMBOO IN CULTURE

For chinese people, bamboo is a necessary and important factor in daily life not only for its beautiful appearance but also for the noble quality it symbolizes. It is one of the most classic spiritual symbol of chinese culture.

十亩之宅，五亩之园，有水一池，有竹千竿。
——中国著名文学家，政治家白居易
House of 10 mu, garden takes a half, A pool of water, accompanied with thousands of bamboo. ——the famous chinese Literati and Politican Bai Juyi

宁可食无肉，不可居无竹。
——中国著名文学家，政治家苏东坡
Rather eat no meat, can not live without bamboo. ——the famous chinese Literati and Politican Su Tungpo

---

the keypoint: regional people! lifestyles! climate! materials!

climate

local life and local history

- Local history and remainings: the Dujiangyan
- Local people: leisure, tea, outside activities, pleasant streets
- Magnificent landscape
- Developed agriculture

location

RESIDENTIAL
The residents of the city is accommodated by the high, bamboo-like buildings.

ROAD & SQUARE
The connections among the buildings are carried on in the ring shape connection body. And the big ones also hold space for squares.

PUBLIC SPACE
The big ones of the ring shape connection body also hold space for commerce service and other public activities.

OVERLAP Overlaps the texture of the cross-section bamboo and the profile of the base.

TRANSFORM Make use of the crosspoint and the different sizes of the texture. Transform them into available shapes for different functions.

INTEGRATE Integrate several parts of various function, and get a complete picture.

MASTER PLAN

PROTOTYPE & ISOMORPHISM
Bamboo is the typical plant of this region. It is a perfect collection of the reflections to the regional factors. Just because of this rationality of the construction of bamboo, we tried to make it a prototype and reply to the morphology of bamboo in as many ways as available. From a single branch to a forest, there exists the isomorphism between the "x city" and the bamboo forest.

CUTAWAY PERSPECTIVE
PERSPECTIVE
SIMILAR IMAGES OF "X CITY" AND THE BAMBOO

Bamboo forests around hills are unique sceneries in this region. The "x city" is surrounded by the fileds and hills is into the whole environment. Also, we spare as much as possible the fileds for farm.

This is one typical unit of our design. The residents share the four suits of transports facilities and the leisure space on the upper air. The plan of each building could be freely designed as long as the vertical transformation can be guaranteed. We try to build a good environment for each household.

step 1
step 2
step 3

CONSTRUCTION
There are various ways to combine bamboo for constructions. Because of the spectacular mechanical properties of bamboo as a building materials, bamboo become a practical choice. It does well in resisting earthquake, refreshing air and energy conservation.

MACROSCOPIC & MICROSCOPIC
The materials and the space form provide the techniques for air circulation.
FRESH AIR & BREATH
The "x city" is a breathing city benefiting from the air-cleaning function of the bamboo.

BIRD'S EYE VIEW
THE SINGLE FLOOR
THE FLOW OF AIR

We hope to make the "x city" dissoved into the green environment of this hilly area, just as the local sea-like bamboo forest.

GREEN VIEW | LOCAL LIFE | BAMBOO CONSTRUCTION | BAMBOO GARDEN

UPWARD VIEW OF THE "X CITY" AND THE BAMBOO FOREST

MODO City

University
University of California (UC) Berkeley

Tutors
Jennifer WOLCH (Professor and Dean)
Mark ANDERSON (Assoc Professor)
Peter ANDERSON (Assoc Professor)

Team A
MOU Yujiang
Michael BERGIN
Alex FENTON

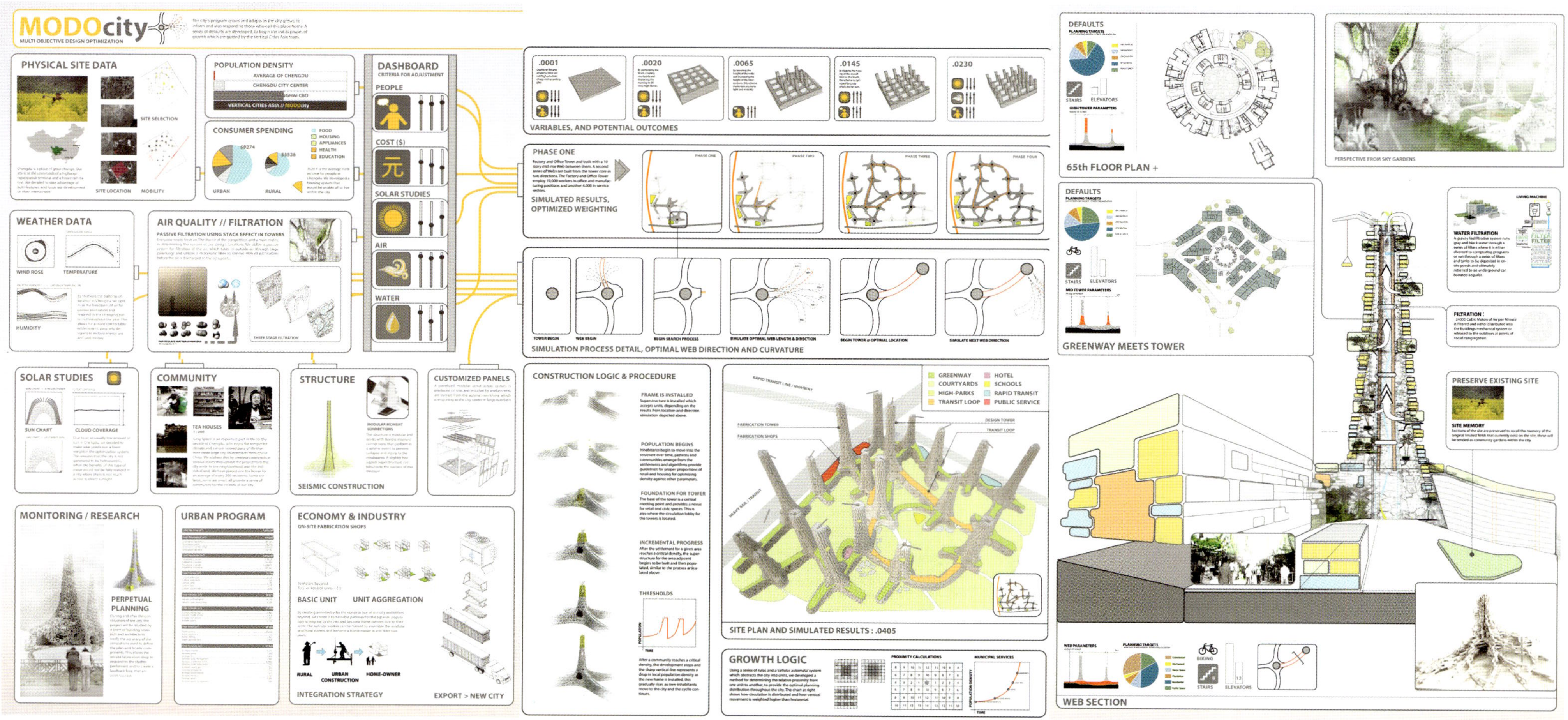
MODOcity
MULTI OBJECTIVE DESIGN OPTIMIZATION
PHYSICAL SITE DATA
SITE SELECTION
SITE LOCATION
MOBILITY
POPULATION DENSITY
AVERAGE OF CHENGDU
CHENGDU CITY CENTER
VERTICAL CITIES ASIA // MODOcity
CONSUMER SPENDING
FOOD
HOUSING
APPLIANCES
HEALTH
EDUCATION
$9274
$3528
URBAN
RURAL
DASHBOARD
CRITERIA FOR ADJUSTMENT
PEOPLE
COST ($)
SOLAR STUDIES
AIR
WATER
WEATHER DATA
WIND ROSE
TEMPERATURE
HUMIDITY
AIR QUALITY // FILTRATION
PASSIVE FILTRATION USING STACK EFFECT IN TOWERS
THREE STAGE FILTRATION
SOLAR STUDIES
SUN CHART
CLOUD COVERAGE
COMMUNITY
TEA HOUSES
STRUCTURE
MODULAR MOMENT CONNECTIONS
SEISMIC CONSTRUCTION
CUSTOMIZED PANELS
MONITORING / RESEARCH
PERPETUAL PLANNING
URBAN PROGRAM
ECONOMY & INDUSTRY
ON-SITE FABRICATION SHOPS
BASIC UNIT
UNIT AGGREGATION
RURAL
URBAN CONSTRUCTION
HOME-OWNER
INTEGRATION STRATEGY
EXPORT > NEW CITY
.0001
.0020
.0065
.0145
.0230
VARIABLES, AND POTENTIAL OUTCOMES
PHASE ONE
SIMULATED RESULTS, OPTIMIZED WEIGHTING
PHASE ONE
PHASE TWO
PHASE THREE
PHASE FOUR
TOWER BEGIN
WEB BEGIN
BEGIN SEARCH PROCESS
SIMULATE OPTIMAL WEB LENGTH & DIRECTION
BEGIN TOWER @ OPTIMAL LOCATION
SIMULATE NEXT WEB DIRECTION
SIMULATION PROCESS DETAIL, OPTIMAL WEB DIRECTION AND CURVATURE
CONSTRUCTION LOGIC & PROCEDURE
FRAME IS INSTALLED
POPULATION BEGINS
FOUNDATION FOR TOWER
INCREMENTAL PROGRESS
THRESHOLDS
POPULATION
TIME
GREENWAY
COURTYARDS
HIGH-PARKS
TRANSIT LOOP
HOTEL
SCHOOLS
RAPID TRANSIT
PUBLIC SERVICE
RAPID TRANSIT LINE / HIGHWAY
FABRICATION TOWER
FABRICATION SHOPS
DESIGN TOWER
TRANSIT LOOP
HEAVY RAIL / TRANSIT
SITE PLAN AND SIMULATED RESULTS : .0405
GROWTH LOGIC
PROXIMITY CALCULATIONS
MUNICIPAL SERVICES
POPULATION DENSITY
TIME
DEFAULTS
PLANNING TARGETS
STAIRS
ELEVATORS
HIGH TOWER PARAMETERS
65th FLOOR PLAN +
PERSPECTIVE FROM SKY GARDENS
DEFAULTS
PLANNING TARGETS
STAIRS
ELEVATORS
MID TOWER PARAMETERS
GREENWAY MEETS TOWER
LIVING MACHINE
WATER FILTRATION
FILTRATION :
PRESERVE EXISTING SITE
SITE MEMORY
WEB PARAMETERS
PLANNING TARGETS
BIKING
STAIRS
ELEVATORS
WEB SECTION

Park City

University
University of Pennsylvania

Tutors
Matthias HOLLWICH (Lecturer)
Joshua FREESE (Teaching Assistant)

Team A
Alexandra VANORSDALE
Mark SHKOLNIKOV
Jeong LEE

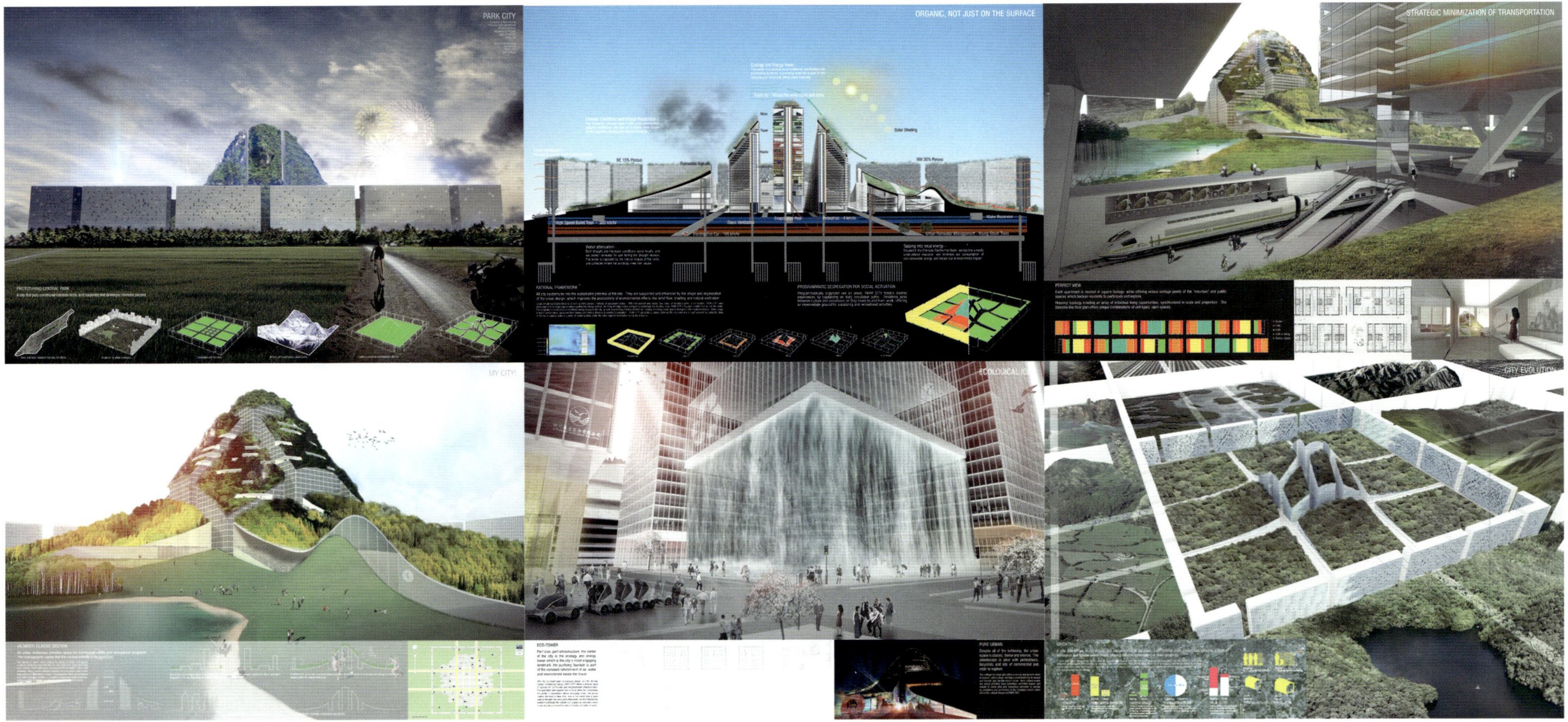
PARK CITY
PROTOTYPING CENTRAL PARK
ORGANIC, NOT JUST ON THE SURFACE
STRATEGIC MINIMIZATION OF TRANSPORTATION
PERFECT VIEW
MY CITY!
ECO-TOWER
PURE URBAN
CITY EVOLUTION

Hover

University
University of Pennsylvania

Tutors
Matthias HOLLWICH (Lecturer)
Joshua FREESE (Teaching Assistant)

Team B
Andreas KOSTOPOULOS
Eva JERMYN
Tia CROCKER

CITY IN THE SKY

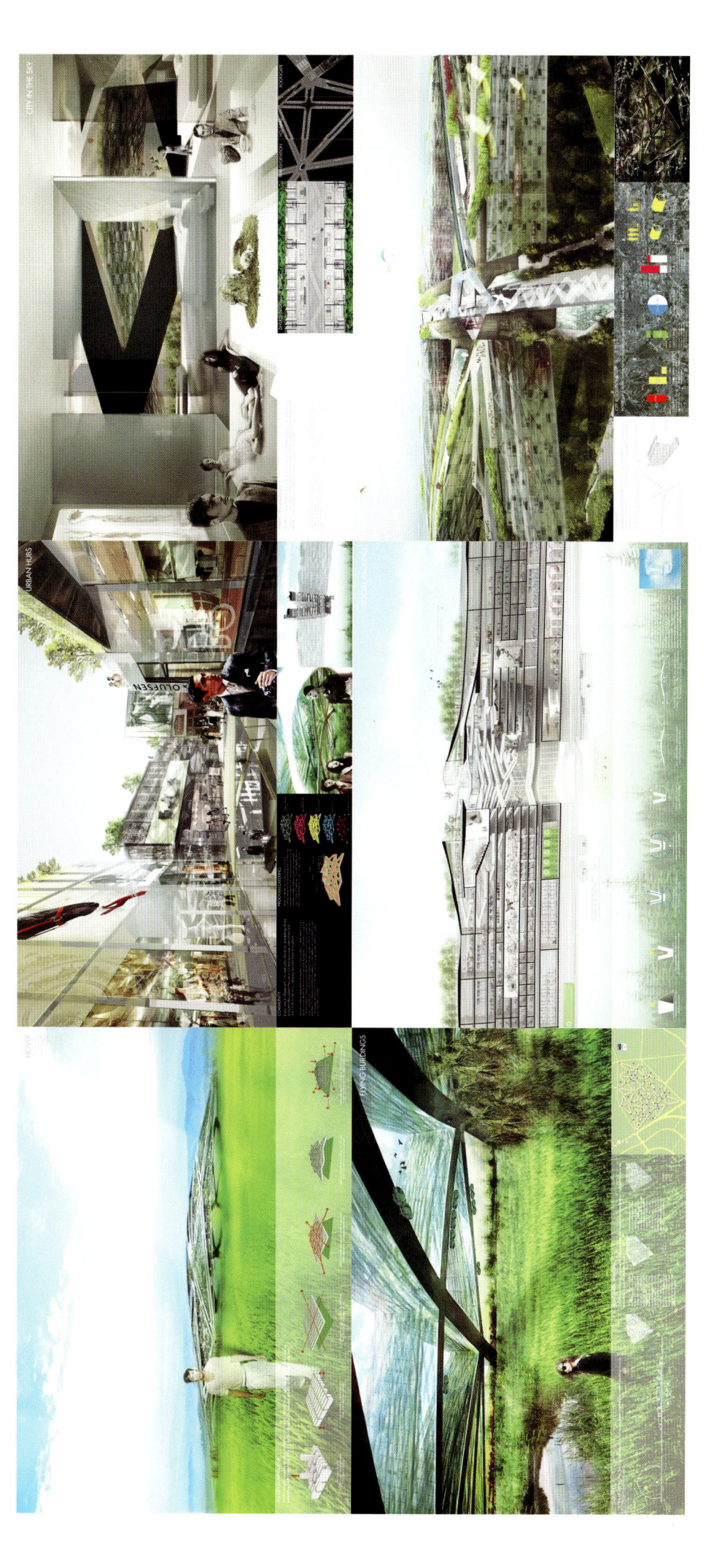

URBAN HUBS

HOVER

FLYING BUILDINGS

Delicate Canyon: Interdependent Urbanism

University
University of Tokyo

Tutor
Ysuke OBUCHI (Assoc Professor)

Team A
Kazami FURUKAWA
Natsuki HIRAOKA
Ioannis POULARAKIS

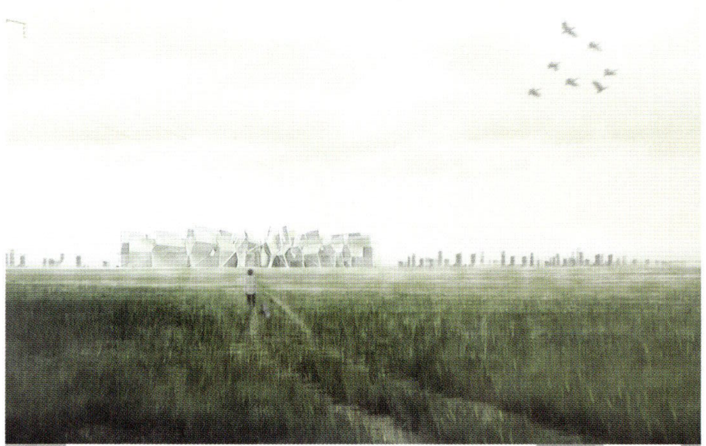

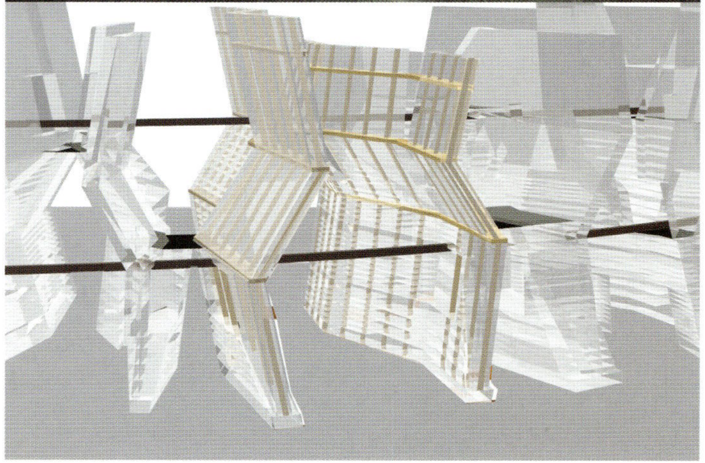

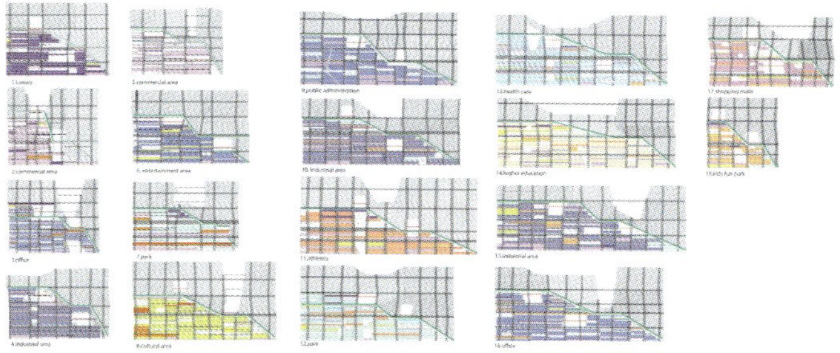

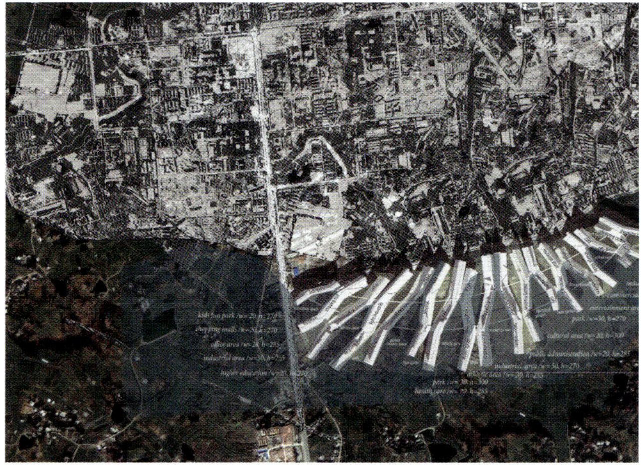

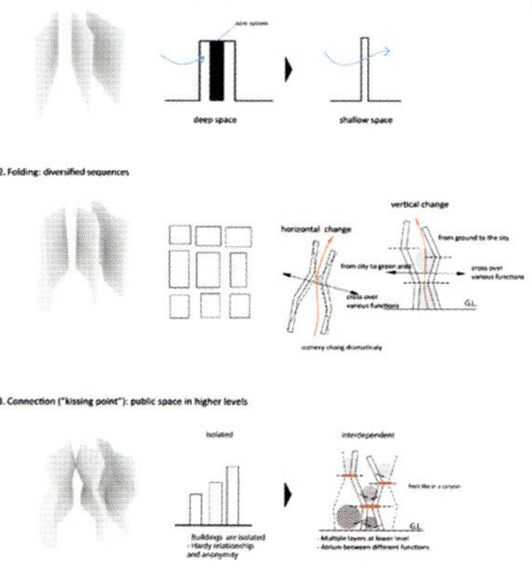

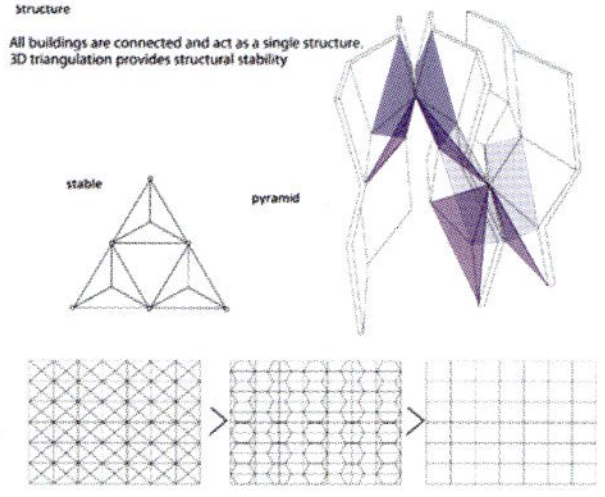

Canyon images

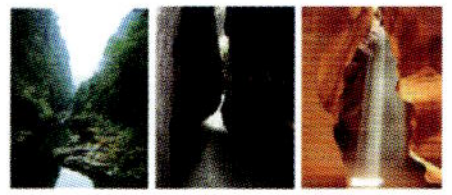

Isolated space

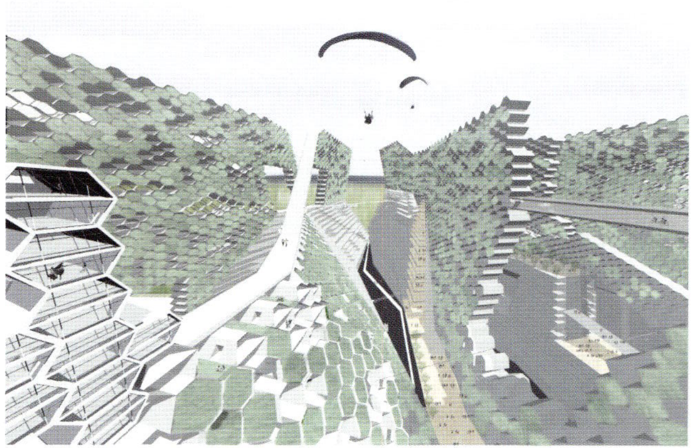

Dragon's Nest: Above the Valley Fog

University
University of Tokyo

Tutor
Ysuke OBUCHI (Assoc Professor)

Team B
Takuya OKUMOTO
Haruna FUKUMOTO

Introduction

We made the concept of urban planning, that is different from existing ways, not division & zoning city but made of architectural scale elements. The way of connecting unit makes different type of space, these spaces become the basic space for urban activity. It can actualize the flexible urban planning by using different existing construction principle, that parallel the out of assumption like the growth of population and energy problems.

Dragon's Nest

Concept

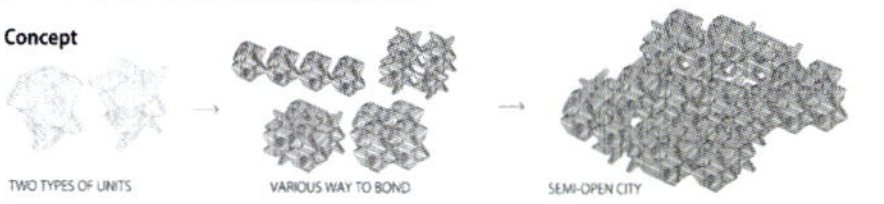

Program

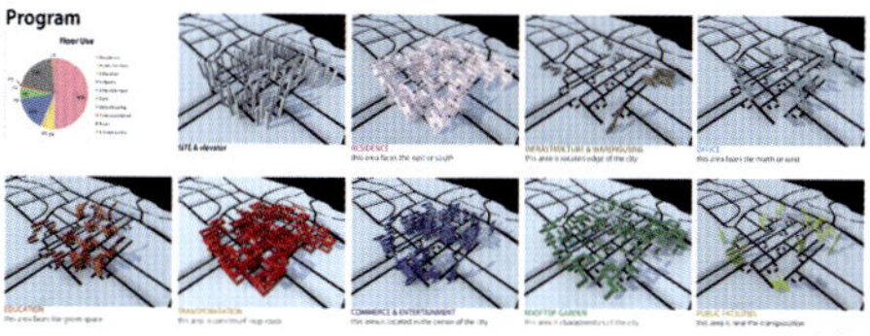

DIAGRAM

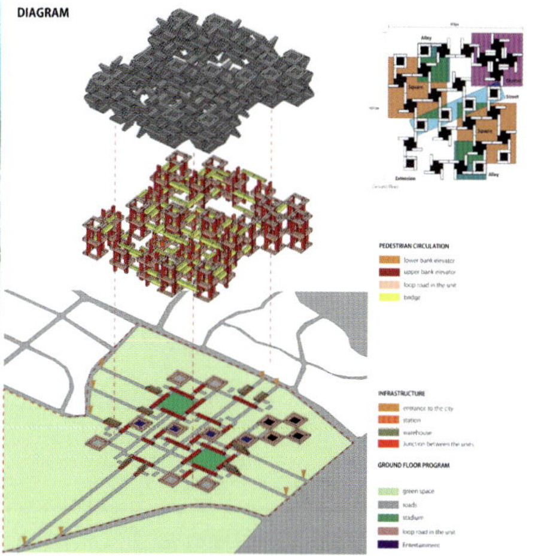

perspective from the north

PROCESS

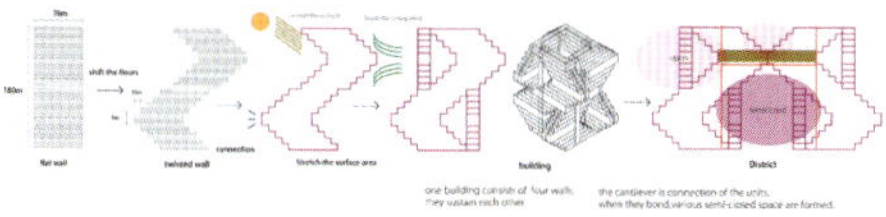

COMPONENT ELEMENTS

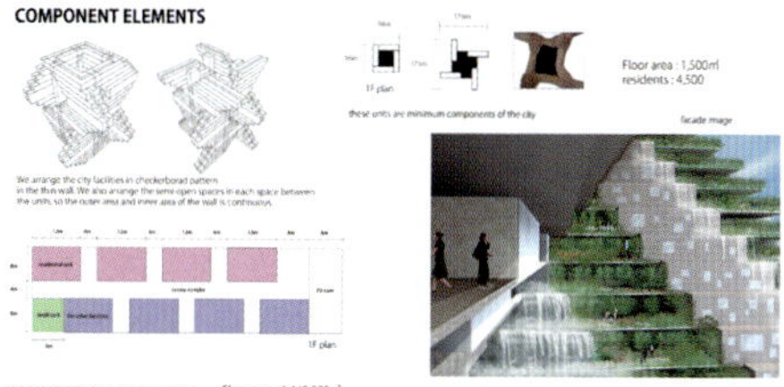

CONNECTION PATTERNS

Floor area : 1,440,000㎡
residents : 18,000

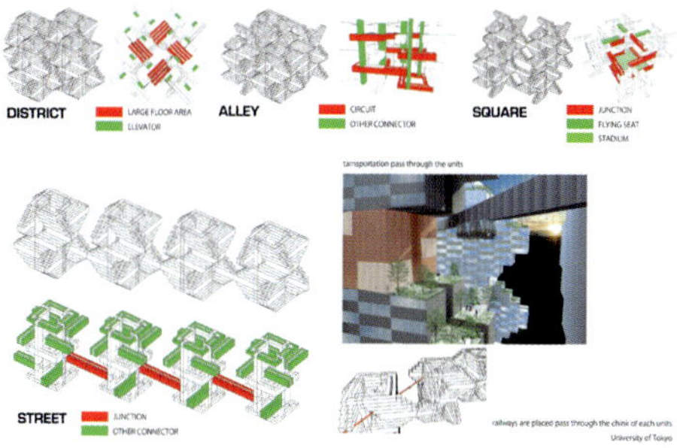

Evolutional Process

Evolutionary tree of the city
The process of making one city by connection of each unit is shown as follows. With the growth of scale, part of the city, such as Activities, Water, Energy and Network change

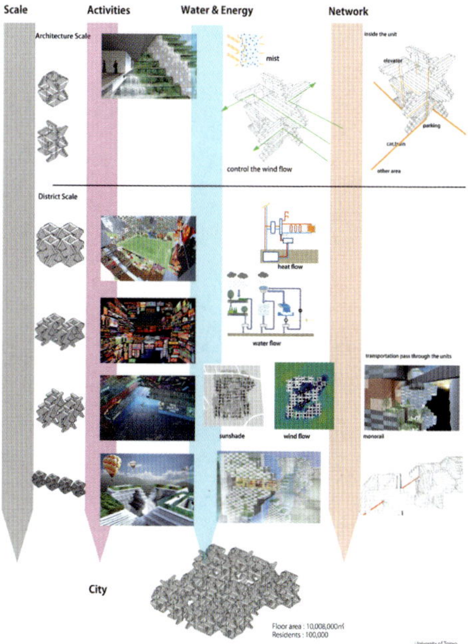

Floor area : 10,008,000㎡
Residents : 100,000

Activities in the city

Easy access to various activities
The merit of high density is easy access to various activities. You can experience the gala while you spend time in your house. The districts of this city are visually connected each other.

Symbiotic program plannning
Generally speaking, the darkness caused by high density is not welcomed. But some programs like commercial facilities and entertainment facilities are compatible with the darkness. We arrange the symbiotic program planning in this city.

perspective of the soccer fileds.

aquarium in the bottom of the building.

sunset view through the downtown

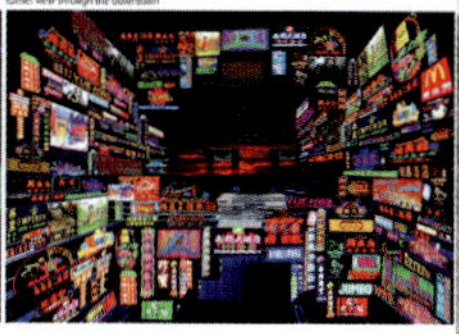

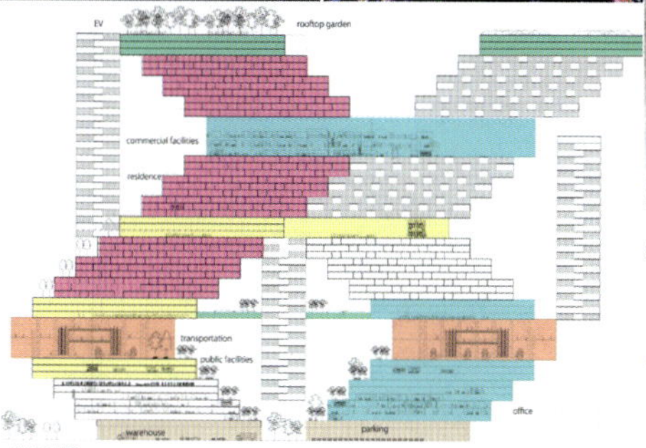

Section 5 = 1:500

WATER & ENERGY

Fresh air solution

Mist

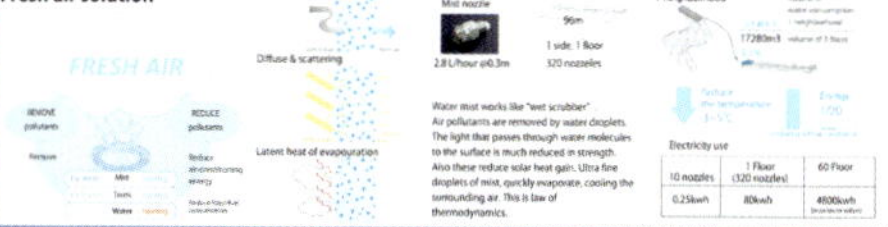

Water mist works like "wet scrubber".
Air pollutants are removed by water droplets.
The light that passes through water molecules to the surface is much reduced in strength.
Also these reduce solar heat gain. Ultra fine droplets of mist, quickly evaporate, cooling the surrounding air. This is law of thermodynamics.

Electricity use

10 nozzles	1 Floor (320 nozzles)	60 Floor
0.25kwh	80kwh	4800kwh

mist is spread by the wind

Flow of water & energy -mist/trees/heating-

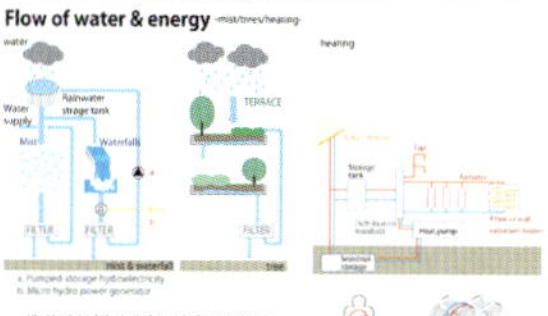

Like blood circulation in the human body, water circulates through the architecture in this city. And water circulation become the flow of generating mist, irrigation system and heating and hot water system.

air temperature

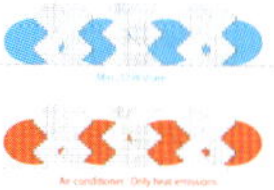

Energy
Mist can reduce the temperature by as much as 3~5 degrees Celsius. Electric use to reduce the temperature is twentieth part of Air conditioner. Mist does not emit heat into the atmosphere. What's more, mist absorbs heat energy from surrounding air owing to latent heat effect. Mist system is better suited for such a high density city.

APPENDIX

EVENT PHOTOS

Deans' Meeting at the National University of Singapore. September 2010.

Jury members deliberating over a competition presentation.

Left to right: Wang Shu, Alan Balfour, Ken Yeang, Joaquím Sabaté Bel and Wong Mun Summ.

Wang Shu, one of five jury members presenting his symposium paper.

Prof Heng Chye Kiang (Dean) and Dr Feng Lun at the award ceremony.

Dr Feng Lun (left) and the Chief Planner (URA) Lim Eng Hwee (right) viewing the competition panels along with guests and participants.

Participants for the inaugural Vertical Cities Asia symposium and competition.

PARTICIPANTS

1. Jury

Alan BALFOUR

Educated at Edinburgh and Princeton and a member of the Royal Institute of British Architects, Alan Balfour is Professor and Dean of the College of Architecture at Georgia Tech. Formerly he has served as dean of the Schools of Architecture in Texas and New York, and was chairman of the Architectural Association in London. Balfour was the year 2000 recipient of the Topaz Medal, the highest recognition given in North America to an educator in architecture.

His most recent book Solomon's Temple is a study of the constructive and destructive power of faith played out in the myths and realities of one place, Temple Mount in Jerusalem; it is due out in the fall of 2011. Though the city is the ostensible subject of Balfour's writing his underlying concern is with exploring the cultural imagination. Creating a Scottish Parliament (with David McCrone, Finlay Brown, Edinburgh 2005) offers an intimate exploration of the conceptualization of the political structure for a devolved Scotland and the architecture that would symbolize and be the instrument for its advancement.

Ken YEANG

Dr. Ken Yeang is a certified architect and planner specializing in the design and the master planning of signature deep-green ecologically-responsive large buildings and masterplans. He is chairman of Llewelyn Davies Yeang (UK) and principal of Hamzah & Yeang (Malaysia).

He studied at the Cheltenham College in Gloucestershire. His architectural education was at the AA (the Architectural Association) School in London. He completed his doctorate at Wolfson College, Cambridge University (UK) on ecological design and planning. He has received numerous awards for his work and authored several books on eco-design and eco-masterplanning.

Joaquím SABATÉ BEL

Joaquím Sabaté Bel is Professor and Chair of Town Planning at the Polytechnic University of Catalonia (UPC). He is the Coordinator of the PhD, Research Master in Urbanism and Regional Design Programmes at UPC. He also chairs the European Postgraduate Masters of Urbanism (Universities of Delft, Leuven, Venice and UPC). He founded the International Laboratory of Cultural Landscapes (MIT-UPC) and is the editor of the journal Identities: "Territory, Culture, Heritage."

Professor Sabaté has lectured widely and his research activities are focused on the study of theories, methods and tools of urban and regional design, and on the relation between heritage resources and local development. In addition, he is Advisor of the Research and Technology Commission of the Catalan Government; of the National University Quality and Accreditation Agency; and also of some Research Councils in Italy, Chile, Argentina and Uruguay. Professionally, he was also responsible for developing urban and regional plans in different European and South American countries.

WANG Shu

Wang Shu and his wife Lu Wenyu founded the Amateur Architecture Studio in 1998. This Hangzhou-based practice has grown into a well-regarded name in China. Wang Shu is also Professor and Dean of the School of Architecture at the China Academy of Art at Hangzhou. The focus of his practice and research is the re-establishment of contemporary Chinese architecture, and this is reflected in projects such as the Ceramic Houses, the Vertical Courtyard Apartment, the Xiangshan campus of China Academy of Art in Hangzhou, the Harbour Art Museum in Ningbo, the Tengtou Pavilion for Shanghai Expo, etc. An important and unique feature of his work is the application of vernacular, traditional, recycled construction materials with modern technology.

WONG Mun Summ

Wong Mun Summ graduated with Honours from the National University of Singapore in 1989. He served on the board of Singapore's Urban Redevelopment Authority (URA) from 1999 to 2005. He is also currently serving on various design advisory panels for the URA and Housing Development Board (HDB).

Wong Mun Summ and Richard Hassell formed WOHA in 1994. The partnership has become one of Southeast Asia's best known and most awarded architectural practices. WOHA has developed vast experience in a wide mix of building types and scales located throughout Asia and Australia, with a focus on innovation and diversity of interests. WOHA's architecture is notable for its constant evolution: no two buildings adopt the same 'style', as each project constitutes a specific response to the potential of the program and the site. The architecture demonstrates a profound awareness of local context and tradition, as well as an ongoing exploration of contemporary architectural forms and ideas, thus creating a unique fusion of practicality and invention. Environmental principles have always been fundamental to WOHA's designs. The partnership has won a large number of local awards and international awards, including the Aga Khan Award for Architecture in 2007, four World Architecture Festival Awards in 2010 and 2009, and four RIBA International Awards in 2010 and 2011.

2. Other Contributors

Mark ANDERSON and Peter ANDERSON

Mark S. T. Anderson
Associate Professor of Architecture,
University of California, Berkeley, 2001–present
Principal, Anderson Anderson Architecture/
Bay Pacific Construction, San Francisco,
1983–present
Fellow, American Institute of Architects

Peter C. O. Anderson
Principal, Anderson Anderson Architecture/
Bay Pacific Construction, San Francisco,
1983–present
Associate Professor of Architecture,
California College of the Arts,
San Francisco
Fellow, American Institute of Architects

Anderson Anderson Architecture
Mark and Peter Anderson's research-intensive architecture and construction work has been recognized with numerous international awards, exhibitions and publications. Based in San Francisco, Anderson Anderson Architecture has designed and built many projects in America, Asia and Europe, ranging in size and place from urban master planning in Wuhan; goat housing in Tuscany; flood control prototypes in Venice and New Orleans; multimedia gallery space in San Francisco; and experimental housing in many corners of the United States and Japan. Their work combines specialized technical experience in construction and prefabrication coupled with a critical eye to broad cultural questions and large-scale environmental issues. Several of their building proposals and a series of short films were recently exhibited at The Venice Biennale and at The Museum of Modern Art in New York. Two recent books on their work are available from Princeton Architectural Press: Anderson Anderson, Architecture and Construction (2001); and Prefab Prototypes, Site-Specific Design for Off-Site Construction (2007). Mark Anderson teaches at the University of California, Berkeley; Peter Anderson teaches at California College of the Arts, in San Francisco.

Alfredo BRILLEMBOURG and Hubert KLUMPNER

Alfredo Billembourg studied architecture at Columbia University and received a second architecture degree from the Central University of Venezuela in 1992. He founded Urban-Think Tank (U-TT) in Caracas, Venezuela in 1993. Since 1994, he has been a member of the Venezuelan Architects and Engineers Association and has been a guest professor at José Maria Vargas University, Simon Bolívar University and the Central University of Venezuela.

Hubert Klumpner graduated from the University of Applied Arts in Vienna and received an MSc in Architecture and Urban Design from Columbia University in 1997. In 1998, he joined Alfredo Brillembourg as Director of Urban-Think Tank (U-TT) in Caracas. He is a member of the German Chamber of Architects, and since 2001, he has been urbanism consultant of the International Program for Social and Cultural Development in Latin America (OAE and UNESCO)

Starting in 2007, Brillembourg and Klumpner have been guest professors at the Graduate School of Architecture and Planning, Columbia University, where they cofounded the Sustainable Living Urban Model Laboratory (S.L.U.M. Lab). Since May 2010, they have also held the chair for Architecture and Urban Design at the Swiss Institute of Technology (ETH) Zurich in Switzerland.

Kees CHRISTIAANSE

Kees Christiaanse was born in Amsterdam in 1953. He was a partner at OMA Rotterdam until 1989, when he founded KCAP Architects & Planners, and has realized multiple buildings and urban projects world-wide. Since 2003, he has been Head of the Institute for Urban Design at ETH Zurich and a Visiting Professor at the London School of Economics. He is involved in the development of docklands in Amsterdam, Rotterdam, and Hamburg, and is designing an "urban breeding ground in London for the Olympic Legacy Masterplan. He was the curator of the 4th International Architecture Biennale Rotterdam 2009.

Richard HASSELL and Alina YEO
Richard Hassell graduated from the University of Western Australia in 1989. He was awarded a Master of Architecture degree from the RMIT University, Melbourne, in 2002. He is currently a board member of both the DesignSingapore Council and the Building and Construction Authority. He has also served on committees for the URA, SIA and Board of Architects (BOA) in Singapore.

Alina Yeo graduated from the National University of Singapore in 2005 with a Master of Architecture degree. She is a project architect with WOHA.

See also WONG Mun Summ (listed under 1. Jury)

Matthias HOLLWICH
Matthias Hollwich is a registered European Architect and cofounder or HOLLWICH KUSHNER LLC (HWKN) and ARCHITIZER. Before cofounding HWKN and ARCHITIZER, Matthias worked at the Office for Metropolitan Architecture (OMA) in Rotterdam, and Diller+ Scofidio in New York. He is currently a Lecturer in Architecture at the University of Pennsylvania, where he created the international conference on aging and architecture: New Aging in 2010. His book, UmBauhau: Updating Modernism, was completed in 2004. Currently he is working on New Aging, a manifest on aging and architecture to be published in the fall of 2011. His work has been featured in the New York Times, Bauwelt, Architects Magazine, Dwell, and many other publications. He has been a speaker at TED_U, TED_X Atlanta, PICNIC in Amsterdam and many more. Matthias is an optimistic and driven to move architecture forward.

Waikeen NG
Waikeen Ng is Associate Professor in the Department of Architecture at the National University of Singapore. He has extensive international experience in urban and spatial planning. Before returning to Singapore at the end of 2010 to take up the teaching appointment, he worked with Scott Tallon Walker Architects in Dublin, Ireland, where he provided input on sustainable urban design, development and planning for a variety of projects. From 1999 to 2007, he was Director of Cities Hub at Fundación Metrópoli in Madrid, Spain, where he was responsible for urban planning research and design projects, both within the country and internationally. Earlier in his career, as an executive architect with the Public Works Department in Singapore, he was involved in the planning, design and construction of educational institutions. Waikeen studied Architecture at the National University of Singapore, and City & Regional Planning at the University of Pennsylvania. He is a member of the American Planning Association and the International Society of City and Regional Planners.

Rosalyne SHIEH
Rosalyne Shieh is an Assistant Professor of Architecture at the University of Michigan, where she was the 2009–2010 Taubman Fellow in Architecture. She received her Master of Architecture from Princeton University, a BA in Architecture from the University of California, Berkeley, and an MSc in Architectural History and Theory from the Bartlett School of Architecture in London. She has taught at NJIT in Newark, NJ and worked in the offices of Abalos & Herreros in Madrid, and ARO and Stan Allen Architect in New York City. She is a founding partner of SCHAUM/SHIEH.

Shieh's research involves issues of representation and urbanism, with a focus on interventions at the scale of the individual building. Current and recent work include a built project in Detroit that responds to the city's changing urban conditions, a funded research project in the form of design proposals for Taiwan's changing urbanism as brought on by the recent completion of the high-speed rail, as well as a proposal for the redevelopment of an urban commercial centre in Houston, TX. Shieh has lectured at the Academica Sinica in Taipei, Taiwan, as well as National Cheng Kung University, School of Architecture in Tainan, Taiwan.

YAO Dong and HUANG Yiru
Yao Dong received his Dr. Eng in Architecture from Tongji University in 2005. After two years as visiting scholar in the United States, he returned to China, and is now lecturing in the Architecture Department in Tongji University CAUP. His current research interests include housing, urban morphology, green building and utopian history.

Huang Yiru received his Dr. Eng in Architecture from the College of Architecture and Urban Planning at Tongji University, where he is currently serving as Vice Dean and Professor-in-charge of Residential Design and Planning. He is a member of the China Housing and Real Estate Research

Council and a member of the editorial board of "Journal of Asian Architecture and Engineering". He is also a member of the Shanghai Real Estate Association Housing Industry R&D expert group.

Marisa YIU

Marisa Yiu is Assistant Professor at the School of Architecture of The Chinese University of Hong Kong, and Founding Partner of ESKYIU. Her academic research is on the cultural and social landscape of cities, specific to Hong Kong and Pearl River Delta. Selected writings include, 'Image Construction: Hong Kong since 1967–8' (LOG journal, NY), and forthcoming chapter in 'Port Cities: Dynamic Landscapes and Global Networks' (Routledge, London); she has also published in A/D, DomusChina, MIT's thresholds, Architectural Record and Journal for Architectural Education.

Recently, Yiu served as the Chief Curator of the 2009 Hong Kong-Shenzhen Bi-City Biennale of Architecture\ Urbanism located at the future West Kowloon Cultural District site. Along with Eric Schuldenfrei they received the 2010 Architectural League Prize, as Founding Partners of ESKYIU. Their selected projects include 'Chinatown WORK' commissioned by the Lower Manhattan Cultural Council; 'Nutritious: an aeroponic facade' exhibited at the Architectural Association, and sustainable installations at the 11th Venice Biennale international exhibition.

Yiu has taught at the Architectural Association; Columbia University Graduate School of Architecture, Planning and Preservation; Parsons School of Design; led workshops at the Cooper Hewitt National Design Museum with the Centre for Urban Pedagogy. She was previously Assistant Professor at the University of Hong Kong (2007–2010). She received her Bachelor of Arts and Sciences from Columbia College, Columbia University (New York) and a Master of Architecture from Princeton University. Yiu is a licensed architect in New York, AIA architect member, an associate of the HKIA and Board member of the Hong Kong Ambassadors of Design Council

3. Participating Universities

The Chinese University of Hong Kong

Tutors
 HO Puay Peng (Professor and Dean)
 Marisa YIU (Asst Professor)

Team A
 LAM Yan-Yu Ian
 LEUNG Yin-Ming, Ivan
 TAM Yin-Shan Isabella
 LI Kai-Min Kenneth
 LEE Kung-Yau
 WAN Ka-Wan, April

Delft University of Technology

Tutors
 Karin LAGLAS (Professor and Dean)
 Henco BEKKERING (Professor)

Team A
 Joeri SLOTS
 Xin DOGTEROM
 Ronald ROELOFS
 Drazen KRICKOVIC

Team B
 Bart van LAKWIJK
 Herman PEL
 Jasper NIJVELDT

National University of Singapore

Tutors
 NG Wai Keen (Assoc Professor)
 LOW Boon Liang (Senior Lecturer)

Team A
 Susanto SOENJOYO
 XIA Wan Nao
 Harvey LUKMAN

Team B
 Welly BUDIMAN
 PING Lei
 Vignesh KAUSHIK

Swiss Federal Institute of Technology (ETH) Zurich

Tutors
 Kees CHRISTIAANSE (Professor)
 Alfredo BRILLEMBOURG (Professor)
 Hubert KLUMPNER (Professor)
 Nicolas KRETSCHMAN (Teaching Assistant)
 Michael CONTENTO (Teaching Assistant)

(continued on next page)

Team A
   Daniel FUCHS
   Sascha TOETLY
   Adrian POLLINGER
   Luis HILTI

Team B
   Carmen BAUMANN
   Alessandro BOSSHARD
   Julianne GANTNER
   NING Hug
   Selina MASE
   Louis WANGLER

Tongji University

Tutors
   HUANG Yiru (Professor and Vice-Dean)
   LI Linxue (Assoc Professor)
   YAO Dong (Lecturer)

Team A
   YAN Wenlong
   LI Jie
   FAN Yinghui
   DING Fan
   LIU Ying

Team B
   WANG Meng
   LIAO Kai
   YANG Xu
   CHEN Xingfeng
   CHEN Jiao

Tsinghua University

Tutors
   WANG Hui (Professor)

Team A
   WANG Shenhao
   LU Chenchen
   LIU Lun

Team B
   WAN Junzhe
   LIU Haijing

University of California (UC) Berkeley

Tutors
   Jennifer WOLCH (Professor and Dean)
   Mark ANDERSON (Assoc Professor)
   Peter ANDERSON (Assoc Professor)

Team A
   MOU Yujiang
   Michael BERGIN
   Alex FENTON

University of Pennsylvania

Tutors
   Matthias HOLLWICH (Lecturer)
   Joshua FREESE (Teaching Assistant)

Team A
   Alexandra VANORSDALE
   Mark SHKOLNIKOV
   Jeong LEE

Team B
   Andreas KOSTOPOULOS
   Eva JERMYN
   Tia CROCKER

University of Tokyo

Tutor
   Ysuke OBUCHI (Assoc Professor)

Team A
   Kazami FURUKAWA
   Natsuki HIRAOKA
   Ioannis POULARAKIS

Team B
   Takuya OKUMOTO
   Haruna FUKUMOTO

4. National University of Singapore

Faculty
   HENG Chye Kiang (Dean,
      School of Design & Environment)
   WONG Yunn Chii (Head,
      Department of Architecture)
   CHAN Kok Hui, Jeffrey
   CHANG Jiat Hwee
   CHEAH Kok Ming
   CHEE Lilian
   CHO Im Sik
   HUANG Yi Chun
   Erik L'HEUREUX
   LIM Ee Man, Joseph
   LOW Boon Liang
   NG Wai Keen
   Tsuto SAKAMOTO
   TSE Swee Ling
   Erwin VIRAY
   Johannes WIDODO
   WONG Chong Thai, Bobby

Staff
   CHENG Zhi Yue
   Katherine CHONG
   GOH Lay Fong
   Cardith HUNG
   LIM Hwee Lee
   Dorothy MAN
   MOHD SAH bin Sadon
   MUJI bin Hochri
   ROZITA bte Ahmad
   SEK Siak Chiang
   Cindy TAN
   Jason TANG
   Philip TAY
   Margaret WONG
   Jessie YEO

IMAGE CREDITS

1. Symposium Papers
All images were provided by the authors unless otherwise stated.

In Search of the Best City Measures: Ten Propositions
Figs 1–4, Ministerio de Fomento, La ciudad Hispanoamericana. El sueño de un orden. CEHOPU, Madrid, 1997.
Figs 5–15 Miquel Corominas.
Figs 16–19 Meta Berghauser Pont and Per Haupt, "Space, Density and Urban Form". PhD dissertation, Technische Universiteit Delft. Delft 2009.

Design Approach for High-Rise and High-Density Living in Tropical Asian Cities
Photographs by WOHA.
Rendered Images by Obilia.

Multitasking Spatial Infrastructures: Slender Urbanism and Mobility Models
Fig 1, Mark Lombardi: Global Networks (2003)
Figs 2–4, Michael Wolf, Hong Kong
Fig 5, photos-hongkong.com/hong-kong-mtr.htm
Fig 6, Michael Wolf, Hong Kong corner houses, Hong Kong University Press, December 2010
Fig 10, Ryan Cheng
Fig 11, Background aerial courtesy of Google Images
Fig 15, Fanny Sze
Fig 17, Ohconfucius (21 June 2008)
Fig 21, MTR

Lessons from High-Intensity, Mixed-Use Urbanism in Singapore's CBD
Fig 1, Atlas of Malaya. 1960
Fig 2, SIT Annual Report 1953 (scan from www.teoalida.net)
Figs 3, 6 & 7, Urban Redevelopment Authority
Fig 8, Housing & Development Board
Fig 10, www.propertyguru.com.sg
Fig 15, National Archives
Fig 19, Singapore National Album of Pictures
Fig 20, www.h88.com.sg
Fig 21, Aung Kiang (via Flickr)
Fig 24, alvinlpc (via media.photobucket.com)
Fig 25, Peggy Loh (via ppunlimited.blogspot.com/2011/01/banquet-in-basin.html)

Key Issues in the Design Approach of Megastructures
Fig 2, Herztberger, H.. Lessons for Students in Architecture. Rotterdam: 10 Publishers, 2005:109.
Fig 3, Wigley, M. Constant's New Babylon [M]. Rotterdam: 010 Publishers. 1999-6-15:210.
Fig 4, http://service.photo.sina.com.cn/orignal/4c5c13f0444529740121a&690
Fig 5, Photography: Kawasumi Architectural Photograph Office. Source: Lin, Z. From Megastructure to Megapolis: formation and transformation of mega-project in Tokyo Bay. Journal of Urban Design, Volume 12: P75, 2007.1.
Fig 6, Sandler, S. Architecture without Architecture [M]. Cambridge: MIT Press, 2009.
Fig 7, Arcosanti: Archology: Theory [OL]. http://www.arcosanti.org/theory/arcology/arcologies/hyperBuilding.html
Fig 8, The conceptual Design of "Urban Stage" by Grade four students DING, HAN, LI (2010).

2. Design Competition
All images are as provided by the respective participating universities.